THE NEW
Building
YOUR MATE'S
Self-Esteem

DENNIS & BARBARA
RAINEY

THOMAS NELSON PUBLISHERS

Nashville • Atlanta • London • Vancouver

Published in Nashville, Tennessee, by Thomas Nelson, Inc., Publishers, and distributed in Canada by Word Communications, Ltd., Richmond, British Columbia, and in the United Kingdom by Word (UK), Ltd., Milton Keynes, England.

Scripture quotations are from THE NEW AMERICAN STANDARD BIBLE, Copyright © 1960, 1962, 1963, 1968, 1971, 1972, 1973, 1975, 1977 by The Lockman Foundation and are used by permission.

Library of Congress Cataloging-in-Publication Data

Rainey, Dennis, 1948–
   The new building your mate's self-esteem / Dennis and Barbara Rainey. — Updated and expanded ed.
     p. cm.
   Updated ed. of: Building your mate's self-esteem. 1993.
   Includes bibliographical references.
   ISBN 0-7852-7824-9
   1. Marriage—Religious aspects—Christianity. 2. Self-esteem—Religious aspects—Christianity. 3. Interpersonal relations—Religious aspects—Christianity. I. Rainey, Barbara. II. Rainey, Dennis, 1948– Building your mate's self-esteem. III. Title.
BV835.R345 1995
248.8'4—dc20   95–6246
                                   CIP

Printed in the United States of America

10 11 12 13 — 00 99 98 97

We dedicate this book to the four people who have had a profoundly positive impact upon our self-esteem—

Bob and Jean Peterson

and

Ward and Dalcie Rainey

Thanks for your faithful care and concern in beginning the process of building a healthy, growing self-esteem in each of us. We're proud to be your children.

CONTENTS

- Be Careful How You Walk
- Values Inventory Analysis
- Responding to Unplanned Difficulties
- Keep Life Balanced
- Esteem Builder Project

Building Block #10: Discovering Dignity through Destiny
- Ask Yourself Some Tough Questions
- Step Out in the Right Direction
- You and Your Mate Are God's Workmanship
- A Man with a Destiny
- Helping Your Mate Gain a Sense of Destiny
- Discovering Your Mate's Destiny
- Leaving a Legacy
- Five Essentials in Leaving a Legacy that Will Outlive You
- Esteem Builder Project

Man to Man: From Dennis
- The Wise Investment
- Wife Builder's Inventory
- Hats a Wife Wears
- Persevere in Your Investment
- Barbara's Tips to Men
- Esteem Builder Project

Woman to Woman: From Barbara
- Understand His Manhood
- Respect His Person
- Adapt to Him and Share His Dream
- Character Inventory
- It Takes Years for Him to Become a Man
- Esteem Builder Project

- Perseverance and Change

FOREWORD

In the wake of a couple's marital spat, I was asked to give comfort to the shaken wife. Neighbors called the police; she called me. As I entered the home, I passed the departing patrolman who said, "It's just a matter of time—they need a divorce."

His conclusion grew out of reality: Half of all American marriages die in divorce courts. Many more hang together by thin, legal threads only. Weddings may be popular, but marriages are *not* alive and well.

While the pessimistic percentages pass in review, a no-nonsense, self-help alternative has surfaced. With *Building Your Mate's Self-Esteem,* Dennis and Barbara Rainey have developed a kind of no-fault solution to the commonest irritant in the Mr. and Mrs. merger. They know the territory and they tackle the tough spots with realism and courage. Esteem Builder Projects and clarity of writing make this book an eloquent source of instruction—and review—for anyone seriously committed to a worthwhile marriage.

Dennis Rainey is no theorist. His FamilyLife Marriage Conferences nationwide have taught him to pick up the marital pulse accurately. He has been used by God as a powerful tool to impact homes and marriages as few men have. His principles are unerringly biblical yet up to speed for our urban pace. From the authenticity of their own relationship, Dennis and Barbara offer not just another book about marriage to set on the shelf, but rather an effective instrument which novice and veteran alike will find valuable.

— Howard and Jeanne Hendricks
Dallas Theological Seminary

ACKNOWLEDGMENTS

Writing a book is enough of a challenge by itself. However, writing at home while faced with the reality of six children and a rapidly growing ministry means this book was a team effort.

Jeff Tikson has brought new meaning to the word *servanthood.* You heroically supplied the leadership to solve a myriad of problems that surfaced while we were submerged in this book. Thanks, Jeff, you've become a trusted friend and co-laborer.

A special thanks to Lori Bricker. We couldn't have done it without you. And we are very proud of the mom you have become after the special training assignment you received in our home.

The FamilyLife Ministry team deserves special commendation. You prayed, encouraged, pitched in, and supported us while faithfully carrying on the task of strengthening marriages and families. You all are a "Team of Destiny"—we've only just begun. Jerry Wunder, you are a gift from God—thanks for being a servant and giving leadership.

A special thanks goes to Fred Hitchcock for all his research and editing. Lynne Nelson, Jeff Lord, and Sue Stinson all helped with the final manuscript.

A special thanks to the team which helped in the initial publishing of *Building Your Mate's Self-Esteem.* Les Stobbe and Jean Bryant, along with Dan Benson and Gwen Waller, were a great encouragement in helping launch *Building Your Mate's Self-Esteem* into a book. We know you guys were as surprised as we were when it took off, but we wanted to again say thanks to you and the entire team of Here's Life Publishers for being difference-makers.

Craig Current, Joe Battaglia, Jane Ann Smith, Randy Marshall, Anne Crow, Dr. George Slaughter, Gay White, and Steve Farrar—thanks to each of you for reading our "stuff" in its raw form and for giving us much-needed advice and balance. Thanks for being friends with a sharp pen.

Don and Sally Meredith have had and continue to have an immeasurable influence in our lives, marriage, and ministry—thanks for discipling us in so many ways.

To our children—Ashley, Benjamin, Samuel, Rebecca, Deborah, and Laura—*thank you!* You are the most understanding and best children a pair of parents could ever hope to have. The little notes, cookies, hugs, and prayers were more meaningful than you know. You are awesome!

A special word to those who helped in the revised edition of Building Your Mate's Self-Esteem:

To Mary Larmoyeux, Sharon Hill, and Mark Crull go a thousand kudos. There is no better support team in the world than you three, and we are deeply grateful for the many ways you support Barbara and me in this ministry to families. Thanks for the encouragement and help. Candidly, we want to thank you for your tremendous heart for families.

To Dave Boehi we give another round of applause and a *big* thank you for your help in revising this manuscript. You once again have proven that your eye for editing and sharpening of a manuscript are invaluable in a written ministry to people. Thanks for your tireless efforts in so many areas here at FamilyLife and for your deep abiding commitment to the Savior. We really do appreciate you.

Bruce Nygren, you are one incredibly patient saint. I am impressed by not only your technical skills in shaping the revision of a nine-year-old book, but even more by the spiritual maturity and commitment you have to God to make a difference in people's lives. Thanks for your heart for families and for your dedication to excellence. And yes, I will do a better job of documenting quotes and statistics in the future! Thanks, too, for finding Steve and Amanda Sorenson, who helped with all the new material that added fresh life and more intensity to an already jam-packed book. They did a terrific job. And to the entire team at Thomas Nelson: You are first rate. Thanks for your commitment to ministry.

Our last thanks go to a man who has enabled hundreds of thousands of families to receive hope and peace in Jesus Christ . . . Merle Engle. Merle, I will not be surprised if I arrive in heaven to find out that you were an angel sent by God. There is no question in my mind that no greater servant, other than the Savior, has ever walked the face of this earth. I so appreciate your pure heart for Christ, your desire to see things done right, and the wind that you have been beneath our wings in multiplying FamilyLife's ministry to families. Thank you for deciding to pitch your tent here in Little Rock and coming alongside us in making a difference in the lives of literally millions of families. May God indeed bring a "Family Reformation."

INTRODUCTION

This is a book on motivating people to believe in people. Both you and your mate need to be believed in. Your mate needs at least one person in his life who will come alongside him and build him up. You are that person. And he is that person for you.

You ask, "Why is this so important?" The reason: We live in an era when personal sense of insecurity has reached near epidemic proportions. Confidence—true bedrock confidence—is rare. Even those people who appear to possess unshakeable self-esteem shock us with confessions of self-doubt. We're puzzled when we see so many high-performance people driven by poor self-esteem—people such as business leaders, speakers, pro athletes, entertainers, and even many Christian leaders.

Surprising as that is, it is in marriage that the "wraps of performance" really come off, revealing our mate's questions about his or her value and worth as a person. The beautiful or handsome, intelligent, gifted person we married admits deep feelings of insecurity. In fact, many people, when they marry, hope their mate will help them by doing the building and reshaping that they couldn't do for themselves.

A wife is stunned when she discovers that her husband, her "knight in shining armor," is really just an overgrown boy with serious questions about who he is as a man.

Or a husband begins to notice that the charming, poised woman who swept him off his feet is painfully insecure in relating to others.

When we marry, we take on the responsibility of helping secure and strengthen our mate's self-image. Unfortunately, we are ill-equipped for such a complex task.

Our staff surveyed 17,000 marrieds and pre-marrieds at our FamilyLife Marriage Conferences by asking them, "In what area would you most like to have further training?" Rated number one by a wide margin, above finances, parenting, fathering, working women, and others, was "how to build your mate's self-esteem." That response confirmed the need for this book.

One of the leading authorities on the family, Dr. James Dobson, underscores the importance of building self-esteem in marriage.

> The most successful marriages are those where both husband and wife seek to build the self-esteem of the other. Ego needs can be met within the bonds of marriage, and nothing contributes more to closeness and stability than to convey respect for the personhood of the spouse.[1]

Not only does the success of your marriage depend upon building your mate's self-esteem, but also your success in rearing children, and in life in general. Two confident partners will be much more effective in every aspect of life than two insecure people could ever be.

Let us outline five reasons we believe both you and your mate will benefit from this book:

1. It will help you focus on your mate's needs and not just on your own. We know that you have needs in this area, too, but as you strengthen your mate's self-image, he will be increasingly free to give to you in return. Far too many marriages consist of two people who are waiting for each other to reach out and meet their needs.

2. Your mate may appear confident today—fully in charge of his life and capable of making wise decisions. But people change. Circumstances change. And changes will affect your mate. One wrong decision in the midst of these changes can crush a person's self-confidence. Your mate needs you to read this book and be able to apply its principles.

3. There is hope. God can and will produce growth in your mate's self-image. He still works in people's lives and He wants to use

you. Far too many people underestimate their role in their mates' lives. They lose hope, and they give up too soon.

4. We believe that confident people ultimately can be released from preoccupation with self to becoming all that God designed them to be.

5. Although the practical principles found in our ten building blocks of self-esteem are written for marrieds, they also apply in our relationships with children, our parents, our friends, and our associates at work. You'll be able to motivate others toward being all that God intended them to be as you apply these basic truths.

The solutions we offer, however, are not the "cookie cutter" variety. Some may be intensely practical for you today, while others may require you to brush the dust off this book a decade from now. We are confident that the discoveries you are about to make can benefit you and your mate for years to come as you build each other's self-worth.

One last word. The Scriptures clearly teach that we are to edify one another. The word *edify* as used in the New Testament comes from two Greek words: *oikos*, which means "a home," and *dimeo*, which means "to build." Therefore, to edify literally means "to build a home." In the process of edifying your mate, a building is formed. As mentioned before, construction of your mate's self-esteem is not for his welfare alone. It will profit you, your children, and others as well.

A NOTE TO OUR READERS

As writers, we face a dilemma. The English language does not contain a one-word equivalent for "he or she," yet we find it cumbersome to repeatedly refer to your mate as "he or she." Therefore, for the sake of readability, we generally will refer to your mate as "he."

CHAPTER 1

Giving Your Mate
a New Image

———◆———

———◆———

HAVE YOU EVER BEEN PUZZLED by your mate's lack of confidence—the evidence of weaknesses and flaws in his or her self-esteem? Have you asked yourself such questions as:

- Why is my husband driven toward accomplishment and achievement?
- Why does my wife constantly compare herself with others?

- Why is my husband so apathetic about life? Why is he so passive about trying anything new?
- Why is my wife so indecisive?
- Why does my husband find it so difficult to admit fault and ask for forgiveness?
- Why is my wife so preoccupied with her past? With her failures and mistakes?
- Why can't my husband relax? Why is he so guarded in relationships?
- Why does my wife appear to be solidly confident in so many areas of life, yet filled with self-doubt in others?

All of these questions represent a deficiency or an erosion in self-confidence. Your mate may appear to have it all together, but you know, as few others do, that underneath that self-sufficient exterior lives a person who needs to be built up and encouraged repeatedly.

Because your mate has these weak spots—these "holes in his armor"—he, like you, needs to be accepted unconditionally. He needs the security of knowing that his wife accepts and believes in him, even when he doesn't believe in himself. And she needs the security of knowing that her husband knows her, yet won't reject her.

Each of us needs someone to tell us we have value. We want to be accepted without mask, facade, or veneer. We want to be loved apart from our performance—totally and completely. As Maurice Wagner, author of two books on self-esteem, writes, "At the heart of personality is the need to feel a sense of being lovable without having to qualify for that acceptance."[1]

In order for your marriage to become a haven for your mate, you must accept him as he is, not for what you hope he will become.

She Loves Him for Who He Is

Dr. Paul Brand, a famous physician and author, knows about

people's thirst for acceptance. Not only does he continue to see this need today among those who have contracted Hansen's disease, commonly known as leprosy, but he also has seen this need for acceptance repeatedly as a surgeon. He wrote about his experience as a surgeon in London during World War II:

PETER FOSTER WAS A ROYAL AIR FORCE PILOT. These men [pilots] were the cream of the crop of England—the brightest, healthiest, most confident and dedicated, and often the most handsome men in the country. When they walked the streets in their decorated uniforms, the population treated them as gods. All eyes turned their way. Girls envied those who were fortunate enough to walk beside a man in Air Force blue.

However, the scene in London was far from romantic, for the Germans were attacking relentlessly. Fifty-seven consecutive nights they bombed London. In waves of 250, some 1,500 bombers would come each evening and pound the city.

The RAF Hurricanes and Spitfires that pilots like Foster flew looked like mosquitos pestering the huge German bombers. The Hurricane was agile and effective, yet it had one fatal design flaw. The single propeller engine was mounted in front, a scant foot or so from the cockpit, and the fuel lines snaked alongside the cockpit toward the engine. In a direct hit, the cockpit would erupt into an inferno of flames. The pilot could eject, but in the one or two seconds it took him to find the lever, heat would melt off every feature of his face: his nose, his eyelids, his lips, often his cheeks.

These RAF heroes many times would undergo a series of 20 to 40 surgeries to refashion what once was their face. Plastic surgeons worked miracles, yet what remained of the face was essentially a scar.

Peter Foster became one of those "downed pilots." After numerous surgical procedures, what remained of his face was indescribable. The mirror he peered into daily couldn't hide the facts. As the day for his release from the hospital grew closer, so did Peter's anxiety about being accepted by his family and friends.

He knew that one group of airmen with similar injuries had returned home only to be rejected by their wives and girlfriends. Some of the men were divorced by wives who were unable to accept this new outer image of their husbands. Some men became recluses, refusing to leave their houses.

In contrast, there was another group who returned home to families who gave loving assurance and continued worth. Many became executives and professionals, leaders in their communities.

Peter Foster was in that second group. His girlfriend assured him that nothing had changed except a few millimeters' thickness of skin. She loved *him*, not his facial membrane, she assured him. The two were married just before Peter left the hospital.

"She became my mirror," Peter said of his wife. "She gave me a new image of myself. Even now, regardless of how I feel, when I look at her she gives me a warm, loving smile that tells me I am okay," he tells confidently.[2]

Mirrors of Acceptance

Did you know that you are a mirror of your mate? You can either reflect the same loving acceptance Peter Foster's wife did, or you can withdraw from your mate and reflect rejection.

When your mate looks into your face—his mirror—what does he see? If your mate sees rejection or any lack of acceptance, the result will be fear. And that fear—the fear of rejection—is one of the most powerful forces motivating and controlling people today.

If you want to see your mate's self-image strengthened, then begin to recognize that the fear of rejection is your enemy. We read in 1 John 4:18: "Perfect love casts out fear." Fear will begin to dissolve in your mate under a steady stream of authentic love.

Give Your Mate the Gift of Value

Love is the most powerful agent for change in the universe—love casts out fear! Perfect love (God's love) is more powerful than the fear of rejection. Perfect love that accepts and embraces another, even in his weaknesses, will win the power struggle against fear every time. Rather than refueling the fear of rejection, you can remove it by accepting your mate. But acceptance isn't always easy, as a young man in his mid-twenties and an attractive young lady discovered years ago.

What You See Is *Not* All You Get

She was as smart as she was pretty. In fact, she was chosen as one of the university's "Top Twenty Freshmen Women."

As a child, she received love and encouragement from her parents, and the community esteemed her family. Her parents modeled a stable marriage. There was little stress for her. Life seemed perfect . . . until she reached junior high. While her friends reached puberty quickly and began to develop physically, she did not. Her chest remained flat, her legs remained skinny, and her hips developed no contours.

Throughout the first six years of school, she felt confident, sure of herself, popular. But as a seventh-grader who was slow to develop, she began to question her worth for the first time. This self-doubt was further fueled by her best friend, who noticed her lack of "physical feminine maturity." One day this friend asked, "Are you sure you're a girl?"

Those words struck her soul like a lightning bolt from an ominous dark cloud. Fear that she would never develop began to whisper in her inner spirit. Her personality changed. She became quiet, reserved, and shy. Constantly comparing herself with others, she always came up short in her own eyes. She felt unpopular, unattractive, and awkward—without personal value, and alone. And no one knew about her fears.

Finally, in her thirteenth year, she began to blossom. In fact, she became very pretty, yet inwardly she had developed a negative view of herself. Throughout high school, she viewed herself as inferior and thought everyone else viewed her that way, too.

Determined to forge a new self-identity, the young woman decided to attend an out-of-state college where she could start fresh. She succeeded. Honor after honor came her way. She earned excellent grades, participated in numerous campus activities, and became very popular. During her sophomore year, she pledged one of the top sororities on campus.

Behind this newly found niche of success, however, was an insecure individual. She became an outstanding performer, yet no one—not even she—realized that at the heart of her performance was a little girl who was afraid to be known because she feared rejection. The accomplishments gave her confidence a boost, but she still needed the acceptance of someone who really knew her. She needed to be accepted for who she was apart from her achievements.

One year after her college graduation, she grew to love a young man who appeared to have it all together. He was the extroverted, confident person she was not. Their whirlwind romance led to marriage after only four months of dating.

She later learned that, although he "appeared" secure, he had needs, too. He was impulsive, brash, and overzealous. Behind his veneer of bravado and pride, he was hiding insecurities of his own.

The Reality Hits Home

After nearly a month of marriage, both began to realize that much more was going on inside the other than they had bargained for. One night, after an evening out with friends, they stayed up talking about how inferior she felt in public settings. Her questions about her worth stunned him. He couldn't believe that this beautiful woman, his wife, could possibly feel that way about herself. He had absolute confidence in her.

After several of these late-evening chats, he finally realized that his wife really did have serious self-doubts. In fact, her withdrawn behavior at social gatherings puzzled him. He silently questioned, *Why does she retreat into her protective shell of silence, when I feel so comfortable with people? Why can't she be like me?*

A Fork in the Road

That young couple was us. And the year was 1972. As we began our marriage, we had critical choices to make. Would Dennis accept Barbara fully and love her during her periods of self-doubt? Or would he join her when she put herself down? Would Dennis be vulnerable and risk being known by a young woman who might reject him? The choices were real. The decisions were tough. Fortunately, we made more right choices than wrong ones.

In retrospect, we believe those days were among the most crucial in our marriage. During those initial months, we laid the foundations of acceptance and the patterns of response for our marriage. As our fears and insecurities surfaced, we also discovered the critical importance of a healthy, positive self-concept to a marriage. We began to recognize the magnitude of the responsibility we each carried in building up or tearing down the other's self-esteem. We both began to see that our own self-image either crippled or completed our marriage relationship.

The Natural Nature of Relationships

A letter that recently came across our desk further illustrates the need for each of us to build our mate's self-esteem. This wife and mother shared with us how her eight-year-old son brought healing to hurts her mate had caused.

MY SON BENJIE IS SUCH A LEADER AND ENCOURAGEMENT. Today is his birthday and he arranged for an old man who lives across the street to buy him a rose. He gave it to me tonight. When I asked what it was

for, he replied, "Today is my birthday and I'm glad you're my Mom."
Now you see what keeps me going—this little man in my life patches
the breaks that the big man causes.

Here was a woman who had experienced rejection, rather than
acceptance, from her husband. Instead of her marriage strengthening
her self-esteem, as God intended, her husband's contempt created the
need for an eight-year-old boy's thoughtful gesture of a rose.

Why aren't we better at building each other's self-esteem? Why is
it so difficult to provide an atmosphere of acceptance for our mates?
In seeking answers to these questions, we studied the conditions in our
world that we believe are largely responsible for the present epidemic
of poor self-esteem. Your mate's evaluation of his self-worth is affected
by four current social trends.

1. A Self-Seeking Culture

We live in a culture of self-fulfillment. Modern men and women
seem more focused on finding individual identity than at any point in
history. Yet to most people, a positive and healthy self-identity
remains an elusive butterfly. We have a restless, self-indulgent society
whose members often use each other to gain the acceptance they feel
they deserve. As a result, we feel used and not genuinely needed,
valued, or appreciated. The sad admission of the late Cristina Onassis,
daughter of the late Greek shipping magnate, Aristotle Onassis, illustrates this feeling of rejection: "My most fervent wish is that I shall
meet a man who loves me for myself and not my money."

People such as Ms. Onassis (and perhaps your mate) feel used
because performance and possessions have become the ultimate
measurement of worth and value. Society applauds people for what
they have *done* and what they have *acquired* but seldom gives an
ovation for who they *are*. Our culture says that self-esteem is built
on self-achievement. We feel we must be production-minded, so
we generally don't cultivate relationships that foster feelings of

8

lasting significance. As a result, we are being "driven" in the wrong direction by a wrong standard of value. (We will look at right values in chapter 4.)

2. Fractured Families

We live in a social structure that also is rocked, if not ripped apart, by divorce. If your mate's parents are not divorced, most likely someone else close to him is. You both certainly feel the effects of a nation plagued with a high divorce rate. A Chinese proverb says, "In the broken nest there are no whole eggs." Broken homes generally do not produce whole people.

It's not that those who come from broken homes do not have great worth. They do. But much like an earthquake, a divorce is followed by years of emotional aftershocks—especially in children. The tremors of fear, anger, and guilt all rumble on, internally deteriorating a young person's self-image. For years, a child may have no idea how long this broken relationship has created internal fissures and fractures in his identity.

Children are affected not only by legal divorce within the family but by emotional divorce as well. Emotional divorce occurs when a husband and wife decide just to "live together," settling for a mediocre marriage. We believe this problem is much more extensive than divorce itself. Even some Christian marriages, it seems, are contaminated with dangerously low, nominal commitments. As a result, the children suffer deeply. An African proverb says it best: "When the elephants fight, it's the grass that suffers."

3. The Fading of Dignity in Marriage

For the better part of three decades there has been a growing disillusionment with the dignity of marriage. The traditional marital relationship is under attack and suspicion, and our civil courts have reduced to rubble the nobility and sacredness of the marriage vows. Because marriage has been robbed of the honor given it by God in the

9

Scriptures, husbands and wives often believe they must look elsewhere for the personal fulfillment and encouragement that builds self-esteem.

Yet marriage hasn't failed, people have.

Because people have failed, marriage has received far too much negative press. Many people have erroneously concluded that marriage itself is the culprit.

The perception of marriage as a consecrated estate has been tarnished by the views of others. One such view is that of Gloria Steinem, who has been an instigator of the attack on marriage. She says, "For the sake of those who wish to live in equal partnership, we must abolish and reform the institution of marriage."[3] This philosophy can cause married couples to feel insignificant, as though they are trapped in a dying institution. The self-esteem of both you and your mate may be bruised by such antagonistic ideologies.

4. Unequipped Brides and Grooms

No athletic team with good judgment would spend most of its budget, energy, or time on a magnificent pregame show and spend little or none on training and preparation. Yet couples today spend an inordinate amount of time and thousands of dollars on the wedding ceremony and very little time or money—if any—on how to complete the cross-country run called marriage. Thus, they are unequipped to meet the unique needs of their mates.

Rather than being able to accept and build up their spouses, these couples generally are burdened by their own fears and insecurities. Under the influence of our culture, and carrying a self-image and value of marriage largely determined by parents, these men and women march off into lifelong relationships with partners who are equally ill-prepared. Weighed down by the past and confused by cultural trends and values, couples are increasingly unqualified to deal with the complex issues surrounding their mates' needs for self-worth. We are convinced that this need to be equipped with the biblical blueprints for building a marriage is why our FamilyLife Marriage Conferences have had over a half million people in attendance since 1976. (For information on these conferences, see address at the end of this chapter.)

The following story illustrates what can happen when a couple enters marriage unprepared.

A Model Christian Couple?

Based on all outward appearances, Laura and Mark were a model couple. With an apparently happy marriage, they enjoyed the benefits of social acceptance in one of the most prestigious neighborhoods in the city, an enormously successful business, and three beautiful, healthy children. Their personal, balanced involvement in an out-standing church formed the wall of protection around their lives. Nothing was missing. Everything seemed to be going their way.

So, imagine the shock when Laura asked us for help. She described her life and their marriage as a "mockery." "We have no relationship," she said. "We can't relax. And the only thing we ever talk about is my husband's business.

"I feel Mark is committed to the marriage, but not to me. He just doesn't want to take on any responsibility at home, especially when it comes to me and my needs.

"I have a growing bitterness toward his work. I see him giving the best of his leadership there. Organizing, planning, and motivating people . . . he's the best. But at home it's another matter. And with me, well, I feel he is growing indifferent. I feel terribly insecure because I don't feel he needs me. As a result, I've grown very critical of him, and of everything he does."

Later, I (Dennis) spent some time with Mark, who admitted that he had not made his marriage a priority. "I never tore her down—I guess I just neglected her. I didn't see why I should open up to her with my problems because she had her own problems. I was in the process of getting my business settled. After we were set financially, I

11

planned to cash in on my family." With a despairing shrug, he added, "Suddenly, it dawned on me there wasn't going to be any relationship at home. I wouldn't have my wife to fall back on.

"As time went on, I grew more and more independent. We became isolated. I watched Laura become fearful and increasingly insecure. She was scared to death, and I wasn't certain I knew how to deal with all of her newly developed insecurities. Her shaky confidence began to infect me. I began to feel shackled by her clingy dependence and need for approval. She became a weight instead of a wife. I lost all desire to build her up."

Mark concluded, "I realize now that our marriage license did not make a marriage. It only gave us the *right* to begin building one."

Laura summed up her feelings, "We're just two outwardly successful people doing our own thing, but independent of one another. *Our marriage consists of each of us trying to get the other to meet our own needs, each waiting for the other to take the first step.*"

Building Your Mate

In these confessions of a successful twentieth-century couple, we find the wife saying, "He's committed to the marriage, but not to me," and "I don't feel needed." Then the husband says, "I didn't see why I should open up to her with my problems . . . she had enough of her own," and "I wasn't sure I knew how to deal with her fears." These admissions are like windows, letting us peek into an outwardly strong house to see the insecurity, fear, and isolation inside. Sadly, many people have come to accept these feelings in marriage as a part of life—like the common cold.

This scene is being played over and over and over, in thousands of Christian marriages today. Perhaps you, like both of us, entered marriage plagued by some degree of personal self-doubt and insecurity, but you carefully masked it behind performance and intense romantic

12

feelings. When your mate's weaknesses surfaced, you felt overwhelmed and at a loss as to what to do.

Often, couples instinctively turn *on* each other, rather than courageously turning *to* each other in order to build confidence and security. Instead of the marriage relationship being a haven in the storm, it becomes the storm itself. Pounded and drenched on the outside by the continual downpour of society's attacks, the marriage now faces a problem of flooding from within. With both partners insecure in their self-esteem and afraid to reach out, they retreat and wait. Unfortunately, many of these marriages ultimately drown and become divorce statistics. And far too many Christian marriages settle for a "negotiated and friendly" emotional divorce.

A Message with Hope

Snoopy, the cherished Peanuts cartoon pet, sat droopy-eyed at the entrance of his dog house. He lamented, "Yesterday I was a dog. Today I'm a dog. Tomorrow I'll probably be a dog. *Sigh*. There's so little hope for advancement!"

Perhaps you feel like Snoopy—hopeless, with very little hope for any change in your mate or yourself. "*Sigh*. There's no hope for my mate in this area." Or, "I'll always be a person with these limitations." You may think your mate's self-image is like hardened cement. It can change, however. Cement can be broken out and repoured, but it takes love, commitment, and diligence.

There is hope. Each of us can overcome failures, past and present. That is one of the encouragements for us as Christians. There is always the potential for change. God has not left us to drift aimlessly without hope or power. The Scriptures offer a powerful promise: "For nothing will be impossible with God."[4] That's exactly what we've experienced in our marriage! Growth and hope. Although it has been difficult at times, we wouldn't trade the growth we've seen in each other's lives for any other satisfaction.

You and your mate *can* experience that, too. We believe your marriage, like ours, provides one of the best possible relationships in which two people can build into one another's lives. The ten building blocks we will share with you will give you the practical help you've needed to see your mate's confidence quotient soar. But first you must understand how your mate established his self-esteem.

For a free brochure and more information on a FamilyLife Marriage Conference near you, contact:

> FamilyLife
> P. O. Box 23840
> Little Rock, AR 72221-3840
> 1-800-999-8663

CHAPTER

2

Slaying the Phantom

———◆———

- *What Is a Phantom?*
- *The Origins of Phantoms*
- *What Is a Self-Image?*
- *The Centrality of Self-Image*
- *Your Mate Needs You*
- *Esteem Builder Projects*

———◆———

E ARLY ON A CRISP SEPTEMBER MORNING *in* 1944, two
cyclists taking cover in a small French town near the Luxembourg
border decided that it was safe at last to venture out into the
countryside. . . . The nighttime rumble of tanks had died away. So the men
mounted up and swept along the road that passed the bivouac. They sniffed
the smoke of cooking fires in the cold autumn air. They noted the usual
scattering of grimy, mud-stained vehicles, partly hidden under tattered
camouflage nets: a couple of trucks, some trailers and a few, big M-4 tanks
with their mighty guns poking out from the cover of trees and netting.

Then, a young American sentry stopped the pair. He was friendly
enough, but firm. They must explain where they were going and why.
The Frenchmen replied as well as they could until, all at once, they
stiffened and fell silent, their eyes wide in astonishment. For over the
sentry's shoulder they saw four GIs in muddy battle jackets and dull-

green helmets walk over to a monstrous tank and, with one man at each corner, simply pick it up, turn it around and set it down again. Thus . . . was the cover of the 603rd Engineer Camouflage Battalion broken and the security of a neighboring armored division imperiled during a critical moment in the Allied offensive. Fortunately, no damage was done.

The 603rd was one of four units that formed what was perhaps the most enigmatic outfit ever fielded in battle, a group called the 23rd Headquarters Special Troops. The 23rd's troops were "special" all right. They specialized in impersonating other troops. . . .With inflatable rubber guns and vehicles, with ever-changing shoulder patches, stencils to make phony signs, and with amplified recordings of heavy equipment in action, the 23rd played role after role. . . .

The purpose of all that razzle-dazzle was to fool the enemy and, by doing so, enable the troops that the 23rd was impersonating to sneak into new positions, to launch a surprise attack, or in some other way to catch the other side off guard.[1]

Forty years ago this phantom division played a role in Germany's defeat. With careful staging and show-business theatrics, they impersonated real troops and created an illusion of military strength. The Germans were fooled and confused. The 23rd was successful.

"Confused" and "fooled" may describe what your mate feels today when he thinks about himself, his identity, and the roles he must play. Unsure of the answers to basic questions such as "Who am I?" and "Am I important or valuable?" your mate, as was the German army during World War II, may be deceived by phantoms and therefore is not living successfully as God intended.

What Is a Phantom?

By definition, a phantom is an illusion—an apparition, or a resemblance of reality. Normally we associate phantoms with Halloween, but did you know that each of us carries a "phantom" within us?

Within your mind you have a picture of how you should act as a husband or wife, father or mother. And, chances are, this image is so perfect, so idyllic, that it is *completely unattainable.* Yet, every day you judge your performance by this phantom! And since you cannot match those standards, your self-esteem suffers.

Barbara sat down one day and described her phantom in writing. Here are the characteristics of this perfect wife and mother:

- She is always loving, patient, and understanding.
- She is well-organized, maintaining a perfect balance between discipline and flexibility.
- Her house is always neat and well-decorated, so she is never embarrassed if friends drop by unexpectedly.
- Her children drop whatever they are doing and obey her every command.
- She never gets angry with her children, even when they forget to do their chores.
- She is serious yet lighthearted, submissive but not passive.
- She is energetic and never tired, even after getting up five times during the night to tend her children.
- She reaches out to her neighbors and takes meals to the sick and needy.
- She looks fresh and attractive at all times, whether in jeans and a sweater, while digging in the garden, or in a silk dress going out to dinner.
- Her hair always does what she wants it to do, and it's never flat.
- Her fingernails are never broken.
- She always plans healthy, balanced meals for her family and bakes everything from scratch. She would never dream of feeding her family prepared foods such as canned ravioli, frozen pizza, or cheap hot dogs.

- She never gets sick, lonely, or discouraged.
- She walks faithfully with God every day, and studies and memorizes Scripture.
- She prays "without ceasing." She prays over flat tires, lost keys, lost teddy bears, and lost blankets. She gives thanks for a husband who is late for dinner and for her son's tennis shoes which the neighbor's dog just chewed up.
- She is never fearful or inhibited about telling others about Christ and speaking the truth to someone who may be in error.

Quite an impressive list, isn't it? With a phantom like that, is it any wonder that it's easy for Barbara to feel like a failure as a wife and mom?

Now look at the list Dennis compiled of the phantom husband and father:

- He rises early, reads the Bible and prays, then jogs several miles.
- After breakfast, he presents a flawless fifteen-minute devotional to his attentive, adoring wife and children.
- Never forgetting to hug and kiss his wife good-bye, he arrives at work ten minutes early.
- He is consistently patient with his co-workers, always content with his job, and devises creative solutions to problems. He works hard, and never wastes time. His desk is never cluttered, and he is confidently in control at all times.
- He is well-read in world events, politics, and important social issues.
- He is a handyman around the house and loves to build things for his family.
- He arrives home from work on time every day and never turns down a request to play catch with his boys.
- He obeys all traffic laws and never speeds, even if he's late for a meeting.

- He is popular with everyone he meets and never tires of people or of helping them in time of need.
- He can quote large sections of Scripture in a single bound, has faith more powerful than a locomotive, and is faster than a speeding bullet when solving family conflicts.
- He never gets discouraged, never wants to quit, and always has the right words for any circumstance.
- His closets are never cluttered.
- He always keeps his garage neat. He never loses things, always flosses his teeth, and has no trouble with his weight.
- And he has time to fish.

The crazy thing about a phantom is that, even though we know we can never live up to this perfect image, we still tear ourselves down when we fail!

The Origins of Phantoms

Where do phantoms come from? They don't appear overnight, as the American 23rd battalion did. Each phantom slowly grows from the seeds of our individual experience.

Our phantoms come from expectations placed on us by parents, peers, employers, coaches, and teachers in school and Sunday school. Dorothy Corkille Briggs, in her classic work, *Your Child's Self-Esteem*, wrote, "Children rarely question [their parents'] expectations; instead, they question their personal inadequacy."[2] Like a child with his parents, your mate typically doesn't question the phantom. Innocently, he accepts the lofty standards and ideals of the phantom just as he accepted his parents' standards and expectations when he was a little child.

Phantoms, with their unattainable attributes, also develop through comparisons. Have you, for example, ever compared your marriage with someone else's? Have you ever compared your mate with someone else's mate? Have you ever compared yourself with someone else? All of us probably have made such comparisons, but when we compare ourselves or our mates to others, we develop unrealistic expectations that we can't attain. These faulty comparisons can be fueled by friends, employers, ourselves, or our mates.

When we make comparisons, we are a bit like Lucy, who one day said to her famous cartoon buddy, "You are a foul ball in the line drive of life, Charlie Brown!" Making comparisons with what we feel is normal and acceptable only makes the unattainable phantom more intimidating. Because he doesn't always compare favorably, your mate concludes that he is a foul ball.

Phantoms come from many other sources as well, including advertisements. Some of you may remember the jingle that went with the ad for a perfume called "Enjolie." It showed a professional young woman at home who was singing these words: "I can bring home the bacon, fry it up in a pan, and never, never let you forget you're a man."

Phantoms like that have colored the thinking of many women today. They hear similar advertisements and messages and think, *Well, I can do it all! I can do all of those things. That's what I should be doing.*

Personal convictions that arise from observing others also feed our ever-growing phantoms.

Perhaps, for example, your wife watches people she admires and assigns the character and personality traits, abilities, and talents she envies most to her phantom. She also may observe the negative side of other women and conclude, "I will never do that." Another standard— that of never failing—is added to the phantom.

The problem of your mate comparing his life with another is that it ordinarily is done from a distance and when the other person is generally at his best. Since your mate is acutely aware of his own flaws and shortcomings, he further depreciates his value by focusing on the apparent best of the other person. Consequently, your mate is destined to feel like a loser even though he may be a winner.

Phantoms can crush your relationship. Since your mate's phantom—the result of his comparisons and others' expectations—is unreachable, your mate experiences failure. These failures stand tall in the corridors of your mate's mind, continually reminding him of his deficiencies. These failures, added together with his successes in life, produce another mental concept—your mate's self-image.

What Is a Self-Image?

Self-image, self-esteem, self-concept—these three terms are used to describe not only how your mate mentally *sees* himself, but how he *feels* about himself and what value and sense of worth he has internally.

Norman Wright, in his book, *Improving Your Self-Image*, writes, "The image we have of ourself is built upon clusters of many memories."[3] Each of us has developed this image over time. Wright continues, "Very early in life we begin to form concepts and attitudes about ourself, other people, and the world. Our self-concept is actually a cluster of attitudes about ourself—some favorable and some unfavorable."[4]

Like a police department's composite sketch of a criminal suspect, your mate's self-esteem is a composite drawing acquired from various sources and firsthand accounts. But the drawing is not a black-and-white, one-dimensional, charcoal sketch. It is a full-color, three-dimensional painting with feelings, a portrait with stereophonic music.

What kind of self-portrait has your mate painted? What kind of music does he hear? Do you really know? When the music of self-doubt is not playing, your mate feels confident, secure, and relaxed. But when the voice and emotions of failure blare in your mate's ears, the self-condemnation can cause paralysis. Feelings of tension, fear, and insecurity can control the way he thinks about himself and his life. Are you aware of what causes these feelings in your mate's life?

Perhaps, however, your mate is so steady that you rarely see him vacillate between confidence and insecurity. The temptation is to assume that he hears no negative music. But your mate may have learned early in life to compensate for feelings of inadequacy by covering them with the appearance that all is well. Inside he may have become accustomed to hearing the condemning music, but he rarely lets you know how he truly feels. Afraid of the rejection of others, he listens to the monotonous, accusing music alone.

Outwardly, his performance may even be flawless, as though he has no needs. Inwardly, however, his secret, inner desire is to have you rescue him by turning off the negative recording and replacing the disk with pleasant music that communicates "well done" or "you are accepted as you are." *His real need is to be built up and loved for who he is.*

We cannot divorce these two: what he thinks about himself (his self-portrait) and his feelings about himself (the accompanying music). They are inseparably linked. They are your mate's self-image. He lives with the music playing and the painting in place. It hangs in the museum of his mind and emotions as either a priceless and original collector's item or as a cheap imitation, accompanied with feelings of worthlessness and insignificance.

The Centrality of Self-Image

Your mate's self-image is central to all he is and everything he does. It will either hinder or enhance his ability to learn, make decisions, take risks, and resolve conflicts with you and others. Your spouse's self-image will either restrain him or refuel him.

Yet in spite of its importance, your mate may not understand how his self-esteem colors all that he does: his behavior, his relationships, and his performance. For some, it is painful even to admit that they have needs in this area.

But they do have needs.

Thomas Fuller said, "A danger foreseen is half avoided." Certainly, admitting your self-image inadequacies to one another is the beginning step to real healing and new intimacy in your marriage.

Your Mate Needs You

Your mate, like the Germans, may have lived in fear for years under the looming shadow of the phantom. Possibly both of you have begun to perceive how the impostor has masqueraded as a reality in your lives, intimidating you almost daily. This, coupled with painful experiences, often results in a poor self-image.

Your mate needs your objective eye and listening ear to help affirm him when he is okay and to correct him when he is in error. Some of the ideals your mate has lumped together in the phantom may not be bad standards. Your mate may merely need your help in balancing the demands of life with those ideals.

The "Esteem Builder Project" at the end of this chapter will assist you in helping your mate slay the phantom and replace negative experiences and images with positive ones. The following two chapters will provide foundational help in building your mate's self-esteem. Chapter 3, "Detecting the Clues," will strengthen your understanding of why your mate acts the way he does. Chapter 4, "Nine Laws that Liberate," will provide some universal precepts that will give you hope as you begin setting your mate free from the shackles of a poor self-image.

Esteem Builder Projects: Essential to Application

The object of Bible study is changed lives. The Christian world is suffering from a deficiency of Vitamin A—Application.

—Dr. Howard G. Hendricks
Dallas Theological Seminary

The objective of this book is to build marriages, not minds. There is a tendency to assume that learning facts and gaining knowledge is the solution, but marriages are built by couples who *apply God's Word together*.

Our hope is that you will convert God's truth into godly behavior. *Building Your Mate's Self-Esteem* is packed with knowledge and information, but your marriage will benefit only if you incorporate the truths into your daily life. We have attempted to emphasize a healthy balance between instruction and application by including "Esteem Building Projects" at the conclusion of nearly every chapter.

The object is to make your marriage all that God intended it to be. These projects are a critical part of that process. Commit yourselves to interact on these projects, and you will build your mate's self-esteem.

ESTEEM BUILDER PROJECT

(Use a sheet of paper if necessary.)

1. Explain to your mate the concept of the phantom, and then ask him to describe his ideal self. Jot down his descriptions and discuss them. Which ones are appropriate and worth working to achieve? Which ones are unrealistic?

2. How has the phantom affected your mate's self-esteem? Ask your mate how he wants you to help him when his phantom is on parade. Discuss this as a couple.

3. Ask your mate to describe what he thinks and how he feels about himself. Record the words he uses. Which are "thinking"

words and which are "feeling" words? Notice any clues that reveal the impact his phantom has on his self-image. This may take some time; be patient and ask plenty of questions.

4. Ask your mate to share with you one way you can be a completer, not a crippler, of his self-esteem. What does he *need* you to do today?

3

Detecting the Clues

———◆———

- *Ten Clues to an Inadequate Self-Esteem*
- *You Are God's Arms of Love*
- *Esteem Builder Project*

———◆———

*A*S A YOUNG GIRL, one of my (Barbara's) favorite pastimes was reading. I spent several summers inching my way up a thermometer in my local library's book-reading contest. Often my mother found me curled up in a hand-me-down chair, or nestled in a corner halfway up the carpeted stairs, with my nose in a book. I was hopelessly lost in those pages, imagining myself a player in the unfolding drama. I didn't like coming back to reality; it was much too boring compared to the adventures of Nancy Drew.

I followed Nancy on most of her heroic adventures and grew in my appreciation of the fine art of careful observation and cautious conclusion-drawing. Other renowned sleuths, such as Sherlock Holmes and, more recently, Agatha Christie's Miss Marple and Hercule Poirot, are also famous because of their eye for detail. They always seem to find the clues needed to solve the mystery.

Just as those super sleuths look beyond the obvious for hints, so you must learn to piece together the hidden and ambiguous clues, along with those your mate conspicuously reveals, in order to solve the mystery of where and how to build his self-esteem.

Becoming a detective does not require donning a khaki trench coat with a turned-up collar and tiptoeing around with a magnifying glass. But it does require some training in observation. You need to look and listen, to evaluate the evidence at hand, and to search for hidden clues. These clues lead you to information that is critical in building your mate's self-esteem.

Ten Clues to an Inadequate Self-Esteem

Silently lurking in the closets and attic of your mate's past and present life are dozens of clues that signal insecurity, fearfulness, or low self-confidence, all of which result from poor self-esteem. You probably have already recognized that your mate has needs in this area, or you wouldn't be reading this book. This chapter will help you better understand your mate and build him up in the areas he needs it most.

The following ten clues will help you understand the origins of your mate's phantom and the experiences that helped to shape his self-esteem. Look closely and listen carefully, for your mate's sake.

Clue 1. Your mate's childhood was marked by parental abuse, parental neglect, parental ignorance, or parents who exercised overbearing authority.

What is your mate's family background? Did his father and mother clearly love each other and their children? Was your mate encouraged as a child? Did his parents instill confidence and a sense of worth and value? Did they believe in him and express it frequently? Were his parents involved in his life? Was he left to cope on his own? Was she abandoned emotionally as she grew up?

Parade magazine featured an interview with comedian Steve Allen and his wife, Jayne Meadows, on their many years together in marriage.

Much of the article focused on Steve's unstable family background. In a final comment, Jayne said, "We are who we are because of where we've been."[1]

Steve Allen came from a family of cynics on the vaudeville circuit. He was left alone and often neglected. He learned to use his natural sense of humor to cover up his deep loneliness and feelings of rejection. Allen's life illustrates the truth that our background largely determines what we will become in personality and, more importantly, in self-esteem.

Your mate's self-esteem is a result of where he has been too. His parents may have been too permissive, too smothering, too strict, too religious, or worse yet, abusive or neglectful. Imagine what your spouse's life was like as he was growing up. How did he feel? How would you have responded in similar circumstances?

If his parents are still living, listen carefully to the way they communicate with their adult child. It may be difficult, but chances are the old patterns of relating are still intact.

Encourage your mate as you begin to learn about his home life. Empathize with him and tell him it hurts you, too, to know that he experienced emotional pain as a child. Your husband or wife needs you to listen and care. But be careful not to become critical of his parents or peers for what they did or did not do. Blaming others does not relieve the problem; it can only increase it by adding the burden of a resentful spirit, which can enslave you and your mate. Give his parents the benefit of the doubt. Assume they did the best they could with what they knew.

Clue 2. Your mate fears opening up, being real, and being vulnerable with you and with others.

Fear is usually embedded in a poor self-esteem. We fear a host of things, yet for many of us the greatest is the fear of rejection. For example, your mate may fear failure or appearing stupid, forgetful, or insensitive. All of these can become grounds for rejection by another—usually someone important or close to him.

The more fears your mate has, the less open he will be in relationships. If the words *withdrawn* and *unexpressive* describe your mate, that's a clue to his insecurity—the blight of actual or perceived rejections in his past. Your mate may be fearful of being known and afraid of being rejected.

Be careful of communicating rejection to your mate in any way, especially if he is not naturally transparent. He may be trying to open up, yet you may fuel the very rejection he fears. Instead, seek to understand him. Ask yourself, *Why is my mate fearful?* Maybe he feels he has tried to be open and it didn't work. Feeling misunderstood, he has given up. You may need to ask his forgiveness for adding to his problem.

What a fearful person needs most from his mate is to be received gently in love when he attempts to express himself. He needs to be heard. Recognize that his fears are real, no matter how inconsequential they may seem to you. To be ignored can make him feel uncared for and unimportant.

James 1:19 says it this way: "Let every one be quick to hear, slow to speak and slow to anger." This is great advice for everyone, but especially for the marriage partner who tends to talk rather than to listen.

In marriage, a delicate balance between being open and stopping to listen must be maintained. The climate of acceptance should be such that each partner feels free to share his thoughts, feelings, and questions without fear of rejection.

If your mate is fearful, it is your responsibility to create quiet, non-threatening, unhurried times for the two of you to be together. Don't be afraid of silence. When your mate does open up, listen and ponder his words. Think about your reply before you give it, and thank him for sharing with you. You may have no idea how deep-seated and painful his fears really are.

Clue 3. Your mate gets discouraged easily.

A mate who is easily discouraged is communicating, "I don't have confidence in my ability. I'm afraid I'll fail. So if I don't try, I won't experience defeat."

What this person needs is a loving, understanding cheerleader to come alongside him and believe the best. As you support your mate, ask questions to help you discover what discourages him and why this pattern is a part of his life. What real or imagined failures in your mate's experiences have led him to develop this facet of his self-esteem?

Clue 4. Your mate lacks confidence, especially in decision making.

Making decisions, especially the critical ones, is difficult for anyone, but for some it can be an excruciating experience. A person who has large doses of self-doubt rarely trusts his own judgment in decision making. Perhaps over-controlling parents made most of his decisions for him, and he never developed a track record of trust in his own decision-making ability. Possibly he was ridiculed for making poor decisions and early in life chose to let others decide for him.

Regardless of the cause, decision making in any area becomes risky when a person has self-doubt and little confidence. Frequently he becomes a follower and finds safety and security in flowing with the crowd.

Here is an opportunity to observe and understand sympathetically so you can come alongside him and begin to rebuild the crumbled wall of confidence. Don't rush in and make all his decisions for him, rescuing him from the pain and, therefore, the risk of a wrong decision. Encourage him to decide and help him in the process. When he is thinking clearly and headed for an accurate decision, verbally praise him for his insight and reasoning. If he makes a poor decision, don't chide him or reject his efforts. Tell him you're proud that he stepped out and decided. Put his decision into perspective. Most decisions are not irreversible or life-threatening.

On one occasion I (Dennis) asked Barbara why she didn't go ahead and discipline one of our six children for what was (to me) clear disobedience. When Barbara responded that she wasn't confident of her judgment, I was semi-shocked! "You're a great mom," I told her. "And your batting average is far better than you are giving yourself credit for. Trust your judgment and decide—God will lead you."

Later Barbara shared with me how encouraging it was to have me believe in her. I was reminded, again, of our need to continually build one another up.

Above all, be patient. A person who does not feel competent in the decision-making process will take an inordinate amount of time to decide. Until he has established a track record of good choices and feels good about himself, you can expect the process to take some time. You may need to remind your mate that to make no decision is often worse than making the wrong decision. Above all, give your mate the freedom to make wrong decisions.

Clue 5. Your mate has difficulty admitting he is wrong, always needs to be right, or is unable to forgive.

We may mentally label this mate as prideful or arrogant, but rarely do we see him as being insecure. Pride gives the air of confidence and great ability. But this person is like a sheep in wolf's clothing. His inability to admit mistakes and ask forgiveness is a mask of protection that covers a fearful self-image. Rather than hide his low self-esteem by being a follower, this individual projects the take-charge, confident exterior he wishes were true internally.

Samuel Butler said, "There is no mistake so great as that of being always right." If your mate has a need always to be right, you know the truth of that statement. It's tough to live with someone like this, and it can create in you a growing feeling of not being able to measure up or of always being wrong.

Give your mate freedom to be who he is. Ask God to give you sympathetic understanding. Maybe as a child, your mate was always told he was wrong, even when he wasn't. Perhaps he felt inferior or was bullied by an older brother or sister. Alone and feeling unworthy, consciously or subconsciously, he may have thought, *Someday I won't have to be wrong anymore.* Perhaps your mate feels that to be wrong is to be a failure, and to admit that is simply too threatening to his needy ego.

Give your mate unconditional acceptance. Never correct him publicly or in front of your children. Be sensitive and advise him privately; he won't feel nearly as threatened with only you in the room. And pray that God will use you to help soften his abrasive attitude.

Clue 6. Your mate is a driven person.

"Drivenness" is a term widely used today to describe individuals who are high achievers outwardly because they are driven inwardly by a deep need for approval. This is a growing problem in our fast-paced culture. A television commercial shows an investments man staying up all hours of the night and getting up before dawn "working for you," and projecting an image of success and prosperity. Another advertisement shows well-dressed, young, urban professionals dashing in and out of taxis, glancing at their watches, looking like VIPs. These vignettes subtly communicate what the insecure person wants most—a sense of importance, of being needed, of having value.

This inner need for significance and personal worth causes people to be driven. They are seeking to gain value through performance, whether it be in the arena of politics, career, athletics, the ministry, or motherhood.

Many who have achieved financial success still feel that they have a long way to go. J. D. Rockefeller, when asked how much money would be enough for him, replied, "One more dollar than I have." Something kept driving him to earn more money, but he never felt satisfied

The symptoms of this common affliction include constant activity—endless meetings, appointments, and emergencies only the driven person can handle. The driven man or woman is habitually overscheduled and usually afraid to say no. Because he gains his importance from others, he becomes a slave to others' opinions. Security and significance, he believes, are to be earned by performance. The driven person won't stop to rest or think. Relationships suffer because there is no time left for them. His life is unbalanced.

Driven people seek the praise of others to affirm their own worth. The problem is, they usually get it. But that acceptance is based on performance and production. It's what they *do*, not who they *are*. *The more they do, the more praise they receive.* But as writer Sidney Harris says, "Self-achievement is no guarantee of self-acceptance."

If your mate is driven or has tendencies to be driven, what he needs most is your acceptance and praise for who he is as a person, apart from his performance. Don't become part of the problem by kindling your mate's need to perform. If you praise him only when he does well and communicate discouragement when he fails, then you are telling your mate that he is acceptable only when he is achieving something important, which is what he has been telling himself for years.

A driven mate needs you to bring balance to a life that is most likely out of control. Help him with his scheduling. Help him say *no* at least once a day. Help him understand how continual overcommitments only increase his chances of failure and can add to his feelings of inadequacy. Help him determine the true measure of success in life.

Clue 7. Your mate is critical of others.

Criticizing others and frequently passing judgment on how things are done or handled are clues to a poor self-esteem. Hiding behind this critical spirit is a self-image trying to lift itself up by pulling others down. It says: "My idea was better" or "My way would have worked" or "I could have done a better job if I'd had the chance." These thoughts and comments are your mate's attempts to give value to his inner person at the expense of others.

Help your mate by being on his team but not taking sides. Help him see the other side without defecting to the other team. And don't join him in becoming critical. Tearing down others yourself will not build your mate's self-esteem; it will only support his weakness.

Clue 8. Your mate is a perfectionist.

A perfectionist is compelled to have things just so, perfectly ordered. He tends to be inflexible with himself and with others. He works hard and accomplishes much, but is rarely satisfied with his work or with himself.

By striving for perfection, he is looking for acceptance and, thereby, inner tranquility. But an orderly life usually eludes him. Because of his high standards, he is especially enslaved to a mental phantom of what he should be. Some people have such perfectionistic standards that if they perform up to the qualifications of their phantoms, they quickly raise the standards even higher. They create "ultra phantoms" and call themselves failures for not achieving the new standards.

Your mate may be too concerned about orderliness, correct grammar, personal appearance and beauty, home decorating, hard work, or financial success. Many of the world's most beautiful people are inwardly the most insecure. Women whose homes are immaculate and look as if they came out of the pages of *House Beautiful* often apologize when you drop in because "the house is a mess."

Perfectionists have difficulty savoring the satisfaction of a job well done. They're always thinking, *I could have done better*, or *I didn't try hard enough*. And they sometimes distrust the authentic praise of others.

Does your mate see himself as a failure in some area, even though outwardly you and others think that he's doing a good job? Are there areas in which he pushes himself and other areas that don't seem to matter as much?

Once again, understanding will allow you to see in your mate a child who was not given complete approval, but was told, "That's nice, but you can do better. Why don't you try again?" Most likely he grew up feeling like a failure academically, physically, athletically, socially, or in whatever area complete approval was withheld. Your perfectionistic mate rarely enjoyed the solid satisfaction of a job well done.

Help your mate believe the truth: that his accomplishments are excellent and that he can do well. Encourage him to relax even though everything is not perfectly ordered. Stop and enjoy his accomplishments with him. Together, seek to understand where he has been in order to unlock the *why* behind his present behavior.

Clue 9. Your mate is self-critical.

Closely akin to perfectionism is the voice of self-depreciation. Continually criticizing himself, the mate who harbors a poor self-esteem desperately seeks approval. Just as this need for approval is the force behind a perfectionist's high standards and hard work, so the same need is the source of endless and varied negative comments about himself. Statements such as, "I can't do anything right," "I'm not very talented," or "I'm not very good at . . ." are clues.

Other signals sent through the fog of bad feelings about self are "fishing-for-compliments" statements. Your mate may ask, "Do you like the way I look in my new dress?" or "How do you like the way I arranged my office?" Are those the real questions? Is your mate looking for your objective opinion, or is your mate secretly hoping for a dose of genuine approval?

Another sign of self-depreciation is difficulty in receiving gifts and compliments. If your mate doesn't feel worthy as a person, he won't feel worthy of material or verbal gifts. He will somehow belittle the gift to make it more appropriate, saying something like, "You shouldn't have," or "This is too much." He might respond to a compliment with, "That's not true," or "You don't really mean that."

Perhaps your mate is self-conscious. He tends to wonder what others are thinking about him. He imagines all eyes are focused on him, and he fears he will stumble. He questions his appearance, his conversational skills, and his mannerisms. He may be acutely aware of every physical blemish.

Gently correct your mate's inaccurate self-assessments. You may grow weary of hearing his negative thoughts about himself, but continue to accept him, affirm him, and praise him for who he is.

Your mate needs to know that those physical characteristics he doesn't like about himself don't matter to you, and that the personality or character traits he dislikes don't affect your love and acceptance of his worth. Offer to help your mate in areas that do need change, but never withhold genuine acceptance. Your mate's self-esteem needs acceptance and love if it is to grow.

Clue 10. Your mate indulges in escapism.

The other day a bumper sticker caught our attention: "Reality is for those who can't cope with drugs."

What a sad commentary on our culture today. We have learned to avoid facing the real issues in life through various means of escape. Your mate may escape from reality through food, material possessions, entertainment, drugs, or alcohol.

Fearful of dealing with inconsistencies, personality defects, character flaws, or just plain pressure, too many people escape to the world of fantasy. They become alien to the real world, denying its realities and responsibilities. They create a fictitious image of themselves that never fails and never lets others down. In this state of denial, they live and take up citizenship.

You must gently bring your mate to the point where he sees that an escape from reality is actually a decision to quit. Organizations that deal with alcoholism and drug dependency may be helpful and perhaps necessary.

Offer your mate a real relationship with a real person and real benefits. Do not underestimate the power of love in bringing another person back from these fantasies.

You Are God's Arms of Love

Having uncovered the telltale fingerprints and shrouded evidence of the past, do you feel you have your work cut out for you? Do you feel you have a mountain to climb or only a small hill?

Hebrews 12:12–13 tells us what to do next: "Therefore, strengthen the hands that are weak and the knees that are feeble, and make straight paths for your feet, so that the limb which is lame may not be put out of joint, *but rather be healed*" (italics added).

Are your mate's hands or knees weak? Is he lame? Part of God's design for marriage is that each partner will be built up and made strong. You are God's physical arms of love and acceptance for your mate.

———————

ESTEEM BUILDER PROJECT

(Use an additional sheet of paper if necessary.)

1. Isolate one or two obvious clues that signal insecurity in your spouse. List the evidence that led you to those clues. What can you begin doing in each area to help create an environment for growth?
2. If you and your mate are reading this book together, discuss which clues best describe each of you and what your mate can do to help build your self-esteem.
3. Take a self-esteem inventory with your mate, using the accompanying form. You may photocopy it if you like.

SELF-ESTEEM INVENTORY

1. Read through this list of descriptions. Using the following scale, rate yourself, then ask your mate to rate himself for each description:

Self	U = Usually S = Sometimes R = Rarely	Mate
	Description	
	Fears change	
	Is introspective	
	Fears rejection	
	Seeks to identify with accomplishments	
	Is critical of self	
	Is easily discouraged	
	Is preoccupied with the past	
	Is defensive	
	Is driven by performance	
	Talks negatively of self	
	Seeks identity through position	
	Lacks decisiveness	
	Is critical of others	
	Tends to question self	
	Compares self with others	
	Fears failure	
	Tends to believe the worst about a situation	
	Can be paralyzed by own inadequacies	
	Seeks identity through accumulation of wealth	
	Has difficulty establishing meaningful relationships	

U = Usually S = Sometimes R = Rarely		
Self	Description	Mate
	Hides weaknesses	
	Attempts to control others to make self look good	
	Is generally satisfied with self	
	Seeks identity through association with significant others	
	Is self-conscious	
	Has negative feelings about self	
	Has unreal expectations of self	
	Worries about what others think	
	Needs continual approval	
	Is insecure around others	
	Has difficulty opening up	
	Takes things personally	

2. Compare and discuss your respective lists with your mate.
3. Which one or two areas tend to be major struggling points for your mate? For you?
4. Write down what your mate recommends you do to help him deal with his major problem area(s).

4

Nine Laws that Liberate

―――――◆―――――

―――――◆―――――

WHEN FBI AGENTS ARE TRAINED to spot counterfeit currency, they do not spend time looking at counterfeits. Instead, they spend hours carefully scrutinizing authentic $1, $5, $10, $20, $50, and $100 bills. Their training is aimed at making them so alert to what genuine currency looks like that an imitation is easily recognizable.

Similarly, your mate needs your help in becoming *alert* to God's truth about himself. As that truth takes up residence in his life, he will begin to spot lies, counterfeit thoughts, and the bogus feelings that deny the truth. These inaccurate assessments will be exposed quickly as forgeries.

A New Standard of Comparison

In order for security to emerge in your mate, he needs a new standard that accurately and authoritatively measures his worth and value. The truth of the Bible is that standard. As established by God, biblical truth is an eternal yardstick of real and lasting value. It does not waver with societal changes.

The concept of truth can engender all sorts of negative responses, including "boring," "dry," "restrictive," "philosophical," and "only for deep thinkers." Yet biblical truth is the only standard by which all people can measure their lives accurately and confidently. It is the foundation upon which you can place the building blocks of self-esteem. Without the foundation of truth, as established by God, all your efforts toward building your mate's self-esteem will crumble when you and your mate inevitably fail each other. Other than the Bible, there is no lasting, permanent criterion by which to know whether a person has succeeded or failed.

Truth Is Powerful

The truth of God's Word promises action—sometimes action that brings pain. As Hebrews 4:12 says, "For the word of God is living and active and sharper than any two-edged sword, and piercing as far as the division of soul and spirit, of both joints and marrow, and able to judge the thoughts and intentions of the heart."

Do you want to help slay your mate's unattainable phantom? Do you want to see his erroneous thoughts about himself whittled down and done away with? If so, the truth contained in Scripture is the sharp sword you need.

Truth Demands a Response

One foggy night, the captain of a large ship saw what appeared to be another ship's lights approaching in the distance. This other ship was on a course that would mean a head-on collision. Quickly, the captain signaled to the approaching ship: "Please change your course ten degrees west."

The reply came blinking back through the thick fog: "You change your course ten degrees east."

Indignantly, the captain pulled rank and shot a message back to the other ship: "I am a sea captain with thirty-five years of experience. You change your course ten degrees west!"

Without hesitation, the signal flashed back: "I am a seaman fourth class. You change your course ten degrees east!"

Enraged, the captain realized that within minutes they would crash, so he blazed his final warning back to the fast-approaching ship: "I am a 50,000-ton freighter. *You* change *your* course ten degrees west!"

A simple message winked back: "I am a lighthouse. *You* change . . ."

Like the sea captain, we may need to change course when confronted with the truth. What we think is true—the phantom—may not be true at all. You or your mate may require more than a minor 10-degree alteration—you may need to change course 180 degrees!

You may conclude that you are going in the wrong direction and handling problems in the wrong way or with the wrong attitude. Without knowing the truths that follow, you may lose heart in seeking to build up your mate. Recognizing these truths is essential for any married partners who wish to help each other construct a positive self-image.

Nine Laws that Liberate

Jesus said, "You shall know the truth, and the truth shall make you free."[1] Perhaps your mate is in bondage to a poor self-esteem because he has chosen (either willfully or out of a lack of knowledge) not to believe the truth.

We want to share nine truths, or laws, that will begin to liberate you and your mate as you build up one another's lives and strengthen each other's self-image. Like water saturating a sponge, these truths should permeate your relationship with your mate. Understanding and applying them is a prerequisite for using the ten building blocks of self-esteem that will follow.

1. The Law of Giving

Jesus said, "Give and it will be given to you; good measure, pressed down, shaken together, running over, they will pour into your lap. For by your standard of measure it will be measured to you in return."[2]

The Law of Giving applies to many areas of life, but is especially relevant to self-esteem. Yet, a prevalent philosophy says, "You can give away only what you have." And the world whispers, "Wait until your own needs are met. Then you will be able to reach out to others and *really* give."

Is that what Jesus meant when He said, "Give"? Did He put qualifiers on this command that excuse the "have-nots"? We think not. Why? Perhaps Jesus knew that, to one degree or another, we all would fall into the category of "have-nots."

Christianity is full of apparent paradoxes, including one that Jesus teaches us: If we give, we will receive. Somehow a transfer takes place so that when we give we are enriched, not depleted, even if we do not see it or feel it at the time.

After hearing some of the material in this book, one woman saw this law illustrated. She wrote, "I have realized that in giving of myself, I am actually getting in return a spouse who feels good about himself, which then makes me feel good about myself."

Perhaps you get tired of giving. You may be thinking, *You don't know my mate. I don't want to give this time.* You may even feel, *I don't care what the Bible says!* We understand. But when truth is not ruling in your life, feelings are. Acting on negative feelings will not build your mate's self-image or your marriage—it will only tear down what you've already built.

Remember, giving is one of the prerequisites of a great marriage. Even if you feel you've given and given and given for years, please don't give up. Your mate needs you more than you realize. Keep on giving. God sees, and He will reward you. As Paul admonished, "Let us not lose heart in doing good, for in due time we shall reap if we do not grow weary."[3]

Theologian F. B. Meyer has said, "He is the richest man in the esteem of the world who has gotten most. He is the richest man in the esteem of heaven who has given most."

Where do you want to be the richest?

2. The Law of Understanding

A story from *Hans Brinker*, a classic in children's literature that is set in nineteenth-century Holland, illustrates the Law of Understanding. It's the story of a band of young teenage boys who took off on a grand holiday adventure. They left their small hometown to skate across Holland's frozen canals and spend a few days sightseeing in the magnificent city of Amsterdam. On their way, the five young men stopped at a small inn to spend the night. After they were refreshed with a hot supper, the boys unwisely emptied their purse on the table in the public dining room and counted their money. After planning the next day's route, they went upstairs to bed.

IN THE MIDDLE OF THE NIGHT, the leader of the boys, Peter, woke to the faint sound of someone sliding across the floor. After a scuffle, the boys bravely apprehended a would-be burglar. The prisoner was taken away by two officers, and the boys and the inn's landlord were asked to appear in court the next morning.

The dialogue in the courtroom was understandably heated. "The scoundrel!" said Carl [one of the boys], savagely. . . . "He ought to be sent to jail at once. If I had been in your place, Peter, I certainly should have killed him outright!"

"He was fortunate, then, falling into gentler hands," was Peter's quiet reply. "It appears he has been arrested before . . . this time he was armed with a knife, too, and that makes it worse for him, poor fellow."

"Poor fellow!" mimicked Carl. "One would think he was your brother!"

"So he is my brother, and yours too, Carl Schummel, for that matter," answered Peter. "We cannot say what we might have become under other circumstances. We have been bolstered up from evil, since the hour we were born. A happy home and good parents might have made that man a fine fellow instead of what he is."[4]

Peter's response is a rare exhibition of what the Bible refers to as understanding. Closely akin to wisdom and knowledge, understanding has traditionally been defined as "the faculty of the human mind by which it . . . *comprehends* the ideas which others express and intend to communicate" (*Webster's Dictionary*, italics added).

Understanding, then, is not just a transfer of information, but an empathy for the other person based on what was shared or communicated. In our marriage, we have found that understanding is essential in building each other's self-image. We are continually seeking to comprehend the context of each other's lives, just as Peter did with the thief. Context helps to explain our self-image, our behavior, and our attitudes.

Applying the Law of Understanding will give you the right to be heard by your mate. Suggestions and attempts to build into your mate will be better received if he senses that you truly understand, or at least *desire* to understand.

The next time your mate expresses a concern, ask him if he feels that you understand it. Practice listening with a sympathetic ear, and look beyond his response to its cause. What has occurred in your mate's life in the past that contributes to his present attitude(s)? Which pressures today may be crushing his self-esteem?

Proverbs 24:3 reads, "By wisdom a house is built, and by understanding it is established." Begin reconstructing your mate's self-esteem, and consequently you will strengthen your marriage by giving him the gift of understanding.

3. The Law of Perseverance

In our marriage, we tend to want instant results. We want to see change yesterday, or at the latest, *now!* However, contrary to our wishes, the positive changes we have seen have occurred slowly. Many are still in process.

Just as your mate's self-esteem grew through a lifetime of experiences, it will be conformed to the truth as he grows in the knowledge of God and experiences His plan for his life. Have faith and hope in Jesus Christ and His sufficiency. Believe that your mate *can* and *will* change.

Paul writes of this process, "We all, with unveiled face beholding as in a mirror the glory of the Lord, *are being transformed* into the same image" (italics added).[5]

We *are being* transformed. We *are being* changed. It's not an instantaneous event; it's a process of *becoming*. The Law of Perseverance warns us not to look for immediate change. An oak tree may take as many as fifty to seventy-five years to become mature. Straw takes only three months. Which kind of growth and maturity do you want in your mate?

But that's hard for some of us husbands to understand. I want to think I've built into my wife's life, and therefore she's complete.

But marriage and life have many phases. In addition, we are in a constant state of change. Life tears us down. As a result, our needs change. The process of building your mate's self-esteem is never over—even for those who write books and speak on the subject!

Charles H. Spurgeon has a word for you as you attempt to build your mate's self-image. He said, "By perseverance, the snail reached the ark." Hang in there. Perseverance will bring reward for you, just as it did for the snail.

4. The Law of Sowing and Reaping

Picture your life, your mate's life, and your marriage when you are in your sixties or seventies. Do you envision a vital, contagious relationship between two people who have climbed mountains together? Do you look with admiration at the one who you can proudly say has grown stronger through the gale-force winds of your lifetime? Or do you hear only the ticking of the clock, the repetitive squeaking of a rocking chair, and imagine an occasional glance into the eyes of your partner, a distant stranger who has never been free to share himself because he was shackled by a poor self-image?

The Scriptures say, "Do not be deceived, God is not mocked; for whatever a man sows, this he will also reap."[6] What are you sowing in your mate and marriage? Are you sowing the seeds of time, creativity, encouragement, and understanding? Or are you sowing seeds of impatience, anger, pretense, selfishness, disregard, and neglect?

If at fifty, sixty, or seventy years of age you expect to enjoy the benefits of a mate who is positive about himself and about life, and a marriage that is alive and rich, then you must aggressively sow positive seeds in your mate's life. A future harvest demands faithful planting and continuing cultivation.

5. The Law of Teachability

The Bible repeatedly teaches that growth cannot occur without a teachable heart. We believe that a teachable spirit is one of the most important components in any marriage relationship and thus in the building of your mate's self-esteem.

When we use the term "teachable spirit," we mean a progressively growing desire to learn. This requires the ability to admit fault and to ask forgiveness. Ultimately, it means a willingness to do what is right and what God wants, regardless of the personal sacrifice or cost. At the heart of teachability is humility.

We've discovered that it is imperative in our relationships with God and with each other to retain our ability to say, "I have not arrived," "I have more to learn," and "Please help me develop and mature in this area." Likewise, we encourage you to ask God regularly to give you and your mate teachable hearts that are willing to do all He has commanded.

Perhaps your mate is not teachable. Begin to pray now that he will hunger and thirst for progress and not be satisfied with mediocrity. Also, model a teachable heart. Teachability can be contagious. You may be the best example of growth your mate ever sees.

6. The Law of Accountability

The Law of Accountability requires you to submit your life to another person's judgment and authority to help you live the Christian life. Paul wrote of this accountability in Ephesians 5:21: "And be subject to one another in the fear of Christ."

Submitting your life to another involves risk and fear. Yet with risk comes the hope of being known and accepted. And with acceptance comes an increase in trust and protection.

Accountability in marriage says, "I need you. You're important to me, and I need you to be my partner. I want to share my life with you because you are a *trusted friend.*" This accountability establishes a partnership of mutual protection for you and your mate. When you become accountable to your mate, you let him into the interior of your life. You may reveal a weakness for which you need advice, a temptation that is plaguing you, or a problem that you need your mate's help in solving.

Accountability works like an umbrella—it protects. Because we are accountable to each other, we feel a part of each other's life. God's design for marriage includes a partnership of accountability for the purposes of growth, protection, and the building of trust. And trust is nonnegotiable if you are to build your mate's self-esteem.

Make your life accountable to your mate in an area in which you need his strength. As a result, watch him beam with excitement. He'll think, *My mate really does trust me! She needs me!* Such accountability will build your spouse's self-esteem.

7. The Law of Risk

Building your mate's self-image—and ultimately your marriage—necessitates taking chances. It's not easy to remove your masks and let another person really know you. It is tempting to retreat from this challenge into the safety of the known and predictable. But remember, taking risks can be rewarding as you gain a stronger marriage. So be willing to risk. Let your mate into your life and encourage him to do the same.

You can help your mate become courageous and vulnerable by honoring his attempts to communicate. Listen and be patient. He is risking your rejection, which may be one of his most controlling fears. Like rappelling off a ten-thousand-foot peak, he is dropping into the unknown, the unexplored, the untried. Encourage these attempts and reward his efforts with approval and affirmation.

8. The Law of God-Given Worth

Helen Keller once said, "So much has been given to me, I have no time to ponder over that which has been denied."

This blind and deaf woman was able to look beyond limiting circumstances and conditions to see that which couldn't be taken away. She realized that God had given her worth and value. Fashioned in His image, she understood that she was the pinnacle of His creation. And she knew that, as Psalm 8:5 tells us, she was crowned with "glory and majesty."

Your mate also has worth. First, God has given him *assigned worth*. He gave value to all people as His creation and to Christians as His children. Just as John F. Kennedy was born into the Kennedy family and thus received a certain type of worth, those who are born again into God's family (through faith in Christ) have been assigned worth. Kennedy did nothing to deserve prestige and position in society, just as we do not deserve our position of right-standing before God. It is a free gift—part of our birthright—when we trust in Christ and ask Him to forgive our sins.

Another illustration of assigned worth is the story of a young man who was kidnapped from his home in Africa and taken to America on a slave ship. After months of experiencing rotten food, disease, the stench of human waste, and seeing the death of many around him, the young man was placed on a platform to be sold. This proud black man stood boldly with his chest out, his chin up, and his eyes fixed straight ahead. The crowd stirred as they quickly noticed that this man was different. But why? The slave trader explained, "This boy is the son of a king in Africa, and he can't forget it!"

Help your mate remember that he is a child of the King. Remind him of the benefits that are his by virtue of the new birth (such as those in Ephesians 1:3–14).

God has also given your mate worth by providing him the ability and responsibility to attain or achieve worth. *Attained worth* is the God-given satisfaction of accomplishing a task, being obedient, or faithfully using one's talents and spiritual gifts. Although achieved by man, these accomplishments are possible only because God gives the ability (the talent), the power (the Holy Spirit), and the opportunity to make it happen.

Lee Iacocca illustrates attained worth. Born the son of an Italian immigrant, Iacocca worked his way up the corporate ladder to second in command at Ford Motor Company. After being fired by Henry Ford, Iacocca went to work for Chrysler as the chief executive officer. Chrysler's turnaround from bankruptcy made Iacocca an American hero. He attained a worth and value in the *world's* eyes that few could ever hope to gain.

A Christian who obeys God and faithfully follows Him throughout his lifetime has an even greater opportunity to attain worth. Although Iacocca's human fame will last only a lifetime, by being obedient to Christ's commands your mate can gain heaven's applause and "lay up treasures" that will last through eternity.

But that's not all. God also gives satisfaction when you fulfill responsibilities on earth. He will grant your mate the privilege of experiencing accomplishment now. The result is attained value.

Buttress your mate's attained worth by reminding him of his faithfulness, his successes, and his contributions—whether they be public or private. Occasionally, everyone loses sight of his personal value and needs to be reminded of past accomplishments. On the other hand, the pleasure of achievement can become one's sole measure of worth. Help your mate maintain a balance between attained worth and assigned worth. This balance will aid him in being content and keep him from being driven.

9. The Law of Divine Sufficiency

This book contains many principles and truths from the Bible. But these valuable principles will be only stale dogma and doctrine to you unless the person of Jesus Christ is at the center of your life. As A. W. Tozer states, "The most important thing about you is what you think about God."

To build your mate's self-esteem, Jesus Christ must be *your* sufficiency. Paul writes, "Not that we are adequate in ourselves to consider anything as coming from ourselves, but our adequacy is from God."[7]

The task of building your mate's self-esteem is not small, nor is it accomplished quickly. Feelings of inadequacy and hopelessness can rise suddenly and envelop you like a thick fog. During these times, the truth may seem painfully distant and even impractical, yet you can keep from being overwhelmed by focusing on the sufficiency of Christ. He is alive today, and He stands ready to guide you along the way.

Paul speaks of this sufficiency as he boasts of the person of Christ being alive and at work in him. "And He has said to me, 'My grace is sufficient for you, for power is perfected in weakness.' Most gladly, therefore, I will rather boast about my weaknesses, that the power of Christ may dwell in me . . . for when I am weak, then I am strong."[8]

Your mate's self-esteem can become a trophy of God's grace and power. No matter how inadequate you feel in helping your mate, or how poor your mate's self-image seems to be, God is completely able to do what appears impossible. His power is most evident when we are weakest. Why not submit to Him today and ask Him to be your sufficiency and your strength? (If you or your mate question your relationship with God and your eternal destiny, please read the Appendix at the end of this book).

Slaying the Phantom with the Truth

The application of these laws can profoundly affect your mate's self-image. His phantom will be exposed in the light of God's truth. No matter how deeply his experience has bruised him, your mate can begin to be healed as you faithfully apply these truths. Your perfection is not demanded; your perseverance is. Remind your mate of these truths as you work to create an environment in your home that nourishes his self-esteem with understanding, giving, patience, and prayer.

Now that the foundation has been laid, the following chapters explain ten practical building blocks that will change your mate's self-esteem.

The Building Blocks of Self-Esteem

1. Accepting Unconditionally

Total acceptance is the most important foundation in building your mate's self-esteem. Without it, your marriage rests on the shifting sand of emotions.

2. Putting the Past in Perspective

Contribute a positive, hopeful perspective to your mate's imperfect past.

3. Planting Positive Words

Your words have the power to contaminate a positive self-image or to heal the spreading malignancy of a negative one.

4. Constructing in Difficult Times

Weather the storms of life by turning toward one another and building into each other rather than rejecting each other.

5. Giving Freedom to Fail

Release your mate from the prison of performance with the golden key labeled "the freedom to fail."

6. Pleasing Your Mate

By focusing on pleasing your mate, you communicate that he is valued, cherished, and loved.

7. Doing What Is Right

Your genuine applause for right choices will motivate your mate to pursue a lifestyle of obedience to God.

8. Helping Your Mate Develop Friends

By encouraging your mate to develop close friendships, you enable others to affirm his value and significance.

9. Keeping Life Manageable

Your role in completing the construction of your mate's self-image requires making tough decisions, knowing your values, thinking prayerfully, and keeping life simple.

10. Discovering Dignity through Destiny

True significance is found as we invest in a cause that will outlive us.

---•►---

ESTEEM BUILDER PROJECT

(Use a separate sheet of paper if necessary.)

The following is a list of the nine laws that liberate. Place a star next to the two or three laws that you feel you need to apply to your marriage. (Don't choose so many that you feel overwhelmed!) Encourage your mate to select and apply several laws too.

1. The Law of Giving
2. The Law of Understanding
3. The Law of Perseverance
4. The Law of Sowing and Reaping
5. The Law of Teachability
6. The Law of Accountability
7. The Law of Risk
8. The Law of God-Given Worth
9. The Law of Divine Sufficiency

Since all of these are attitudes and perspectives, think of concrete ways in which you can demonstrate these attitudes toward your mate.

BUILDING BLOCK # 1:
Accepting Unconditionally

*T*otal acceptance is the most important
foundation in building your mate's
self-esteem. Without it, your marriage
rests on the shifting sand of emotions.

5

Dealing with the Good, the Bad, and the Otherwise in Your Mate

———◆———

- *A Word from God to the Audience*
- *The Fatal Choice*
- *Creating a Garden Experience in Your Marriage*
- *What about Differences?*
- *Living with Your Mate's Differences*
- *Continue to Verbalize Commitment*
- *Accept Your Mate Unconditionally*
- *Esteem Builder Project*

———◆———

IN THE FAMILIAR BIBLICAL ACCOUNT of God's gift of Eve to Adam, we find the basis for unconditionally accepting your mate. In scene 1, Adam, although secure in his self-esteem and knowing his worth and value, makes a discovery: He is alone. God allows Adam to feel that aloneness in order to prepare him for His plan.

The stage is set for scene 2: the crucial introduction and first meeting. The curtain rises. The audience, heaven's angels, slide forward on the edge of their seats and fall silent.

God and Eve enter the scene, where Adam is already on location.

God presents Eve to Adam as His perfect provision for Adam's need. She is God's solution to Adam's problem. Then the climax occurs: Adam completely accepts God's gift—Eve.[1] The audience cheers. The curtain falls.

Before we yawn over the familiarity of the story, let's think for a minute about this crucial scene. What if Adam had said, "She's not what I had in mind, but there's no other choice, so I'll take her"? How would Eve have felt? Would she have felt accepted? But Adam's response exhibited complete acceptance. There was no rejection. No conditions.

What about Eve? Was she just a puppet in this play? We don't think so. Eve made a choice, too. What if she had rejected Adam in any way? She had no way of knowing what kind of husband he would be to her. She couldn't ask his parents about his bad habits or talk to his friends about his manners.

Adam and Eve made commitments to receive and to accept each other as God's gift and provision for their need on the basis of faith in God. They knew their Creator. They knew that He was loving and could be trusted.

We have had the privilege of experiencing this "acceptance by faith" with each other. In a similar way, we have received six children from the hands of God. Before our last child was born, we both guessed it would be a boy. With all our experience, we expected our intuition to be accurate, especially since we had agreed all this time. But on a cold, clear, January evening, three hours after we arrived at the hospital, the doctor held up our new baby and said, "It's a girl!"

Suppose we had immediately held a conference—just the two of us—and the following conversation had transpired:

"There must be a mistake—it was supposed to be a boy."

"She looks a little blue, don't you think?"

"You're right, and I wonder if she'll be a good baby."

"You never know."

"Well, what do you think? Should we keep her?"

"Let's vote."

Obviously, that conversation never took place. We never asked a question, never expressed a doubt. We received Laura Victoria and accepted her as God's gift to us without knowing anything about her. We did, however, know and trust the God who gave her to us. So we reached out and took her and, holding her during those early moments of her life, began to build a relationship. We knew this was the child God had given to us.

Accepting your mate as God's gift is very similar. That unconditional acceptance is based on a belief in God's ability to provide what's best. By reaching out and receiving Eve from God's hand, Adam made a commitment to her. Because of that commitment, Eve experienced acceptance and thus the freedom to be who God had created her to be. She felt no pressure to become like anyone else.

We are amazed at the number of Christians who wonder if they made a mistake and married the wrong person. If you're one of those who is sometimes plagued by doubt, you will never be able to express acceptance until you have settled the issue that God sovereignly brought you and your spouse together.

As Barbara and I were revising and re-writing this book, a woman attended one of our FamilyLife Marriage Conferences in Washington, D.C. She tearfully confessed that, for more than a dozen years, she had wondered if she had married the wrong man. She had never shared her doubts with her husband, fearing it would hurt him. But through the process of our weekend conference, she realized that God had provided her husband for her.

With tears of joy she shared with one of our speakers how liberated she felt now that she had received her husband as God's personal provision for her needs. Her love for her husband grew immediately as she expressed her acceptance of him.

My ability to receive Barbara and Barbara's to receive me were rooted in our ability to believe that God is sovereign. Our confidence in God and how He brings people together supersedes circumstances because God is a God who rules 100 percent.

You have a choice. Are you going to receive your mate as God's gift to you? As Paul said in Philippians 3:13-14, ". . . forgetting what lies behind and reaching forward to what lies ahead, I press on toward the goal." You can put the past behind you once and for all by deciding that God has brought you together, and state to your spouse with firm conviction, "Yes, I believe God has brought us together, and I receive you as His gift to me."

A Word from God to the Audience

At the end of scene 2, after the curtain closes, God steps out of the action to address the audience: "For this cause a man shall leave his father and his mother, and shall cleave to his wife; and they shall become one flesh."[2]

Thus, God has given us, as observers of Adam and Eve, a mandate describing how two people are to become one. Here are the three steps He outlines in His Word:

Step one is to *leave*. We tend to think of leaving as a physical move, which most of us made when we married. We left our parents' homes (or the apartments we shared with roommates) and moved into our own homes. But God has much more in mind. The old adage of "cutting the apron strings" is closer to the truth than a move with Mayflower Van Lines. To leave means "to sever dependence upon." It means to cut the lines of emotional and financial support from our parents and to tie those lines into our mates.

Yet, for many of us, the apron strings are not cut; they are only lengthened. It's called "Project Rescue"—with good old Mom and Dad coming to rescue their distressed child! Your mate may feel that he (or she) has to compete with the in-laws for your dependence and loyalty.

"To sever" does not mean to terminate the parental relationship, but it does mean that your dependence and allegiance are given, first and foremost, to your mate. Your mate is to demonstrate that same "severing" and "dependence" for you. Leaving parents should always be done within the context of honoring them. Some couples have used a concept I share in my book, *The Tribute:* a written tribute acknowledging their parents' impact upon their lives and, at the same time, clarifying this new step of cleaving to one's spouse.

In step two, God commands us to *cleave* to one another. To cleave means "to form a permanent bond, to make a commitment." It's similar to the process of combining two different metals to make a new metal, an alloy. This commitment between a man and woman was designated by God to be irreversible—a permanent arrangement called marriage, with no escape clauses and no pre-nuptial agreements.

This explicit, bonding commitment is essential. It is only as you absolutely and resolutely commit yourself permanently to your mate that you give him the freedom to be real and to experience acceptance.

The third step—the result of leaving and cleaving—is to *become one flesh*. It begins on the wedding night with physical intercourse and continues throughout the years of marriage. Becoming one—becoming that new alloy—is a process. Oneness takes time, but it can't happen without the leaving and the commitment of cleaving.

The Fatal Choice

As the play continues onstage, we watch Adam and Eve enjoying a perfect relationship as a result of their unconditional acceptance of one another. In Genesis 2:25, we read that "the man and his wife were both naked and were not ashamed." That's a picture of total transparency. Adam and Eve didn't have anything to hide. They knew each other and accepted each other. But as their story develops, we observe in scene 3 the fatal encounter with the serpent, Satan (Gen. 3:1–5).

The couple made two choices to disobey God, and all of history was forever marred.

Notice that Adam said to God, "I was *afraid* because I was naked; so I hid myself" (italics added).[3]

Fear was the first fruit of sin. Adam and Eve had never felt fear before, but that feeling compelled them to do something foreign. They covered themselves from each other. Then they hid again, from God. Sin and fear had distorted their perception of their Creator and His love.

Adam and Eve once knew perfect acceptance in their relationship with each other and with God. Now, because of their sin, they lived with only the memory of perfect acceptance. In addition, they experienced a new companion—fear. The fear of rejection now plagued their fellowship with God and with each other. So fear, even at the very beginning, hindered the marital relationship.

The most profound fear is the fear of rejection. All of us feel it in our marriage relationships. We think, *If you really knew me, you wouldn't accept me. If you really knew what I was like on the inside, who I was as a person, you might reject me. You might not love me anymore.*

It's risky to be seen and to be known by our mates. Because of the depth of intimacy in the marriage relationship, there is greater potential for pain and rejection. Today we know fear but have no idea what that perfect acceptance was like. We're born on this planet with the image of God implanted within us, but as we look at our lives, we become more and more convinced how sinful, how unacceptable we truly are at our core.

Yet God, in His grace, has given us—as husbands and wives—the opportunity to taste some of the freedom that Adam and Eve experienced in their pre-Fall days: complete, untainted acceptance.

Creating a Garden Experience in Your Marriage

How do you experience freedom from fear in your marriage relationship? First, receive your mate as God's gift to you. Don't focus on the imperfections or the differences. Focus on the Giver, the One who is sovereign, the One who doesn't make mistakes. Sincerely thank God for your mate, just as Adam and Eve did.

Make a commitment to one another. Tell your mate that you see him as he is and accept him as God's gift. Acknowledge that truth verbally to each other: "I accept you as God's gift to me. I trust Him in His choice of you for me." This commitment will do a lot to build worth in both your mate and yourself.

The most important step in building your mate's self-esteem and self-worth is to accept him unconditionally. This is not a resigned, defeated acceptance; it's an acceptance that embraces your mate with expectancy, excitement, and great hope for the future. That's how Adam received Eve. He accepted her based on his knowledge of God. Adam had a friendship with God, and because he knew he could trust God as his provider, he accepted His gift.

Second, commit to valuing your mate. Think for just a minute of one valuable possession you own. How do you treat that possession?

Often we put valuable possessions in special places—on a pedestal or in a vault that's really secure. We handle those possessions carefully. We're gentle with them, so as not to damage them, and we take pains not to lose them.

The parallel for marriage is clear. Do you value your mate? Do you take good care of your mate? Are you gentle with your mate? Do you respect him or her?

The attention we give to one another communicates, nonverbally, how much value we place on our mates. If we pay attention to our mates—giving them respect, honor, and time—then we prove that we value them. If not, our actions communicate that we don't value our mates.

Perhaps you made your foundational commitment to your mate with relative ease and set out to do right, but along the way you stopped accepting your mate. You now find yourself subtly trying to change him. When you concentrate on changing your mate, you focus on his negative qualities (from your perspective) rather than on his positive ones. You put yourself in an authoritative position in your mate's life. You actually try to take God's place and orchestrate change. Your mate then becomes defensive, and suddenly the marriage is no longer a partnership—it's a civil war.

If this is your situation, it is time to renew your commitment and to remember that only God can change lives. He may change those "negative" qualities in your mate, or He may not. Either way, your unconditional acceptance is vital to your marriage and to your mate's self-esteem.

What about Differences?

Emperor Wang Tee of China is reported to have said to his wife, See Ling, "I have a problem. I'm noticing that our mulberry trees are being damaged. I'd like for you to go and find out what's wrong with them."

So the empress discovered that a small, drab-colored moth was laying eggs on the leaves. The tiny eggs would hatch into little worms, which after a few days would spin cocoons and damage the leaves.

Wondering if she could destroy the little cocoons, she dropped one of them into a pot of boiling water. To her surprise, the cocoon began to slowly unwind. As it unwound, she saw, glittering in the water, a silvery thread. Upon further inspection, the thread proved to be a half-mile long!

Thus, through the process of solving a problem, See Ling discovered something beautiful: silk.

Likewise, we discovered the beauty of acceptance early in our marriage when we began to deal with some difficulties in our relationship. A couple of things—our differences and our personal insecurities—were eating away at the joy of our relationship, much like those little worms had eaten away at the mulberry leaves.

The old adage that "opposites attract" was really true for us. We were very different in many, many ways. For instance, Dennis was impulsive. He'd get an idea and, man, he'd be gone. I (Barbara), on the other hand, tend to be very disciplined. I like to think things through and evaluate what we're going to do before we act. Often, during our first year of marriage, I found myself being left in Dennis's dust.

We also discovered other differences. Dennis was expressive; I tended to be quiet and cautious about what I said. Dennis wanted to spend money on fishing; I wanted to spend money on furniture.

In addition, both of us lacked self-confidence in certain settings. I was not good at meeting people at large social gatherings and tended to cling to Dennis. And he had some weaknesses that his boss pointed out to us one day during lunch. When I heard that, I remember thinking, *Now what am I going to do with this information about my husband?*

Like See Ling, we began to realize that we had a problem and we'd better find a solution if we wanted our marriage to be secure and happy.

We are not alone. Like flies at a summer picnic, differences buzz in the ears of many couples, threatening to rob their relationship of its peaceful, accepting love. As humorist Sam Levenson once said, "Love at first sight is easy to understand; it's when two people have been looking at each other for a lifetime that it becomes a miracle!" Someone else said, "Love is blind, but marriage is an eye-opener." As you move past the honeymoon stage, all those differences—those little "eye-openers"—begin to affect your marriage.

Ironically, differences are those wonderful qualities that attracted you to each other when dating. He was outgoing; she was shy. He was a big spender, which made her feel special because she was a tightwad. He was a hard worker; she was impulsive and fun-loving. Or, the reverse may have been true. Either way, opposites attract like iron filings to a magnet.

When the honeymoon fades and reality sets in, those attractive "uniquenesses" are often viewed as aggravating weaknesses. The very traits that initially drew you to your mate may now repel or frustrate you.

As a result, you may be faced with several decisions. First, you must ask yourself, *Will I continue to accept my mate in this particular area of difference, or will I withdraw a portion of my acceptance, thereby driving a sliver of rejection between us?* Ignoring the question doesn't work because differences don't go away. If you can't accept that annoying quality, you are actually rejecting your mate (either silently or verbally), and his self-image will suffer. Your only two options are to accept him or to reject him.

Living with Your Mate's Differences

If you choose to pursue acceptance, then another question arises: *How do I live with this difference?* The answer is multiple choice, with more than one, or possibly all, of the choices being correct in any given situation.

1. Pray for yourself.

Ask God to make you content with your mate as he is. Pray, too, that God will show you the positive sides of your mate's differences.

As I mentioned earlier, Dennis and I are extreme opposites on the impulsive/disciplined scale. When we were first married, his impulsiveness tended to drive my disciplined nature crazy. I *felt* that we had no order, no schedule, no budget, and no regular devotions.

I remember praying diligently for God to change all the things in Dennis I didn't like. Then I realized what really needed to be changed was *my attitude.* God did change my perspective, and in time I began to see how much I needed Dennis's spontaneity to balance my more rigid control.

Ask God to examine your attitudes and your motives and to give you a greater capacity to understand, accept, and even appreciate your mate's differences. This step may be necessary before God can use you to elevate your mate's self-esteem.

2. Talk about it with your mate.

Ask for the privilege of being heard. Tell him you are not rejecting him and that you remain committed. Assure him that he is loved, no matter what. One thing we have learned in our marriage is that we are teachable at some moments but not at others. Unless it is obvious, we ask whether or not the time is opportune for "learning."

If you find that your mate is not emotionally prepared to discuss a touchy issue, leave the subject alone. Don't try to force a confrontation.

You also may discover that the territory you are about to encroach upon is marked: NO TRESPASSING. It may be off limits at this point in his life. If so, be satisfied with exploring small bits of turf at a time. Do not expect (or try) to cover the whole country in one evening. Go slowly.

If your mate is willing to talk about a difference that is bothering you, share your feelings without accusing him and pointing the finger of blame. Don't be critical. Let him know you realize that you're not perfect and that you understand him, or want to understand him, in this area. Realize, too, that we all have weaknesses or tendencies we will never completely conquer. Because of our fallen nature, we'll never achieve perfection until we reach heaven.

If your mate considers a difference to be a weakness, ask if you can help. Then, at the end of your discussion, remind your mate again of your commitment and acceptance. We call this the "bookend principle." Just as bookends are used to prop up books that contain truth, so your reminders of love and complete acceptance at both ends of the discussion will support the truth of what you have said. And it makes the truth a whole lot *easier* to hear!

3. Tutor your mate (with his permission).

As a couple, we continue to assist one another in many areas, such as punctuality, patience with children, planning, feelings of discouragement, anger, and worry. We have discovered that the many opposites that attracted us to each other when we were dating—and later became repellents—are the very things that have provided balance in our marriage. Our differences have made us more effective as a couple than we ever could have been individually.

One area in which I have assisted Dennis is in his public speaking. Early in our marriage, I noticed that he was making obvious grammatical errors as he spoke. I felt free to offer help because, on more than one occasion, I also told him honestly that he communicated well.

So, one evening after a speech, I asked Dennis if I could make a suggestion that might make him more effective as a speaker. He agreed to hear me out. Although my critique was a little threatening, he confessed that he had not done well in English in school and he welcomed my suggestions.

Some months later, on the way home from another speaking opportunity, Dennis told me, "I still want you to help me with my speaking, but I'd like you to wait a little while before you tell me the cold, hard truth."

I realized then that my technique needed refinement. I had been too quick to tell him the "truth," and my "help" had become a discouragement because it wasn't seasoned with enough praise or separated long enough from the actual event. Had I not modified my recommendations, I would have crossed the fine line separating acceptance from rejection.

If your mate grants you permission to help, ask God for wisdom in *how* to help. Offer your assistance in such a way that your mate experiences your acceptance and in no way senses rejection.

4. Ignore certain differences.

Some of the annoying differences in your mate may not be weaknesses. Commit those differences to the Lord in prayer, asking Him to give you peace and contentment to live with them, even if your mate never changes. It is important to accept him "as is," without pressuring him to change. Choose to ignore the differences that are off-limits and seemingly beyond change, and rejoice over the many benefits you enjoy because of your partner's strengths.

Continue to Verbalize Commitment

Several years ago, God gave us the wonderful privilege of helping a couple resurrect a marriage that seemed to be beyond hope. The changes were dramatic. Their commitment to Christ and to each other was real, and they grew steadily in their relationship.

But one day the wife came in, discouraged once more about their marriage. Apparently she and her husband had reached an impasse. Each time they argued about the problem, the husband threatened to leave—a tactic from the past. Unwisely, he was saturating their relationship with the fear that maybe he would follow through this time.

One of the Ten Commandments of Marriage should be: "Never threaten to leave." This threat creates cracks in the commitment, erodes the security of total acceptance, and fuels fear.

In addition, threats rarely cause a person to change. They only communicate rejection. Rather than threaten to leave, each of us should creatively and continually express our commitment and acceptance to our mates. God gave us an example to follow. He didn't tell us only once that He loved us; He told us often and in many ways. He even sent His Son to demonstrate His love, and He gave us His Word to read over and over so we wouldn't forget it. He continues to show us His love today through His Holy Spirit.

Our mates need to hear words of commitment and acceptance from us, not just once but many, many times. Tell your mate often how much you love him. Then tell him that you accept him just as he is.

Each time a difficulty arises in your relationship—a misunderstanding, a difference, or a clash of wills—remind your mate (even in the heat of battle, if necessary) that you intend to remain loyal to him. Assure him that your commitment will not change because of this particular situation. Those infusions of truth will become the rein-forcements you both need to work through difficulties in your mar-riage. Total acceptance will motivate you to persevere.

Also, tell your mate occasionally that you'd choose to marry him again. This declaration will give him value and approval and build his self-esteem. It will remind him of the truth—that he is accepted.

Throughout our years of marriage, we continue to see potential threats surface unexpectedly. Attitudes, ideas, fears, temptations, and old memories all arise to threaten our mutual acceptance. We may wonder, *What would he think if he knew this thought?* or, *What would she think if she knew how I felt?*

Experiencing acceptance is a process. Just as a swimmer tests the water temperature of a swimming pool before diving in, so marriage partners test each other before revealing themselves. The revelation is sometimes risky, but necessary. Learn when to speak, what to say, and how much to say. Communicate with wisdom.

Accepting Your Mate Unconditionally

Why is unconditional acceptance so important? Because if you accept only in part, you can love only in part. And if you love in part, your mate's self-esteem will never be complete. That area of rejection will keep your mate from becoming all that God created him or her to be.

A great illustration of why unconditional acceptance is so crucial to a marriage is found in the story of Charlie and Lucy Wedemeyer. Charlie, a high school football coach was diagnosed with amyotrophic lateral sclerosis, commonly called "Lou Gehrig's Disease" at age thirty. The doctors gave him one year to live. But, with Lucy caring for him, driving him up and down the sidelines in a golf cart, and even reading his lips and relaying his instructions when he no longer could talk, Charlie continued to coach for seven more years.

In their book, *Charlie's Victory*, the Wedemeyers describe the crisis which occurred when Charlie realized he was losing the strength to continue as head coach:

> AS LONG AS I COULD COACH, I'd been able to use my mind, feel a part of something bigger than myself, focus on what I could do instead of worry about my limitations, and contribute something to the people closest to me. Without coaching, I would have nothing to give; I'd lose one of the biggest reasons I had to go on living.
>
> Lucy tried to encourage me by being her usual, upbeat, and optimistic self. But by this time my spirits were as hard to prop up as my body.

Some friends came to visit, and Charlie needed to use the bathroom before seeing them.

> She held me tight and we began a tediously slow shuffle into the bathroom. We were barely through the door when I began to cough. My knees buckled and I would have crashed to the floor if Lucy hadn't instantly tightened her grip on my arm and wedged me against the wall with her body. I felt her muscles strain and tried to stiffen my legs to help, but with each cough I could feel another bit of strength seep from my body. When the first spasm of coughing passed, it was all Lucy could do to move me over and ease me onto the seat.
>
> At that moment, I sensed the utter futility of my life. While thoughtful friends waited nearly an hour in the living room to see me, and my exhausted, loving wife stood watching over me, I sat hopelessly on a [toilet] seat, too weak to move and too discouraged to keep on fighting.
>
> Tears of humiliation and frustration welled up in my eyes as I looked up at Lucy, sighed in resignation, and said what I'd felt was true for a long time: "You and the children would be better off if I died."
>
> I'll never forget Lucy's reaction. Later I learned my words had so startled her that she silently prayed, "Please God, give me the words to

say." Slowly, deliberately, she straightened up as she gathered her thoughts and looked right at me. In an almost angry, don't-you-forget-it tone tempered by the love in her eyes, she said, "We would rather have you like this, than not have you at all."

I was suddenly overcome by emotion, overwhelmed by the love of this woman who had already been through so much with me. I'd never in my life felt so loved by her. I began to sob. She put her arms around me and we sobbed together. And after a time we regained enough composure and strength to get to the living room for a short visit with our guests.

I had no idea how long I would continue to live. But I knew I'd never forget Lucy's words that day. What I didn't know was how many times the memory of those words would help keep me alive by giving me the will to continue fighting for my next breath.[4]

Lucy's love and unconditional acceptance literally kept Charlie alive. Isn't that what marriage is all about? Marriage is another person being committed enough to you to accept the real you.

The hope for marriage is that we can each find the security to dare to be real. That security can come only from complete acceptance by another. It gives us the confidence to say, "The whole world may reject me, but my mate won't."

Remember that complete, unconditional acceptance is a process. As you build, build, and build into your mate, your acceptance will begin to set him free from self-doubt, fear of failure, and an incorrect self-image. Your acceptance will release him to be his best. It will build self-confidence and hope. Your faith and belief in him will help him see himself as God does—worthy and valuable.

A familiar saying states, "He who knows you best loves you most." As you grow to know and accept your mate, your love—as well as his self-esteem—will grow.

ESTEEM BUILDER PROJECT

(Use a sheet of paper if necessary.)

1. What are the greatest "fears" in your life? How do they affect you?
2. List below any areas where you are afraid to be transparent, afraid of being rejected, or don't feel fully accepted by your mate.
3. List any areas in which your mate may be afraid to share his innermost thoughts with you and where he may be fearful of being rejected—areas where you feel he intentionally keeps you at a safe distance.
4. How have you contributed to his covering up in these areas (threats, lack of love, manipulation, rejection, etc.)?
5. Will you accept your mate as being God's provision for you? Write out a commitment and contract with God stating that you will strive to accept your mate fully.
6. How can you pray positively for your mate? List at least three qualities that you will ask God to develop in his life.

BUILDING BLOCK #2:
Putting the Past in Perspective

Contribute a positive, hopeful perspective to your mate's imperfect past.

6

Helping Your Mate Clean Out
the Attic of the Past

———◆◆◆———

———◆◆◆———

S A FIVE-YEAR-OLD BOY growing up in a small, white, two-story frame home, I (Dennis) was terrified of one place— the attic. An eerie stillness enveloped me whenever I ventured into this hot, creepy, windowless room. The scent of mothballs perfumed the air. The attic was laced with invisible threads of spiderwebs that feebly attempted to capture me if I got too near. Mysterious shapes, covered by sheets and blankets, crouched in corners, casting suspicious shadows on the plank floor. A solitary lightbulb swung from the ceiling. It was *always* burned out.

I just knew that attic contained more than discarded junk. *Something* was living up there, *something* that would mercilessly defend its territory against weaker, pint-sized trespassers. I never saw this creature, but I knew it was there. And I feared I would get locked in that dark, dusty, despicable garret, alone with the "thing."

Everyone has an attic in which the past is stored. It's a place where emotionally-charged relics still live under sheets and in boxes, tucked into the corners of our minds. Those memories—of when we failed others and when others failed us—haunt and accuse. They also contribute significantly to the makeup of our self-image.

As a child, I feared going into that attic alone, but when accompanied by another person, I became downright courageous. That dark, scary spot in my home became little more than just another room. Sure, my heart still quickened a bit as I opened the door, but somehow fear was put to flight when a trusted friend stood beside me.

Likewise, your mate may be extremely fearful of visiting his attic of the past alone. But his confidence will grow if you go with him and uncover together the musty relics that assault his self-image. Your mate needs your help in sorting out the genuine antiques—the good esteem-building memories—from the counterfeit junk produced by past negative experiences.

The Past and Your Mate's Self-Esteem

It has been said that the person whose problems are all behind him is probably a school bus driver! Seriously, no one can say that he is totally free from his past. Problems we encountered as children most likely still confront us as adults. Things we were told we couldn't do right as children probably have become the things we can't do right as adults.

Today, many Christians are imprisoned by the attics of their past and need to break free. Your mate may be one of them. To help release him, you must first help him determine which items fill his attic and which things from the past affect his self-esteem.

When you married, you probably underestimated the impact of the past on your mate's life. Consequently, you may often be surprised or perplexed by his decisions, attitudes, or actions.

No one has a flawless past. All of us have suffered from our mistakes and the mistakes of significant others—our parents, peers, coaches, teachers, and family members. The pain of the past has damaged the way your mate views himself and the way he handles life today.

I met a young man several years ago at a Christmas party who told me something fascinating about himself: "I'm married, I have three children, I like my job, and I'm really very happy in life." Then he added, "But you know what's interesting? I still find myself trying to compete with my older brother. He was always better than I was in sports. He always beat me in grades and was ahead of me in school. For some reason, even though I know it's foolish, I still find myself wanting to beat my brother as an adult."

The Influence of the Past

Dan Allender, speaking to Christians during his seminar on sexual abuse, said:

> MANY MEN AND WOMEN TODAY live out their Christian lives unaware of their past, of their past history of abuse and how it influences them. They do not see how a past event that occurred years ago has much influence on current patterns of living. This blindness to the past saps their energy of the present, leaving many people drained by the demands of helping keep in place the patterns of denial. This robs the church of liveliness, passion, and depth.

It takes a lot of time for you and your mate to deal with your past. So each needs to be patient with the other. We can't change the past, but we can lessen the influence and control (especially the negative control) it has on our lives.

In an interview conducted by *Tabletalk* magazine, Larry Crabb was quoted as follows:

FIRST OF ALL, sin has terrible consequences, and there simply is not going to be an easy way out of it. When a husband unburdens himself and makes known what he has done, and his wife forgives him, they cannot expect that they are just going to go back to their respective lives as if nothing had happened. A real struggle has come into their lives which needs to be acknowledged.

Look at the patterns in the relationship, patterns where the wife has been guarding herself, saying, "I've been hurt so bad as a kid," or "I've been sexually molested," or "My father never really loved me." As a result of wounds such as these, she has a lifelong pattern of protecting her soul, which means she is probably not giving herself as a woman to her husband, so he feels cheated and lonely and he goes somewhere else.

On the other hand, the man may believe that he's failed in the past in significant ways and now he feels locked into a subtle pattern of self-deception where he says, "I'm not going to give all of myself to my wife because if I did and I failed, I couldn't stand the pain."

When a couple begins to recognize these patterns, then they begin to realize the walls they've built up between themselves. You must have the courage to examine the relational patterns in your marriage in order to gain a new sense of trust. . . . It takes more than just memorizing a Scripture verse.[1]

You Are of Incalculable Value in Your Mate's Life

Vonette Bright, wife of Campus Crusade for Christ founder and president Bill Bright, has said, "No one, man or woman, can reach his full potential without another giving his life up for that person." That is really true in marriage. Don't think for a second that you're not needed. You need to get inside your mate and find out what makes him tick, what makes him the way he is today.

You don't have to be a trained counselor to be of value in your mate's life. You can give what your mate needs most—acceptance, love, and the freedom to fail. Your mate needs that from you more than from anyone else.

A recent article in a sports magazine gave some statistics on the accomplishments of NBA players. One of those statistics applies to marriage as well: "Seventy percent of all the points scored in the NBA over a period of a year are assisted points. Only 30 percent of those total points that are scored are unassisted."

Your mate needs your love and acceptance to assist him in dealing with his past. Remember, you are valuable in your mate's life. First John 4:18 reads, "There is no fear in love; but perfect love casts out fear." That is your goal in dealing with the past—to cast out that fear that controls your mate today.

The Dark Corner of Parents' Mistakes

Probably no human relationship evokes more emotional response—good and bad—than one's relationship with his parents. Unquestionably, your mate's parents were the most influential people in developing his self-esteem. Their attitudes, feelings, and actions were recorded in your mate and formed the basis for his self-image.

"As the twig is bent," the poet Virgil wrote, "so the tree inclines." The messages our parents send us—whether they were messages of love and security or of criticism and blame—have played a critical role in determining how we view ourselves today.

Pleasing the most important people in our lives should give us a feeling of worth and value. Yet a child needs to feel valued not only for his performance and his accomplishments but also for who he is. Parents who withhold this unconditional acceptance create an adult who must perform in order to gain value. He looks to others for the missing parental approval.

One Woman's Story

Sue and Rich dated and grew to love one another during college. Soon they were engaged, and finally married. Although Sue had openly shared many things about herself with Rich during their courtship, he had no idea how the lack of her father's unconditional approval had shaped her self-image and influenced her life.

When Sue was six years old, her militaristic father inspected her bedroom every Friday evening. In preparation, she would balance one chair on another to dust the tops of the window and door facings, which her father routinely examined. He scrutinized any other work she was required to do just as intently. On one occasion, she was grounded for two weeks for missing two sprigs of crabgrass when she weeded the lawn.

When Sue was eleven, she had to carry two cases of bottled soft drinks down the basement stairs, although she could barely manage to pick them up. Halfway down, she tripped and fell head over heels to the concrete floor. She was lying in the midst of broken glass and spilled liquid when her father jerked her up and, without inquiring about her well-being, yelled, "You dummy, I told you not to drop them!"

Not surprisingly, Sue was left with an impoverished self-image. At times during her marriage, her insecurity surfaced in the form of emotional withdrawal. When she and Rich argued, she would give him the "silent treatment."

Rich was often caught off guard, but he encouraged Sue to share her feelings. He rarely said, "You shouldn't feel that way." Instead, he acknowledged her emotions as true feelings, although not always the truth. He remained committed to helping her resolve, not repress, her feelings about her parents. As a result, her self-esteem has improved, and she has a positive perspective on things she once considered to be negative.

Another woman never received her mother's approval. She tells how she feels as an adult today: "Just once I'd like to hear my mother compliment me on something. I'd be elated if she would say something nice about the wife and mother I am. But there's seldom a kind word. I'm fifty-five years old," she went on, "and you'd think that what I do would be good enough. It depresses me so. I feel so low."

Warning Signals from Your Mate's Home Life

The following series of warning signals could indicate that your mate's self-image was adversely affected by his relationship with his parents:

Characteristics of home life:
- A home where mistakes weren't tolerated.
- A home where the father was distant, aloof, and authoritative.
- A home where to admit need was to be weak.
- A home where either the father or mother was absent physically, emotionally, or mentally.
- A home where there was any form of abuse: sexual, emotional, or physical.
- A home where worth was tied to performance.

Characteristics of parents:
- Parents who were so self-sufficient they never admitted their need of anyone.
- Parents who never admitted that they were wrong, nor asked for forgiveness, nor expressed love and affection.
- Parents who didn't allow their children to be children, but expected them to behave as adults.
- A parent or parents who habitually expected too much and seldom expressed satisfaction for a job well done.

Characteristics of life now:
- A feeling that your mate could never please his parents even as an adult.
- An abnormal feeling of need for parental approval or a preoccupation with what "Mom and Dad think."
- Feelings of resentment toward a parent(s) and a refusal to try to honor them.

Your mate also may be striving for the parental approval and acceptance that he missed as a child. Assisting him in dealing with his past is the pivotal point between healing a damaged self-image and leaving it needy and incomplete.

A Reprieve for Parents

Before you accuse us of being too harsh on parents and laying all the blame on them, let us assure you of three important facts.

First, everyone is born imperfect. Because we're descendants of Adam and Eve, all of us start life with the seeds of negative self-worth already planted within us. Nothing your mate's parents could have done would have changed this fact.

Second, no parents are perfect. No one sets out to ruin his child, but all parents make many, many mistakes in raising their children. Some do a better job of parenting than others in certain areas, but no mother or father does it perfectly. More than likely, your mate's parents did the best they could.

Some of us have placed unreal expectations on our parents. We expected them to provide for us perfectly and to be what only our heavenly Father could be. Because they failed to live up to those standards, we have become critical of them. J. Wesley Brown wrote some years ago in *Christian Century:* "Perhaps the greatest honor we can do for our parents is to let them down off the pedestals of our imaginations, where we are inclined either to idolize them or to flog them as gods who failed, as indeed they must fail."[2]

Brown is right. We need to accept our parents as people—people who need forgiveness as well as respect—people who need honest relationships with their children perhaps more than with anyone else. This begins when you and I take our parents off the pedestal, realize that they are real people, and relate to them as human beings with unique needs that only their children can meet.

Third, we can't blame our parents for what is our responsibility today.

Too many of us expend far too much emotional energy casting blame on our parents when we should be taking responsibility for our own lives. Although your mate's parents made errors, your mate is now responsible for himself as well as for his present response to his parents.

Consequences to Your Mate's Self-Image

As a result of his parents' mistakes, your mate may feel somewhat insecure about himself. He may also experience guilt, fear, and anger toward his parents.

Does your mate feel guilty because he didn't fulfill his parents' expectations? Is he plagued by guilt over something he said or should have said, or something he wishes he'd never done? Is he still looking for parental approval he never received as a child?

Perhaps your mate feels intimidated by authority figures, and the implied failure they represent, because he had no loving relationship with his parents. This fear of failure may dominate his life, leading him to live cautiously and never take unnecessary risks.

Or, he may be angry, full of resentment toward his parents. Your spouse may refuse to forgive them in hopes of punishing them for what he suffered as a child. Yet, holding on to bitterness and anger is more detrimental to him than to the parents he seeks to punish. Dr. Paul Meier, one of the founders of the Minirth-Meier New Life Clinics, once told us that 95 percent of all Christians carry some anger or bitterness toward their parents. That's an astounding statistic.

One young man revealed his insecurity, which he traced to his father's neglect of him as he grew up. "My father traveled a lot," the young man explained. "He was always gone and was too busy to write or call. He completely neglected me. I never knew if he would be proud of the way I was growing up or not. Today, I still feel directionless. I'm sad for me, bitter against him, and scared about my future."

Getting Out of the Corner

Getting your mate out of this dark corner of his parents' imperfections is essential if you are to help him build a positive self-esteem. If you and your mate do not put the past behind you, then you will always be behind your past. The following are some tips for helping your mate in this area.

First, begin to work with your spouse to get the problem fully out in the open. Talk about how your parents treated you, and ask your mate to share his experiences. Be patient. Talking about these things can be very painful. Affirm and strengthen your mate by listening and verbally expressing encouragement and acceptance.

Second, help your mate understand his parents. Proverbs 24:3 reads, "By wisdom a house is built, and by understanding it is established." Understanding is essential in your mate's relationship with his parents.

Talk together about your mate's parents and seek to put their lives in proper perspective. Consider the homes each of them came from and begin to appreciate the obstacles they have had to overcome. Understanding their backgrounds will result in viewing parents with compassion.

Third, remind your mate that God's grace and power are greater than his parents' mistakes. No matter how poor a person's home life may have been, God delights in resurrecting a damaged self-image and restoring dignity to that wounded person. Point your mate toward Christ and the hope He offers by verbally drawing his attention to Christ and expressing your confidence and belief in the greatness of God.

Fourth, help your mate determine how he will respond to his parents. He has no control over how he was treated as a child, but he does have control over how he will relate to his parents today. Bring into focus what his parents did right by pointing out some positive things about your mate and how you are the benefactor of those good traits. This is important even if your mate's parents are no longer living. The memory of a deceased parent can be powerful, especially if the memory harbors bitterness.

Fifth, help your mate experience all that God has for you both in your marriage by clipping any ties of inappropriate dependence. As stated in Genesis 2:24, he is to "leave" his parents, thus no longer being dependent on them for money, an undue amount of emotional support, or acceptance.

Sixth, encourage your mate to make the choice to forgive his parents—completely. Oscar Wilde has said, "Children begin by loving their parents. After a time, they judge them. Rarely, if ever, do they forgive them." Unfortunately, that's true for many people, but it doesn't need to be true for Christians.

Paul implores each of us to forgive "each other, just as God in Christ also has forgiven you."[3] To forgive someone means to give up the right of punishment. Patiently and gently, urge your mate to deal with his past constructively—to put away his punishing emotions and replace them with an attitude of love and understanding.

Perhaps, after several conversations about his parents, you could schedule a weekend getaway or an evening alone in which he could think about and deal with his feelings toward his parents. Encourage him to empty out that dark corner of his past by listing on a piece of paper everything he can think of for which he may resent his mother and father. He may need to add the wrong attitudes he has held toward them. A qualified counselor may be necessary if you feel you cannot help your mate get on top of this emotionally charged area and be able to forgive his parents.

As you and your mate discuss parental issues, remind him of 1 John 1:9: "If we confess our sins, He is faithful and righteous to forgive us our sins and to cleanse us from all unrighteousness." Your mate may find it helpful to write this verse across his list and then to tear it up, symbolizing the forgiveness and erasing of these wrongs from his life.

After confessing these sins to God, it may be appropriate for your mate to ask his parents' forgiveness for wrong attitudes. But he should *not* expect anything in return. Be sure your mate isn't planning to point out how his parents' wrongdoing, expecting them to "see the light" and ask his forgiveness, too!

Although you can do much to encourage your spouse in this area, you can't remove the sting of his past relationship with his parents. You can't make him believe what God says about His grace and healing power. Nor can you force him to go through the process of forgiveness. It must be his choice, his belief, his conviction. Pray diligently for him.

A letter that I (Dennis) received from a young woman in a graduate class I was teaching demonstrates the power of forgiving one's parents. This letter illustrates the effects of a parent-child relationship and the positive results of dealing with the past as God directs:

Dear Mr. Rainey,

MY FATHER PHYSICALLY ABUSED ME when I was a child. He would beat me so badly that at times I didn't think I was going to live. At other times, my mom was in such fear for me that she would call the police.

But perhaps even worse than the physical abuse was the mental abuse. Oh, how he hated me! He would cuss and scream at me every possible word you could think of and a lot you probably couldn't think of. When he was silent, the raw hate in his eyes spoke almost louder than words.

Also while growing up, I was sexually abused by my two older brothers. If I had told anyone, they would have beaten me up, and who would I tell anyway? Finally we got caught; how thankful I was! Then someone hugged me and assured me it wouldn't happen again, right? Wrong. I was beaten again, told it was my fault and lived with dirty, obscene comments about it for months.

During my freshman year in college, I became a Christian. My life began to change rapidly. Over the next year and a half, God took me from tremendous hate toward my father, to a dislike, to a like, until I could say I loved my father.

Then I began to find out certain things. My father was abused as a child. No one ever told me that before. His father kicked him out when he was seventeen. That must have been hard. Well, what about my mom? How come she stood by and let my father abuse us? Her first husband was an alcoholic and beat her, so she left him. Even though she worked two jobs, on many evenings there was nothing to eat for her and the three boys. That must have been hard. Then, she had to stay awake at night to guard the baby crib or else the rats would eat on the baby all night. No wonder she was scared to leave her second husband.

Does this excuse what happened to me as a child? No. Does it make it more understandable? Yes.

My father still yells and cusses at me, but you know what? Not quite so loudly. I call him on special occasions. I share my life with him and ask his advice. His response? Not so good, but that's okay. The other day I heard he was bragging about me at work. There's hope.

This young woman came from one of the most difficult backgrounds imaginable. She suffered much. Yet she *chose* to be set free from her understandable, but nonetheless wrong, response to her father by giving forgiveness.

Seventh, as a couple, aggressively begin to honor your mate's parents. Honoring parents makes our forgiveness visible. It not only will bring blessing to his parents, it also will give you and your mate a sense of well-being about life and thus a positive sense of self-worth. This truth is captured in one of the Ten Commandments: "Honor your father and your mother, as the LORD your God has commanded you, that your days may be prolonged, *and that it may go well* with you on the land which the LORD your God gives you" (Deut. 5:16, italics added).

Look for ways to help your mate honor his parents. Honor starts with a heart of compassion. Colossians 3:12 instructs us to "put on a heart of compassion." The word *compassion* means to feel with someone, and to accompany that feeling with action.

Your mate's parents need to see that he has compassion for them. They need to be hugged. They need your mate to see them as people who have needs and struggles. Just as a parent will hug a child and bandage his skinned knee, your mate can come alongside his parents and stand with them.

There are many practical ways in which your mate can honor his parents. He can spend time with them. He can send them encouraging and thankful letters or call them regularly. He can do what he can to meet their needs as old age takes its toll.

He can also write a Tribute—a written document thanking his parents for what they've done right. Maybe it won't be easy for him. Maybe he will sit for hours trying to think of something to say and how to say it. It may be particularly difficult if, in his home, emotions weren't discussed. To give you an idea of what you could say, allow me (Dennis) to share a part of what I wrote to my mother. I had my Tribute to my mom typeset and framed. Today it hangs right above the table where she eats all her meals. It's entitled, "She's More Than Somebody's Mom":

WHEN SHE WAS THIRTY-FIVE she carried him in her womb, while he did his best to kick her ribs out. It wasn't easy having a baby in 1948. There were no dishwashers, no paper diapers, only crude washing machines with clotheslines hanging in a musty basement to dry an endless mound of laundry. . . . She always offered a chilled washcloth for his forehead whenever his fever was high. Her steamy hot potato soup was always best to eat when propped up against a pillow in bed. Her warm kitchen was her trademark, the most secure place in her home, a shelter in the storm. . . . She always came to rescue the sunburned boy with soothing ointments. She read him books, taught him how to organize, make lists, how to make his bed, pick up clothes, catch crawdads and minnows, bake cakes from scratch, and how not to leave water-filled glasses on wooden tables . . . it makes rings. . . . She went to church faithfully. In fact, she led this six-year-old boy to Christ in her Bible study class one Sunday evening. She is truly a woman to be honored. She is more than somebody's mother . . . she is my mom. Mom, I love you.

Instead of recounting meaningful incidents from his childhood, your mate may want to thank his parents for various gifts: a strong work ethic, common sense, compassion, the example they set in their marriage, their patience. . . .

Once the Tribute is written, encourage your mate to read it to his parents personally. Although that may also be difficult, it may lead to precious moments of sharing, openness, and thanksgiving.

Through the process of writing a Tribute, your mate may notice more of the things his parents did right. This may free up some of his emotions, which can lead to healing.

As you support your mate in dealing with his attitudes toward his parents, it is imperative to realize that the choice of forgiving and honoring is his, and it most likely will take time. We are human creatures, at times enslaved to our emotions. Give your mate the freedom, the space, the grace, and the time to work through his feelings toward his parents. It may take months, or even years, for all of the hurt to be brought out into the open. Your mate needs your patient understanding, particularly in this area of his life.

(For a more detailed discussion of the subject of honoring your parents, see *The Tribute*, by Dennis Rainey with David Boehi, Thomas Nelson Publishers. The book contains a process that many have found helpful.)

BUILDING BLOCK #2:
Putting the Past in Perspective

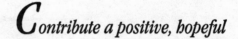*Contribute a positive, hopeful*
perspective to your mate's
imperfect past.

CHAPTER

7

Helping Your Mate Clean Out
the Attic of the Past, II

———— ◆ ————

———— ◆ ————

AS YOU HELP YOUR MATE clean out the attic of his past, you'll find that his relationship with his parents is only one of many "things" that can harm him.

Second only to the home in influencing our lives is our relationship with peers. These were the people we tried to impress the most. And, depending on whether we were inside or outside the "in-group," our self-image either soared or sank.

The Dark Corner of Peer Pressure

I (Dennis) will never forget how, as a young boy in first grade, a few friends and I began to choose who would be "in" and who would be "out." One of the first "outs" was Lois. She came from a very poor family and couldn't dress as well as the others. She was also slow in class, which didn't help. So we quickly excluded her.

The "in" group rejected Lois as a person—slowly at first, but ruthlessly as the years passed. By the time we reached high school, she was the butt of countless jokes. When we were seniors, she had such an inferiority complex that I don't recall seeing her look up from the floor that entire year.

Some eight years later, when I read Dr. James Dobson's book on self-esteem, *Hide or Seek*, I recognized my false values and my haughty, foolish evaluation of Lois. I wept when I thought about my cruelty to her. I asked God to forgive me for my arrogant, childish behavior. She was made in the image of God every bit as much as I was.

Peers can have poisonous tongues. William Hazlitt wrote at the turn of the nineteenth century: "A nickname is the hardest stone the devil can throw at a man." Some never forget the names they've been called. Do you know what your mate was called while growing up? Do you recall some of the names you were called?

Here are a few nicknames we've come across: Dummy, Pit-i-ful Paul, Messy, Fatso, Peewee, Runt, Brick-Brain, Ornery, Grasshopper Brain, Yo-Yo, Troublemaker, Slow Learner, Bones, Motor-Mouth, Sloppy, Sleepy, Devil's Daughter, Nerd, Turkey, Lardo, Bird Legs, Space Cadet, Rebellious, Simple Sally, Buzzard-Beak, Metal-Mouth, Freckle-Face, Weirdo, and Geek. Names like these can really hurt.

If your mate's peers called him a name, they may have helped tear down his sense of worthiness. And the damage was done during a very crucial time in the formation of his self-esteem.

Even today, your mate may be very peer-dependent. He may self-consciously wonder if he's wearing "just the right" outfit or using "just the right" lingo. He may doubt his ability to relate to your friends. Or he may need to lose a few pounds and feel self-conscious about his less-than-flat stomach. Many adults are still influenced by the pressure to conform to the values of their peers.

Getting Out of the Dark Corner of Peer Pressure

Those haunting songs peers sang about your mate and those grinning faces he just knew were laughing at him all echo in his mind, leaving him feeling less than acceptable. But you can help free your mate from those feelings by taking a few key actions.

Begin by deciding on your own value system. What is truly important to you both, and why? By which values and standards do you want to measure your lives? It's important for you to recognize the false value system through which your peers either granted acceptance or rejection to another person.

If you and your mate do not have your own set of convictions—your own scales of worth and value as defined by the Scriptures—then you will end up using the world's scales. You will be peer-dependent, and what the world calls valuable will be the vacillating standard by which you will measure your lives. So begin to speak the truth about how you and your mate have the image of God implanted within you.

It's one thing to put our past behind us. It's another to go back to the slavery of wrong value systems, of living life as a pleaser of men, depending upon the opinions of others to determine your joy. If your mate does that, continue to remind him of the truth of God's Word. He is not meant to please people but to please God.

As a couple, study the Scriptures together. Learn what God values: loving Christ, obeying Him, and serving others. By bringing your lives into conformity with God's values, you will gain a unique set of convictions that give both of you ultimate value. Your *convictions* will determine how you live and how you feel about yourselves.

Paul gave us critical instruction when he encouraged us to break away from the world's mold and conform ourselves to God's value system. "I urge you therefore, brethren, by the mercies of God, to present your bodies a living and holy sacrifice, acceptable to God, which is your spiritual service of worship. And do not be conformed to this world, but be transformed by the renewing of your mind, that you may prove what the will of God is, that which is good and acceptable and perfect."[1]

It is so important to invest your life in values that will last. Pour yourself into God's unchanging, eternal values, and teach others to do the same.

A few convictions that have allowed us to "break from the herd" are: the value of our family, doing what's right, ministering to others' spiritual needs, helping the poor and the hungry, and sharing with others the good news of Jesus Christ. These all bring ultimate value, worth, and divine purpose to our lives.

Also, discuss with your mate his past relationship with peers and try to understand how they have affected his self-esteem. Do some scenes that play over and over in his mind remind him of his inadequacy? Ask him to share these painful memories with you, and then discuss the false values that his peers were perpetuating. As a couple, compare those values with God's.

In your marriage relationship, it's important to talk about these things. As you expose them to each another, you will receive the love and acceptance you so desperately need, and you both will be free from the influences of the past.

Then encourage your mate to forgive those who may have rejected him in the past. Forgiveness of peers is as important as forgiveness of parents. Forgiveness means to put away the right that you or your mate have to punish another person.

Does a certain name cause your stomach, or your mate's, to tighten? Do you or your spouse get angry at the very mention of a person's name? If so, it may be that you have not put away the right of punishment.

Since the heart of Christianity is forgiveness, none of us has any right to hold onto thoughts of revenge, whether they be toward a brother, a sister, a mother, a father, a friend, a peer, a coach, a Sunday school teacher, or anyone else who has harmed us through word or deed. The apostle Paul wrote, "Be kind to one another, tender-hearted, forgiving each other, just as God in Christ also has forgiven you."[2]

Part of our heritage as Christians goes back to the Cross. There, God put on Christ all of the punishment we deserved so that we would be forgiven. Now, as we relate to brothers or sisters who may not have been kind to us, we have an opportunity to demonstrate grace—to put away the right of punishment. It is our responsibility to forgive again and again, to join what Christ called the "seven-times-seventy" club in which members forgive an infinite number of times.

Skeletons in the Corner

A third monster—following parents and peers—that lurks in the corner of your mate's attic comes from the *past*. It may be a mistake that accuses and condemns, telling him that he does not merit your love and acceptance. Perhaps it is a series of wrong choices, poor judgment, or some secret sin that haunts him. Is he burdened by guilt over a sexual experience from his childhood or adolescence, or possibly a willful rebellion against God in which he broke one of God's laws?

If your mate has been divorced, he carries a certain sense of failure and rejection from that experience. Or, if you have been divorced, your mate may fear the unknowns of your past. Divorce is never easy, never painless, never simple. Its effect cannot be ignored. This skeleton from the past must be met and reckoned with repeatedly.

Bitter memories of past failures can vandalize your mate's self-concept. Tearing and ripping his self-portrait, these failures attack and retreat, but they never leave. Your mate's inner beauty is smudged by the guilt attached to these scarring memories of failures, foolishness, and folly.

Such guilt can be domineering. One woman confided in me

(Dennis) that she and her husband of one year had not yet sexually consummated their marriage relationship. Although her husband had remained very patient, she was suffering from extreme self-condemnation.

She went on to share how she had been sexually assaulted three times during her early adolescent years and had told no one until now. She had convinced herself that it was her fault and that she should bear the consequences. Now she was frozen in guilt and fear in her relationship with her husband. She wondered, *If he knew, would he truly accept me?*

With my encouragement, she finally shared each of the traumatic experiences with her husband. His acceptance of and patience with her changed her life. Slowly her fear melted and, with it, much of her self-condemnation. Her understanding husband was instrumental in delivering her from the captivity of the past.

Cleaning Up the Past's Dark Corner

Many of us continue to feel negative emotions and replay pictures of past mistakes. It has been said that we are worn down less by the mountain we climb than by the irritating grains of sand in our shoes—sand from the past. We must help our mates take off their shoes and dump out those little pieces of gravel and dirt.

Robert Schuller once said in a speech:

> NO ONE PUTS GOD'S PEOPLE DOWN more than themselves. . . . Instead, we need to find somebody who'll believe in us and lift us up. It's my personal opinion that God can always deal with pride in our lives. He can always reduce us. What we need is someone to come alongside you, alongside me and to believe in us, to help pull us up out of the quicksand of the past.

You hold the keys of love, acceptance, and forgiveness that can unlock the prison of the past and let your mate experience love and acceptance. God can use you to help release your mate from the haunting memories stored in his attic. Prayerfully consider the following five ways in which you can help your mate clean out the dark corners of his past:

First, never pry about the past, but let your spouse know you are always available to listen. Unfortunately, most people tend to have a morbid curiosity about the failures of others. Yet there is no need to have the gory particulars brought into your marriage relationship. Details serve only to kindle the imagination, causing you to replay a scene or an event. They could tempt you to condemn your mate.

Second, if you are aware of something in your mate's past that continually troubles him, find a biblically-trained Christian counselor who can help your mate work through his difficulty. This will not be necessary in every situation, but it could be one of the best investments you could ever make in your mate's self-image.

Third, assure your mate of your "over-acceptance," regardless of what he has done. One of your mate's greatest fears may be that you will find out who he is and what he's done, and then reject him. Your mate's greatest need is to be assured of your steadfast commitment and love. An environment of "over-acceptance" provides a climate for healing and growth.

Be sure to back up your promises with actual acceptance. Never throw the past up to your mate. Never. It will only communicate rejection and plant the seeds of mistrust. Instead, cultivate his self-esteem by your continual acceptance.

Fourth, if he has confessed his past failures to God (and to you when appropriate), help your mate understand that he has been forgiven. Romans 8:1 reads: "There is therefore now no condemnation for those who are in Christ Jesus." Some people still condemn themselves, not believing that Christ took the punishment we all deserve. But when Jesus died on the cross, He paid the price for all our sins—no exceptions—so there is no need to remain in guilt and self-condemnation. You have such a privilege of being able to remind your mate of this truth. Model forgiveness by continuing to give it.

Early in our marriage, I (Barbara) experienced some difficulty with depression and low self-esteem. There were days when I would feel like such a failure because I had done things that I felt were really wrong. I believed I had blown it. I remember feeling unlovable during those times and would think to myself, *I'm just not a good wife. I'm not a good mother. I'm not worthy.*

Then Dennis would come to me and say, "It's okay. I love you, and God loves you."

But that seemed too good to be true. I'd look back at him skeptically and say, "You can't love me. I'm just not good enough for you to love me." Then I'd argue with him, allowing my feelings to overrule the truth.

One day, after a number of these discussions, Dennis finally said, "Barbara, I want you to know that I love you and God loves you, and it's the truth. Now, you have a choice as to whether or not you will believe it."

The light came on in my mind, and I thought, *You know, he's right. I'm calling him a liar by saying that he doesn't love me because he does, and God loves me as well.* That was a real turning point for me in acknowledging the truth, regardless of how I felt about myself.

Poet Edwin Markham has said, "Choices are the hinges of destiny." For me, the choices I began to make that day have influenced my whole life and our relationship. As I slowly began to choose to believe in Dennis's love for me, my poor self-esteem began to lose its grip on my life.

Fifth, help your mate understand that he has no business remembering what God has already forgotten. Many Christians live as if they're trying to drive a car by looking through the rearview mirror. Focusing on where they've been, they move forward at a snail's pace rather than at the brisk velocity God intends. They allow the past to overshadow the present. If this describes your mate, then help him put aside the past and allow God to do something new.

One woman had been in a dating relationship she knew was not morally right. She and her boyfriend had experimented sexually. Finally, she broke off the relationship. During the next year Isaiah 43:18–19 became very real to her: "Do not call to mind the former things, or ponder things of the past. Behold, I will do something new, now it will spring forth; will you not be aware of it? I will even make a roadway in the wilderness, rivers in the desert." What a promise! Encourage your mate to memorize this passage.

Paul also writes, "Forgetting what lies behind and reaching forward to what lies ahead, I press on toward the goal for the prize of the upward call of God in Christ Jesus."[3] Paul wasn't looking in his rearview mirror, even though he had assisted in the murder of Stephen. He was looking forward—at the Person of Christ. Help your mate do the same.

Be on Guard against Unseen Forces

Each of us lives in the midst of an unseen spiritual world as real as this book. Just as God with His angels is accomplishing His work on earth, Satan and his demons are seeking to undermine God's work in you and your mate.

You will encounter some of your most difficult warfare as you begin to build into your mate's life, for it is then that your marriage becomes a threat to what Satan is attempting to do. Satan wants to discourage and dissolve your mate's self-confidence. And he wants you to lose heart in your responsibility of building into your mate's life.

We are not extremists. We are not suggesting that a demon is behind every bush, but Satan *is* a very real enemy and should be taken seriously.

Consider the following verses. Peter writes, "Be of sober spirit, be on the alert. Your adversary, the devil, prowls about like a roaring lion, seeking someone to devour."[4] Lions in the forests and plains of Africa prey upon the weak, the unsuspecting, the unprotected, and the stragglers who wander from the safety of the herd. Similarly, Satan looks for marriages with weak spots, mates with unprotected self-esteems, and spouses who live independently of each other. Likewise, he wants to discourage you from building into your mate's self-esteem. Be advised, and be on the alert.

Paul also admonishes, "Be strong in the Lord, and in the strength of His might. Put on the full armor of God, that you may be able to stand firm against the schemes of the devil."[5] Standing firm in Christ means living obediently. It means believing that what God says is more true than how you feel. Strengthen yourself with faith in God, the promises of His Word, and with prayer.

Remember, "the accuser of our brethren" is at work among Christians, seeking to confuse, discourage, and deceive us, and to tempt us to believe a lie instead of the truth about ourselves, our mates, and our marriages.[6] All of these affects your mate's self-esteem.

Keep Your Own Attic Clean

We've talked about your mate's past, but what about *your* attic? Is it clean? Is your daily life free from the ridicule of the past? Or are you bitter over something or someone and are therefore controlled by anger?

If you feel emotions from the past welling up inside you, consider completing a project we gave a woman a number of years ago. You may find that this exercise for *yourself* is necessary before you can begin to build your mate's self-esteem.

Mary was bitter. She was angry at her parents for the neglect she felt as a child and at her husband for his inconsistencies. At first, she had difficulty admitting her resentment, but finally she was able to do it.

To help Mary put aside her resentment and bitterness, we told her to begin by writing a detailed explanation of how her parents had wronged her and how that had made her feel. She also listed disappointment after disappointment in her relationship with her husband.

When she finished her list of grievances, she read it aloud. Seeing her anger on paper and hearing it in her own words gripped her, and she began to cry.

Through her tears, Mary bowed her head and prayed, "Forgive me, God. What I've written here is sin. You've commanded me to honor my parents. I haven't. Instead, I've harbored anger against them for twenty-five years.

"Forgive me, too," she went on, "for my lack of a loving spirit toward my husband and my critical attitude toward him."

When she finished, a great relief swept over her like a gentle, fresh, spring breeze. Mary then took a large, red, felt-tip pen and printed across each of the three pages in bold letters the words of 1 John 1:9: "If we confess our sins, He is faithful and righteous to forgive us our sins and to cleanse us from all unrighteousness."

She smiled as she crumpled those sheets of paper in her hands. Then she walked outside, dug a shallow hole in her flower bed, and dropped the sheets into it. She lit a match and set the pages on fire. Watching the flames turn the paper to ashes became symbolic of what God was doing in her life—transforming something bad into something good. Mary then covered the ashes with dirt until the hole was filled and piled seven softball-sized rocks on top.

Today, when the old bitterness attempts to burst through the soil of her life and she is tempted to look back, she looks out her kitchen window and sees her rock pile. It remains there as a reminder that her past is gone—her sins are forgiven and buried.

What about you? Does your past need to be buried and remembered no more? You'll never be able to build your mate's self-esteem if you are controlled by your own past. But once you are free, you can help him recognize and deal with the effects of his past on his self-esteem.

When to Seek Professional Counseling

Occasionally, outside help or professional counseling may be necessary in order to help your mate get beyond a particular problem. Dr. Frank Minirth, of the Minirth-Meier Clinics, says that the following half-dozen observations may mean that you should encourage your mate to seek a biblically trained counselor:

1. Physical Symptoms

An abrupt weight gain or loss, frequent headaches, complaints of poor physical health, or a loss of sleep or appetite could be a signal that your mate needs help.

2. Mental Symptoms

Observed mental anxiety, sadness of appearance, a confused state of mind, or prolonged or frequently repeated depression could mean that qualified help should be sought.

3. Frequent Complaints of Emotional Pain

A person who is suffering emotionally through a recent traumatic experience or one who continues to have difficulty with an emotional problem from the past should consider getting an opinion from a competent counselor.

4. Impaired Basic Functioning

If your mate is having a difficult time coping at work, socially, or at home with the most basic responsibilities, it may mean that you should seek outside help.

5. Dependence upon Drugs or Alcohol

Severe feelings of insignificance frequently result in chemical dependence. These can be accompanied by thoughts of suicide and need to be treated by a professional.

6. Irresponsible Behavior

Inconsistent or immoral behavior may mean that your mate is not coping well with some internal struggles.

Obviously, if, over a period of time, you feel that the problem(s) is much larger than your capability to help resolve it, you should seek the advice of a trusted counselor who points people to the Scriptures and Christ.

For further information on counseling call The Minirth-Meier New Life Clinics at 1-800-NEW-LIFE.

ESTEEM BUILDER PROJECT

(Use a sheet of paper if necessary.)

1. Do you need to empty out one of the three "dark corners in your attic"? Parents? Peers? The past in general? Follow the suggestions at the end of the appropriate section in order to begin the process of healing.
2. Suggest that your mate read this chapter, then discuss how it may apply to him. Remember, don't pry. Let him share what he feels comfortable discussing.
3. Perhaps you will want to suggest to your mate that he follow the steps outlined after each section. Be careful not to *push* your mate, however.
4. Describe your relationship with each of your parents. What are your fondest memories? What would you change? Describe the impact each parent has had on you.

Dad	Mom
Words that describe	Words that describe
a.	a.
b.	b.
c.	c.
Major impact on me:	Major impact on me:
a.	a.
b.	b.
c.	c.

5. Describe the emotions you feel today as you think of each of your parents.

Dad	Mom
a.	a.
b.	b.
c.	c.

6. Do you presently hold any bitterness, resentment, or unresolved anger toward either or both of your parents?

    ___yes   ___no

If yes, explain why in the space below. (Be specific about whom and what.) Then take time right now to write out a statement of confession and confess that to God in prayer as sin.

Let all bitterness and wrath and anger and clamor and slander be put away from you, along with all malice. And be kind to one another, tender-hearted, forgiving each other, just as God in Christ also has forgiven you.

(Eph. 4:31-32)

7. Describe the impact that peers, past and present, have had on your self-esteem both for good and for bad.
8. Looking at your past relationships with peers, are there any incidents or events that you need to put behind you? Get the monkey off your back by forgiving them now and putting the past in perspective.

Brethren, I do not regard myself as having laid hold of it yet; but one thing I do: forgetting what lies behind and reaching forward to what lies ahead, I press on toward the goal for the prize of the upward call of God in Christ Jesus.

(Phil. 3:13-14)

9. Are there any present relationships with your peers in which you are conforming to wrong values and thus not fulfilling God's standard for you? If so, what are they and what do you need to do about it?

I urge you therefore, brethren, by the mercies of God, to present your bodies a living and holy sacrifice, acceptable to God, which is your spiritual service of worship. And do not be conformed to this world, but be transformed by the renewing of your mind, that you may prove what the will of God is, that which is good and acceptable and perfect.

(Rom. 12:1-2)

10. Are there any incidents or vague feelings from the past that continue to haunt or condemn you? If so, how are they affecting you today?

11. List practical ways you think your mate can help you move beyond this problem.

BUILDING BLOCK #3:
Planting Positive Words

Your words have the power to contaminate a positive self-image or to heal the spreading malignancy of a negative one.

CHAPTER 8

Words Are Seeds

———— ✦ ————

———— ✦ ————

IKE THE AVERAGE AMERICAN FAMILY, we have moved a number of times and have lived in several areas of the United States. We've been homeowners in Boulder, Colorado; San Bernardino, California; Dallas, Texas; and Little Rock, Arkansas.

Our Southern California house came complete with a small, picture-perfect lawn. It was a beauty to behold—the kind of lush, soft, green carpet you enjoyed mowing in broad daylight on a Saturday morning while your neighbors looked on in envy. But it was quite a different story in the other places we have lived. Those lawns were well established, but with weeds. The worst stand of weeds was in Dallas, where we unsuccessfully fought nut grass.

When freshly mowed, our yard of weeds looked pretty—from a distance. But within a few days, it sent up strange seed pods. The runners, growing unnoticed underground, threatened to choke not only our sparse clumps of grass but also the few trees we had. We began to suspect that this weed had mutated into a new, invincible breed, destined to take over the yards of the world. To avoid ridicule, we mowed our lawn at night!

From our experience with lawns, we've learned that weeds come from seeds. Weed seeds primarily come from the soil or a neighbor's yard, or are carried by the wind. It can be a full-time job keeping them at bay. Predictably, we have gained great respect for the potential of seeds.

Words Are Powerful Seeds

Words are like seeds. Once planted in your mate's life, your words will bring forth flowers or weeds, health or disease, healing or poison. You carry a great responsibility for their use. As Proverbs 18:21 warns: "Death and life are in the power of the tongue." Your words have the power to contaminate a positive self-image or to heal the spreading malignancy of a negative one.

In the book of James, we see other word pictures. James says that the tongue can be like a bit that directs a horse, or a rudder that controls the course of a ship. It can be like a fire or a poison, both of which create destruction. Or it can be like a fountain or a fig tree, from which either good or bad may spring.

You are not the only one who plants "word seeds" in your mate's life. In fact, many of his mistaken perceptions about himself have sprouted from the negative words of others. These weed seeds, which have been around since Adam and Eve sinned, have been passed through the soil of humanity. In your mate's lifetime, some have crept across his property lines in the form of jokes, criticisms, and innuendos from close friends and peers. Many have germinated to blight his self-esteem. As his partner, however, you have the power to arrest the growth of negative words by sowing your own positive words.

Planting Good Seeds

When God created the universe, He used a unique vehicle—words. The psalmist records how God created all that we see: "By the *word* of the LORD the heavens were made. . . . For He *spoke*, and it was done; He *commanded*, and it stood fast" (italics added).[1]

Life was conceived in the mind of God and given birth by His words. He could have fashioned creation gently in His hands, yet He chose to use words. He spoke, and it "stood fast."

In a similar way, we share in God's creative handiwork when we use words that give life to our mate's self-esteem. In marriage, one of the most important things about a couple is *what they say to each other*. When positive words flow, the relationship is robust and flourishing. If the lines of understanding and positive communication go down permanently, it is only a matter of time before that marriage dies. We can create life in our mates with our positive words, or we can inflict destruction with our negative or neglectful words.

Perhaps some of you remember when many factories in the United States were turned into manufacturing firms producing ammunition, ships, and other products during World War II. Posted throughout those factories were little signs with these words: "Loose lips sink ships." Today in our homes, we need little signs that read: "Loose lips sink partnerships."

Pulling Weeds and Planting Seeds

One of our children's favorite songs is from the children's cassette tape, "Ants'hillvania." It is about a prodigal ant, Antony, who became an "independ-ant." Through his newly found independence, young Antony left the anthill and went off to do his own thing. He was going to be greater than all the great ants before him: Alex-anter the Great, Michael-ant-gelo, and Napole-ant.

Through various songs and riddles, Antony's friends plead with him to come home. One song, titled "Seeds," has application for building your mate's self-esteem. Read the lyrics and think about what kind of seeds you are sowing in your mate:

First you pull the weeds, then you rake and hoe,
Then you plant some seeds, that's the way you sow;
Just you wait and see, everyone will know
What you've planted there, when they start to grow.

Every plant has little seeds
That make others of its kind;
Apple seeds make apple trees,
And they'll do it every time

Seeds make flowers and shrubs and trees,
Seeds make ferns and vines and weeds. . . .
What you plant is what you grow,
So be careful what you sow.[2]

Antony concludes that he has been sowing the wrong seeds in his independence. The parable ends as he becomes a "repent-ant" and decides to come home. His family, thrilled that the prodigal ant has come home, kills the fatted aphid, throws a big party, and lives happily ever after.

Sow the Right Seeds; Avoid the Bad

Like Antony, your mate may need a good word. Proverbs 12:25 has some good advice: "Anxiety in the heart of a man weighs it down, but a good word makes it glad." Notice the impact of a "good word." Gladness comes not from a sentence or a paragraph, not from an entire message. Gladness comes from just one, well-placed, positive word.

Be sure to appreciate the power of words. They can assault our mates or honor them as valuable people who have God-given worth and assets. Efforts to understand the past and give unconditional acceptance will be quickly negated if we sow pessimistic, critical, or unsympathetic words into our mates' hearts. *The Living Bible* says it well in Proverbs 11:9: "Evil words destroy. Godly skill [wisdom] rebuilds."

Heed the warning of the children's song:

> *You must choose your seeds with care;*
> *What you sow will blossom there. . . .*
> *What you plant is what you grow,*
> *So be careful what you sow.*[3]

Few things are more difficult than observing someone who is careless with words—sowing "weed seeds" in his mate's life through words of criticism, accusation, sarcasm, and judgment. We know of one husband, for example, who feels his wife needs to become more organized. She is people-oriented, known for her compassionate spirit, but she is not a natural housekeeper. In addition, she has her hands full taking care of their four children.

The husband writes up lists of tasks for her to complete and calls her several times a day to check on her progress and also to add to her list. If she falls behind, he hits her with a barrage of withering criticism. He often loses his temper when she fails to complete her tasks. Worse, when they visit friends' homes, he asks, "Why can't you keep our place as clean as this?"

What do you think has happened to this woman's self-esteem over a decade of marriage? The person she loves most will not accept her for what she does best. She is loved by her friends, and could have a wonderful ministry helping others in need—if only her husband would set her free. His words of criticism and control have left deep wounds which may take years to heal.

With our mouths, we have the ability to plant weed seeds—critical comments, cynical statements, angry words—that can choke out the good fruit. So choose with wisdom and care the "seed words" you speak to your spouse. These are critical to his self-esteem, for in them he sees himself.

One final warning on weed seeds: Don't expect an immediate "crop failure" of weeds if you've been planting negative words in your mate's life for years. Asking your mate's forgiveness may hasten the process of killing the weeds, but the seedlings of carelessly spoken words may take years to die out. Ask God to make you mindful of the power of your tongue and to make you aware of the words you speak to your mate.

Words, however, are not the only source of weed seeds. Your negative attitudes toward your mate also have a devastating effect on his self-esteem. Nonverbal cues or ignoring your mate can plant seeds, too. You may be habitually sowing negative words or attitudes without realizing it.

But remember, God delights in changing lives and giving new beginnings. Your marriage can become a healthy, productive garden where two people generously express to one another gratitude, appreciation, belief, and praise.

Sow Seed Words of Praise

Everyone loves to be praised, and your mate is no exception. William James wrote: "The deepest principle in human nature is the craving to be appreciated." And Mark Twain said, "I can live for two months on a good compliment."

Praise is valuable because it is a virtue seldom practiced! We seldom praise our employees, we seldom praise our kids, and we seldom praise our mates. Yet, our homes ought to be a haven where praise is liberally applied.

Carefully read this definition of praise: "to give value, to lift up, to extol, to magnify, to honor, to commend, to applaud." If you give some creative thought to this definition, you can come up with hundreds of ways to praise your mate. Since building your mate's self-esteem is basically a matter of helping him to feel valuable, praise is a necessary tool in that process. The more you verbally express your appreciation (praise), the more secure your mate will become in his self-esteem.

Have you ever asked someone to repeat a compliment? We have. "Oh, you really liked our FamilyLife Marriage Conference? Tell us what meant the most to you." Inwardly, we are saying, "Yes, we need to hear this! Would you tell us one more time so we can relish your comments for a few seconds longer?" Life can seem intolerably heavy at times, and a good, encouraging word can help to lighten the load and lift your mate's spirits.

Arnold Glascow has said, "Praise does wonders for our sense of hearing." It also does wonders for our sense of sight. When you praise another person, you take your eyes off yourself and focus on someone else for a few, brief moments. This positive focus on another not only helps to put *his* life in perspective, but *yours* as well. Here are three ways to praise your mate and put life into perspective:

1. Praise specifically.

Give your mate value and honor through the gift of praise. Your mate needs you to praise him specifically for who he is as a person. This helps him to see his uniqueness. He also needs praise for those things he does—his effort and work—for you and your family's benefit. Sow the good seeds of praise in his life with statements such as:

"I appreciate you because you . . ."

"I admire you for your . . ."

"Thank you for . . ."

To appreciate means "to raise in value," while to depreciate means to "lower in value." You can watch your mate's value appreciate because of your verbal appreciation of him!

Think about it for a moment. What do you really appreciate about your mate that you haven't said "thank you" for in a while? Which good qualities, good deeds, or good attitudes can you think of? Take a minute or two right now and list five. Make them as specific as possible. Why not share them during your next meal together? Praise not only is "becoming," it is infectious—others might join in.

Your Husband	Your Wife
1.	1.
2.	2.
3.	3.
4.	4.
5.	5.

Don't forget to praise your mate for those mundane daily duties. Tell him *why* you appreciate the tasks he performs and how you benefit from them. Make a mental note of those unpleasant, difficult tasks, and give a verbal reward of encouragement the next time he completes one. It may motivate him to do it more often.

Anytime Dennis fixes something around the house, I (Barbara) am quick to express my appreciation. I know how inept he feels in this area and what it takes for him to crank up the courage to at least try! I also thank him often for working hard and providing for us as a family.

Robert Louis Stevenson said, "Make the most of the best and the least of the worse." Far too often, we reverse what Stevenson said. But if you follow his advice, you will inspire your mate to keep on trying, and you will bring out his best.

2. Praise wisely and truthfully.

When a marriage relationship hits a trouble spot, it may be difficult to find much to praise. Yet those are the times we need praise the most. So initiate praising your mate. Bring relief to him in the midst of trouble.

Solomon wrote: "The words of wise men are like goads, and masters of these collections are like well-driven nails" (Eccl. 12:11). When you choose to encourage and praise your mate, your words can prod or goad him in the right direction. Notice the result: Well-driven nails secure all kinds of building projects. Our words can be used like nails, to secure our mate's self-esteem. Your wise and truthful words will bring perspective to his life, to your relationship, and to your situation as a couple. Finding a solution may even be easier.

But what if all this praise goes to my mate's head? you may be asking. *Won't he become prideful?* There is a difference between truthful praise and flattery. Flattery gratifies a person's vanity. Praise, however, is based on a person's character and deeds. When you truthfully praise and applaud your mate's choices, you help him build godly character.

Paul exhorts, "Speak truth, each one of you, with his neighbor" (Eph. 4:25). At the center of these words is "truth." Once again, we find the standard for bringing value to another person. Truth results in assurance and security, worth and value. It becomes the compass during the storm that confidently steers us in the right direction.

Praise your mate in all situations, using wisdom to meet the need of the moment and speaking truthfully to help construct his character.

3. Praise generously.

Your praise can be excessive only if your words are insincere. Genuine, heartfelt praise cannot be overdone. Besides, your mate gets plenty of criticism and correction from others and from himself to offset your praise. And if he does get a big head, God is fully capable of shrinking it back to size!

During the early months of our marriage, we spontaneously complimented and praised each other for newly discovered characteristics. It became almost a game to see who could find another good quality to praise. We named our exclusive "club" the Mutual Admiration Society. It remained quite active for several years and provided much of the basis for the great beginning of our marriage.

Today, with a houseful of children and new discoveries about one another coming less frequently, the situation is not quite the same. But the Mutual Admiration Society does reconvene. Some evenings at the dinner table a question is raised, such as, "What do you appreciate most about Dad?" We then go around the table and answer. We've heard such classic, and truthful, comments as: "He goes fishing with me"; "He goes on dates with me"; or, from our daughter Rebecca when she was just five, "He sneaks chocolate with me." It's very difficult to be depressed when a chorus of youngsters, who are mostly blind to your faults, cheers you on.

William James said, "All of us, in the glow of feeling we have pleased, want to do more to please." Thus, you can help to motivate your mate toward excellence in his character and his performance by giving generous, liberal, and fervent praise.

Sow Seed Words of Belief and Affirmation

In our self-centered culture, you will rarely find others who unequivocally believe in your mate. You have the main responsibility for sowing words of belief and affirmation in your spouse.

One of the strengths Dennis brought into our marriage was a steady belief in me (Barbara). When I am tempted to become overwhelmed by self-doubt, he rarely, if ever, joins me in my self-deprecating accusations. Instead, he reminds me of the truth. He tells me what he thinks about me—positively, of course, without lying or flattery. He also praises me for the things I do right. His words help to turn my focus from a negative view of self toward a positive one. His unwavering belief in me has given me the much-needed confidence I lacked.

Words that communicate belief and affirmation are important to your mate's self-esteem. He needs your unparalleled belief in him. You have been drafted to play on his team, to be the coach who believes in him, and to be the cheerleader who gives praise even when he loses. He needs you to be his biggest fan, not his sharpest critic.

117

One woman we know uses words extremely well. Recently, when her husband was in the middle of some pressure-packed situations at work, her words of reassurance kept him going. "You're all right. I believe in you. I'm confident you will make the right decision," she assured him. "This will soon pass, but I'm ready to talk about it anytime and help in any way I can."

Expressing belief in your mate assures him of your faith in him as a person and in his ability to perform in your marriage, your family, and his job. Remember the bonus: When your words of belief communicate to your mate that he is trusted, he will be motivated to prove himself worthy of your trust.

One of the best stories about believing in someone else is a story of two boyhood friends, Johnny Echols and Marty Marion. These two boys loved baseball. It was their passion. They played day after day. In fact, they made a pact that they were going to play baseball together forever.

As time went on, Johnny became quite good at baseball. In fact, he soon became the star of their hometown team and was the talk of Atlanta. Everyone knew who Johnny Echols was because he always made the outstanding plays; he always hit the home runs.

One day, the coach called Johnny to the locker room and said, "I need to talk to you, Johnny. There's going to be try-outs for the minors, and I think you've got enough talent to make it."

"That's great!" Johnny exclaimed. "Marty and I will go. We'll pack up, and we'll be on that bus tomorrow!"

"But Johnny," the coach replied, "I wasn't talking about Marty, I was talking about you! Marty's an ugly duckling. He can't field, he can't hit, and he's just not going to be good at baseball. But you have talent, Johnny. You have great potential, and you need to go try out."

Johnny was adamant. "Well, Marty and I will go anyway."

When Marty's mother found out about this decision, she tried to discourage Johnny, too. "Please don't take Marty with you, Johnny. He's not as good as you are. You know he'll be rejected, and that will just cause him pain and hurt. Don't make him go through that."

"No, I want to because I believe in Marty," Johnny insisted. "I believe he has potential."

So Johnny and Marty went to the try-outs. After a few days, the coach offered Johnny a contract. He was elated. "That's great! Marty and I will sign up and play on your team."

The coach looked embarrassed. "No, I'm not talking about Marty, I'm talking about you. We want you, Johnny, but we don't want Marty."

There was a long moment of silence before Johnny spoke again. "Well, if you don't take Marty, then you can't have me. It's either both of us . . . or neither of us."

Needless to say, the coach was baffled. No one had ever said anything like that before. Everybody just looked out for themselves, for number one.

But Johnny stuck by his guns. The coach thought about it for a long time and finally decided that Johnny was valuable enough that the team would offer a contract to Marty as well. So both of them made the minor league teams.

In his third year in the minors, Johnny washed out. That was the end of his baseball career. But by now Marty had learned what Johnny had done for him and had become motivated by the belief that Johnny had in him.

Deciding to prove that Johnny was right, Marty began to improve. He started hitting better and fielding better. Before long, Marty became a rising star.

Soon Marty was called up to the majors and made the St. Louis Cardinals team as a shortstop. Not long after that, he became the team leader. In fact, in 1944, Marty Marion was the most valuable player in the World Series!

Years earlier, when Johnny had talked to Marty's mother, he said,

"Love is a kind of belief. I believe in Marty, and we're friends. I believe he has potential, and I'm going to stick by him. Believing in someone is the best kind of love."

We think Johnny was right. He knew the value of believing in a friend. Likewise, God has called us to believe in our mates.

Write a statement of your mate's value to you. Maybe it's a note in his lunch. Maybe it's a note packed away in the suitcase. Let your mate know how much you appreciate and value him.

Weeds or Fruit Trees: Take Your Pick

Years ago we took a fall vacation to New England, where we picked apples for five dollars a bushel one frosty morning. The "pick-your-own" orchard of mature Cortland apple trees covered the rolling hills like a patchwork quilt stitched in rows. The limbs were heavily laden with the ruby-red fruit, which we picked and ate for the better part of two hours.

As we were leaving, we met the owner of the orchard. We complimented him on the condition of his trees and the delicious fruit. He received our praise but quickly added his perspective. He told us about bitter New England winters and about fighting bugs and weeds for years to bring the orchard to its present level of productivity. It had taken hard work and perseverance, but it was beginning to pay off.

In a similar way, you have been entrusted with a plot of soil: your mate. You have also been given seeds: your words. The choices you make today—to plant good seeds in your mate and to avoid planting bad seeds—will guarantee a fine future harvest. In the meantime, however, you must weather the onslaught of changing circumstances, unexpected difficulties, and life in general as you love and live with him. But faithful tending will result in the roots of his self-esteem going down deeply into the truth of God's Word.

As Paul writes in Galatians 6:9: "And let us not lose heart in doing good, for in due time we shall reap if we do not grow weary." That's quite a promise! You *will* reap a good harvest if you don't grow weary and quit, but the kind of harvest really depends upon you. Will you help to grow weeds or fruit trees? Take your pick.

ESTEEM BUILDER PROJECT

(Use a sheet of paper if necessary.)

1. List some "words" (and attitudes and actions that accompany them) that you plant in your mate's life which produce:

Weeds	Fruit/Flowers
1.	1.
2.	2.
3.	3.
4.	4.
5.	5.
6.	6.

2. Are there any "weed seeds" you've planted in your mate's life for which you need to ask forgiveness?
3. What words encourage you and lift your spirit?

   1)   4)

   2)   5)

   3)   6)

4. What words or actions bring you down and discourage you?

   1)   4)

   2)   5)

   3)   6)

5. Complete the following sentences with one or more conclusions.

My mate can express belief in me by . . .

My mate can encourage me when I'm discouraged by . . .

6. Write some positive words to your mate. Pick one of the following formats:
   - a letter of praise
   - a letter of encouragement
   - a letter of appreciation
   - a statement of belief

Be specific. Avoid generalities.

As you write this letter, be sure to express your unconditional love and acceptance for your mate. Why not start by thinking of the two or three most important times you have had together. IMPORTANT: Be vulnerable and transparent in your letter. If this is difficult, let him know at the beginning of the letter. Your mate will respect your openness even more.

Then, read your letter to your mate, looking into his eyes. Make a mental note of how he responds when you read your letter to him and how it makes you feel when he reads his to you. CAUTION: Encouraging each other in this way can become a healthy addiction. Don't hesitate to repeat this project often!

BUILDING BLOCK #4:
Constructing Self-Esteem
during the Difficult Times

Weather the storms of life by turning toward one another and building into each other rather than rejecting one another.

CHAPTER

9

Building during the Storm

———◆———

- *Life's Difficulties Can Erode Your Mate's Self-Confidence*
- *Suffering Is Universal*
- *Daily Stress May Undermine Self-Esteem*
- *Building Your Mate during the Storm*
- *Weather the Storms Together*
- *Esteem Builder Project*

———◆———

FOR SOME REASON THAT ONLY GOD KNOWS, I (Dennis) did not leave for work on time that June morning. I had just finished tying my tie as Barbara began doing her exercises. Suddenly, I noticed that she had stopped and was sitting on the bed with her head between her knees.

"Are you okay?" I asked.

"No, I don't think so," she said weakly, her face white. "I feel like I'm going to faint."

Since her pulse was high from the exercise, she rested a few minutes, waiting for her heartbeat to return to normal. I had experienced an abnormally high heartbeat that winter, so when her heartbeat failed to slow down, I assured her that I knew exactly what to do. I put my arm around her and suggested that she get up and walk around with me.

After I helped her up, Barbara took only a couple of steps before turning around, collapsing on the bed, and nearly losing consciousness. When she complained again that her heart was really pounding, I began to become frightened, too. She had never experienced anything like this before.

I placed my fingers against Barbara's neck and attempted to check her pulse, but her heart was racing so fast I was unable to count the beats. "I'm calling an ambulance," I told her. Then I called a neighbor, who agreed to take care of our two small children.

When the ambulance arrived, we sped to the hospital where the heart monitor told the story: Barbara's heart was pounding at a rate of three hundred beats per minute. For the next six hours, the medical team did all they could. Barbara's bed in the coronary intensive care area literally shook from her fast-beating heart. Her pulse remained unchanged.

I had begun praying for Barbara the moment I recognized her problem, but I felt so powerless. After hours of waiting outside the care unit alone, I called Kitty Longstreth, a widow who had become a close friend, and asked her to pray and to call others who would pray. Shortly after noon, "Miss Kitty" (as she is affectionately known to the Rainey family and many others) got down on her knees and started praying for Barbara.

I was allowed to see Barbara once every two hours, and then for only five minutes. So I had plenty of time to pray, read the Scriptures, and think. I recall wondering early that afternoon, *What will I do with two children under three years of age? I need my wife.* Those were grim moments.

At 2 P.M., Barbara's lungs started to fill with fluid. At five beats per second, her heart did not have time to fill up with blood and completely pump it out, so her blood pressure was dangerously low.

125

At 3 P.M., she began to have difficulty breathing—asthma. By now, she was sick from all the medication the doctors had tried, and the pain was intense. The doctors warned me that now, more than ever, coronary failure was a real possibility. And I couldn't even communicate with her.

At 4 P.M., the cardiologist began preparations to use an electric shock to stop her heart and try to restart it at its normal rate. At the same time, five miles away, Miss Kitty finally felt the freedom from the Lord to get up off her knees. She later told me she *knew* everything was okay.

"I knew that either Barbara had died and gone to be with the Lord, or her heart rate had returned to normal," Miss Kitty said. "God gave me a peace to stop praying." Her clock read a few minutes past four.

The doctors told me they never had to use electric shock because Barbara's heart rate returned to normal "on its own." The time was 4:05 P.M. I had an incredible sense of relief and thankfulness as I walked into her room. The fear melted away as we embraced and wept.

Although a previously undiscovered congenital heart defect was still present, the doctors gave us hope that Barbara would lead a long, normal life. They released her from the hospital five days later.

After that experience, Barbara understandably became very introspective about anything going on inside her body. Concerned that her condition might recur, she became acutely aware of every heartbeat and physical ache. Then we found out she was pregnant.

During the next eight months, we learned to live with questions—questions about two people, a mother and a baby, rather than just about Barbara. These were heavy, thought-provoking months. There was little romance, little laughter, and little emotion left for anything or anyone else. It was an oppressive time, especially for Barbara. Yet together we moved through it.

When Barbara gave birth to Samuel, a healthy, nine-pound-five-ounce boy, it was God's signal to us that there was hope for the future.

We had no idea how much we would need that hope during the years to come.

Life's Difficulties Can Erode Your Mate's Self-Confidence

When we said our marriage vows, neither of us thought we'd have a year of suffering like the one we experienced in 1977. Today we are more realistic about life. We have learned that suffering comes to all of us at different times in our lives. We also have seen that one's self-image becomes fragile when the storms of life strike.

Some marriages crumble during life's storms. One spouse blames the other, or they refuse to communicate at all. If they fail to turn to God—lock-arm and lock-step together—they begin to drift apart or become combative.

It happened to us. After Barbara returned from the hospital in 1977, we felt an incredible closeness and bonding from having shared that experience. During the months that followed, however, she grew lonely, fearful, and anxious.

She questioned her relationship with God, asking, *Am I not praying enough? Am I not trusting Him right? What's wrong? Why can't I lick this thing? Why can't I bounce back and feel normal like I used to feel? Will I get sick again today?*

Barbara's introspection over her health was at times overwhelming. Occasionally, I wanted to tell her to "just move on." I felt that she was too preoccupied. I wanted to let her know that the children and I needed her to be with us—mentally as well as physically. But she couldn't just flip a switch and go on. She had to process things at her own rate.

Most important, however, was how these circumstances affected Barbara's self-esteem. Suddenly faced with her own mortality, she felt expendable.

A confident self-esteem is largely dependent on that feeling of being needed—of having something to offer—and one's personal ability to perform. With both of those pillars shaken, Barbara entered a state of bewilderment and discouragement. She became a little fatalistic about life. And although we knew God was still sovereignly in control of all that had occurred, we had to reckon with these disturbing thoughts.

At times, we seemed to drift toward isolation in our marriage because I didn't comprehend what she was going through, and she couldn't understand my feelings. I wanted a whole wife back, and Barbara thought she deserved to feel normal again.

Suffering Is Universal

God is gracious and doesn't often allow couples to experience suffering as painful as Job's, but He does allow measured doses of trouble at sovereignly ordained intervals. We have shared with you a bit of our trouble, but we are not alone. We have watched dear friends bury their seven-year-old boy two days before Christmas. We have helped others during business disasters and job losses. Other couples we know have experienced suffering from infertility, repeated illnesses, aging, midlife crises, problems with parents, teenage rebellion, death of parents, financial setbacks, the divorces of grown children, or children who disgrace the family name.

All of these people have experienced loss. Some have endured earth-shaking blows. Many, if not all, have questioned their self-worth and self-confidence. The difficulties have produced strength in many, but others have never quite seemed to recover.

How we respond to trials and loss is important. Trials either bring you and your mate together as one, or they drive you apart. Isolation is the natural result of trials if you do not take appropriate action to strengthen your relationship.

When you and your mate drift into isolation, one of two things typically occur. You may go through a silent divorce in which you remain married but depart from intimacy, or you may call it quits and go through an actual divorce.

Daily Stress May Undermine Self-Esteem

Suffering is not limited to times of tragedy. Affliction, heartache, and trouble visit almost predictably during different stages of life, usually during times of change and stress. One occupation that has plenty of scheduled and unscheduled trials is the job of being a mother.

The average mother today is often not esteemed by society for her contribution to the next generation. Instead, she may be told that mothering is a menial task that anyone could do.

Because she may not derive adequate esteem from her role, the mother is often unprepared and worn out when her children hit adolescence. As we all know, most teenagers are not gentle on their mothers. They have a way of questioning parental decisions, judgments, and authority on almost every issue. And most are oblivious as to how their attitudes and actions chip away at their mother's self-esteem. She feels attacked in this battle of the wills and finds herself questioning her worth and value. At one point we had four teenagers in our family, so we experienced firsthand how brutal life can be for a mom during those years!

If you are a husband and father, come alongside your wife to protect and support her. Crossing the turbulent waters of child rearing together will strengthen your mate's self-esteem and bring you to the empty nest united. I (Dennis) have realized that I had a responsibility to protect Barbara from the emotional attacks of our teens. On more than one occasion, I have had to step in and say to a teenager, "You cannot treat or talk to your mom in a disrespectful way."

Building Your Mate during the Storm

The storms of life will affect you and your mate differently. You may be tempted to turn away from one another. Don't! Turn toward one another in total commitment and provide a shelter during the storm. There are many ways to do this.

First, recognize that suffering is going to occur. James 1:2 says, "Consider it all joy . . . when you encounter various trials." The passage doesn't say *if* you encounter trials, but *when* you encounter them. So trials will come. Life will deliver unkind messages. Life is not fair.

When a good friend lost a son in a tragic plane crash, he said, "Life is overrated. It wouldn't be so hard if we didn't think life should be so easy."

We think this is one of today's problems: We don't anticipate suffering, so we're caught off guard when it comes. Couples should anticipate possible challenges and freely share their feelings about suffering. If you have a plan and know scripturally how to view adversity when it comes, then it won't cause you to go to war with one another. Indeed, you can turn troubles and trials into something that is purposeful, meaningful, and an opportunity for growth in your marriage.

Second, give your mate the freedom to process what's going on in his life. Don't expect him to flip a switch and just "deal with the problem and move on." It's not usually that easy.

If your mate's suffering doesn't diminish after a reasonable time, resist the temptation to make such statements as: "Snap out of it and trust God!" or "Quit acting like a big baby. You're more mature than that!" or "We've spent enough time talking about this. I think it's time we just put the whole matter to rest."

We've found that, to arrive at the end product God wants to develop in our lives, we must go through a lifelong process of becoming like Christ. Trials and tragedies should force us to turn to God, but one person may take longer than another to come to that point. Men and women do process suffering in differing ways.

Here is where your mate's self-esteem can benefit from a large measure of your understanding and longsuffering. True love doesn't quit just because its object doesn't respond quickly enough.

Third, find out what your mate needs. We have discovered that it is best to simply say, "I want to meet your needs and be the best possible partner I can be, but at times I don't know how. Would you tell me how you want me to love and encourage you in this situation?" Talk about your feelings and give your spouse the freedom to feel whatever he is feeling.

Your mate *may* desire to solve the problem. For example, if you have a difficult child, your wife may want you to join forces with her in loving and disciplining him. In other situations as well, your active involvement in problem solving may be just the encouragement your mate desires.

At other times, your mate doesn't want any advice, but would prefer for you to come alongside and listen compassionately. After you've listened and listened, it may be appropriate to say to your mate, "You're okay. You're going to make it because I know that you will ultimately do what's right. I believe in you. And I'm praying for you."

Fourth, build your marital foundation on Christ. In Matthew 7:24–25, Jesus says, "Therefore, everyone who hears these words of Mine, and acts upon them, may be compared to a wise man, who built his house upon the rock. And the rain descended, and the floods came, and the winds blew, and burst against that house; and yet it did not fall, for it had been founded upon the rock." This passage speaks about building a home on a foundation that can withstand trouble, trials, and tribulation when they come.

Jesus goes on to explain what happens to someone who doesn't build on this foundation: "And everyone who hears these words of Mine, and does not act upon them, will be like a foolish man, who built his house upon the sand. And the rain descended, and the floods came, and the winds blew, and burst against that house; and it fell, and great was its fall" (vv. 26–27).

Luke records the same parable and provides a different play on words: "He is like a man building a house, who dug deep" (6:48a).

This same principle is at work as you build a Christian home. You can't build it overnight; it requires a lifetime. When the floods come and the winds beat against your home, it will stand firm if you are in the process of building upon the Rock.

It was already hot early that Texas summer morning when Dave met with a land developer to talk about a zoning issue. August 25, 1977 would be a day that neither he nor his wife, Carol, would ever forget. She had left her two boys—Ben, almost twelve, and Tom, eight—at home to play while she ran to school to prepare for a class she would begin teaching the following week.

Dave finished his meeting with the land developer and almost stopped by his home, but he decided against it and drove on to work. So neither Dave nor Carol were home that morning when the two boys pulled out their dad's deer rifle.

The night before, finding a shell, they had put it into the chamber. This morning, when they decided to play with the rifle again, they forgot about that shell. The gun went off, killing eight-year-old Tom instantly.

The months that followed were characterized not only by emotional pain, guilt, and grief, but by physical pain as well. Dave said he felt as if a hay hook had sunk into his stomach and then ripped out a piece of it. Carol fell into deep introspection. Both asked, "Why?"

Although this level of suffering seldom strikes repeatedly during one's lifetime, we are all likely to experience painful times when we are forced to hold onto God and to each other for survival. These times strike like a flash flood, without warning.

Unlike many couples who experience a tragedy of that magnitude, Dave and Carol moved through that loss and today have a strong marriage. Their stability and strength came as they built into one another's lives through prayer and complete dependence upon Jesus Christ.

Dave prayed daily for Carol and for himself. He prayed for

understanding of his wife and for knowledge of how to help her. He renewed his commitment to her and pledged a renewal of their wedding vows. She knew he had resolutely decided to endure and persevere. She felt he cared deeply for her, and he proved it as he helped her look to the future, without pushing or being impatient with her.

Carol spent enormous amounts of time reading the Bible and shared Scriptures with Dave. She focused on things that were "worthy of praise"[1] and expressed them to Dave and to her son Ben. Although it took nearly all of the energy she had, she sought to make dinner a happy time. She started exercising with Dave—it relieved the stress and gave them time to think and talk.

As a couple, they forced themselves to focus on others and to stay involved in their church. Together, they wrapped their arms of love around Ben and helped him work through his grief and guilt. Above all, their commitment to Jesus Christ and to one another was strengthened beyond measure. They built their home upon the "Rock."

Fifth, buoy your mate's confidence during these times by offering perspective. The preacher in Ecclesiastes penned these famous words: "There is an appointed time for everything. And there is a time for every event under heaven—a time to give birth, and a time to die; . . . a time to weep, and a time to laugh; a time to mourn, and a time to dance."[2]

You will gain perspective by looking up from the stones and boulders that are tripping your mate along the way so that you can grasp the whole panorama of life. Use your words to lift life's pain up against the backdrop of God's sovereign control. All that happens in life is sifted through the all-knowing, all-loving hands of the Father. Recognizing that may not make the pain any less intense for your mate, but it will offer hope for the future.

Bring balance to your mate's assessment of his own life by recalling God's faithfulness in the past. Point out, too, that he is valuable, although he may be tempted to feel otherwise during the midst of difficulty. If he is suffering for doing wrong, direct him to the graciousness of God, who wants to forgive his worst mistakes.

Our perspective on circumstances is aided when the Scriptures permeate our thinking. Often, during difficult times, our ears are more keenly tuned to hear God's voice. Your mate's spirit may be lifted if you read him an extended portion of Scripture (such as Psalm 23, 31, or 34) at the end of a stressful day. At other times, a single verse or your own paraphrase of biblical truth can bring light to the darkness that has enveloped him.

Ecclesiastes 3:7b reveals that there is "a time to be silent, and a time to speak." Depend upon God to give you the wisdom to know when to be silent, when to speak, and which words to use to bring perspective to your mate. God promises to give wisdom if we will ask in faith.[3] One of the greatest feelings of satisfaction comes from knowing that God has given you the right word at the right moment for your spouse. And He *will* do just that.

Sixth, for Christians, suffering precedes fruitfulness. One prerequisite of bearing fruit in the Christian life is the painful process of "pruning." Jesus said, "Every branch that bears fruit, He prunes it, that it may bear more fruit."[4] God is lovingly ordering events, circumstances, and relationships in our lives for the purpose of helping us to become more and more like Jesus Christ. Personal godliness is His primary goal for us. The pruning He must do seems at times to be severe—even too painful to bear. But there is little fruitfulness without pruning.

One of the great privileges of marriage is that we do not have to go through these pruning periods alone. God has provided a partner with whom you can share the pain of the process. If your mate is in the midst of a season of pruning, come alongside him and gently remind him of the hope of becoming more Christlike through the suffering.

Seventh, aggressively make your relationship with your mate a priority during times of strain and struggle. Build times to talk into your schedule. If possible, take walks together. Schedule a weekend to get away and minister to your mate in his area of personal struggle. You may wish to work together toward solving the problem. Above all else, pursue your mate. Don't let him become isolated by the crisis. It affects you both.

After Barbara's initial heart episode in 1977, she had three more similar "attacks" in the next ten years. We finally learned she had Wolfe-Parkinson-White Syndrome, which means that an extra pathway in the heart conducts electricity. In layman's terms, this could be compared to an interstate bypass. The electrical impulses that caused Barbara's heart to beat would go around the regulator in circular fashion. Surgery would be required to correct the problem.

A physician who specialized in this congenital defect told me, "You've got six kids and a lot of responsibility, but I want you to know that your wife could drop dead instantly!"

His words pressed us into fervent action. We searched from one coast to the other to learn how to take care of the problem. Our search led us to Oklahoma Memorial Hospital in the spring of 1991. A doctor there explained three possible complications that could occur during the operation: a stroke, damage due to surgery, or sudden death. His sober explanation, which he was required by law to give us, cast a dim light on the rest of the evening and throughout the next morning during Barbara's surgery.

After over thirteen hours, she was wheeled out of the operating room. Although she had undergone extensive heart catheterization, the physician said she would be all right. I took her in my arms and said, "You're okay, you're okay. The doctor says you're going to be fine."

God used this experience in our marriage to cement us together. It has affected many areas of our lives even today: our schedules, how we view each other, and our preoccupations.

Weather the Storms Together

A little girl was sitting on her grandpa's lap, listening to some sage advice. As her blue eyes peered deeply into his, the silver-haired man said, "Sweetheart, remember, life is like licking honey off a thorn."

It's true. Life is bittersweet, but the hope for you and your mate is not having to "go it alone." God has called you to weather the storms together. Build into your mate's life so that the world might see Jesus Christ more clearly in his life and yours. And remember, as Ray Stedman, the late pastor and author, said, "The ship won't sink, and the storm won't last forever."

Consider what Job says to God after all the trials he has experienced:

> *I know that Thou canst do all things, and that no purpose of Thine can be thwarted. Who is this that hides counsel without knowledge? Therefore I have declared that which I did not understand, things too wonderful for me, which I did not know. Hear, now, and I will speak; I will ask Thee, and do Thou instruct me. I have heard of Thee by the hearing of the ear; but now my eye sees Thee; therefore I retract, and I repent in dust and ashes.* [5]

In the midst of his sorrow, Job found God. And that may be the purpose of it all.

───────◆───────

ESTEEM BUILDER PROJECT

(Use a sheet of paper if necessary.)

1. Is your mate presently being pulled down by something you are not sharing together? Why not ask him if you can be a part of this time in his life and be the person he needs you to be?
2. Discuss with your mate what he needs from you:
   • Help with a solution.
   • Compassion, patience, and understanding in the process.

- The perspective that biblical truth provides.
- A reminder of God's provision from the past.

3. Today, begin to ask God to help you pursue your mate and know exactly what to say and do to build self-esteem into his life. Be honest with God.

4. Pray together that God will enable you to stand together during this time of suffering.

5. Be sure you are an active member of a Bible-believing church. A church is an absolutely essential component for any marriage that wants to experience all God intended. Find a kindred-spirited couple in your church who will allow you to be real and bear your burdens with you.

BUILDING BLOCK #5:
Giving Your Mate the Freedom to Fail

*R*elease your mate from the prison of
performance with the golden key
labeled "the freedom to fail."

CHAPTER

10

Down, But Not Out for the Count

- *Hope for Your Mate*
- *Failure's Effects*
- *An Anatomy of Failure*
- *Why We Fail*
- *The Antidote for Those Who Fail*
- *The Suspender Principle*
- *Esteem Builder Project*

HAVE YOU EVER WONDERED WHY your mate:

- finds failure so threatening, even frightening?
- has difficulty admitting that he's wrong or that he has failed?
- is paralyzed at times by the fear of failure?
- experiences internal feelings of failure despite outward appearances of success?

If you answered *yes* to any of those questions, you are seeing the symptoms of an insecure individual who has difficulty dealing with failure. Your mate isn't alone. All of us are prone to fail, and no marriage is exempt from failure's influence.

In a performance-oriented culture such as ours, failure belts us like a punch in the stomach. Repeated failure often results in a knockout blow, and many people give up altogether.

Emotionally, failure is extremely costly. It leaves us with feelings of guilt, self-condemnation, and doubt. It's no wonder that failure is feared and risk is so frightening.

Hope for Your Mate

Perhaps your mate has been shattered by past failures and, consequently, has a fragile self-image. By slowly forging in your mate the freedom to fail, you'll help him become more open to change, more willing to take risks, and more confident in decision making.

Giving your mate the freedom to fail communicates that you are on his team, regardless of the outcome. It tells him that even if he makes a mistake and fails, you will be there to help him up, dust him off, and encourage him to try again. The issue is not whether he will ever fail, but rather whether he will get back up and whether you will be at his side.

In an address to a nation divided by the Civil War, Abraham Lincoln underscored the need to persevere in spite of failure. He said, "I am not concerned that you have failed. I am concerned that you arise." The following excerpt, which appeared in an advertisement in the *Wall Street Journal*, also emphasizes this point:

> YOU'VE FAILED MANY TIMES although you may not remember. You fell the first time you tried to walk, didn't you? You almost drowned the first time you tried to swim. Did you hit the ball the first time you swung the bat? Heavy hitters, the ones who hit the most home runs, also struck out a lot. R. H. Macy failed seven times before his store in New York caught on. English novelist John Cracey got 753 rejection slips before he published 564 books. Babe Ruth struck out 1330 times, but he also

hit 714 home runs. Don't worry about failure. Worry about the chances you miss when you don't even try.

Failure's Effects

Failure, a strict taskmaster, accompanies us all too frequently during the journey of life. After failing, we usually attempt to avoid any future mistakes by walking one of two paths. The most commonly followed path is accelerated performance. Our failures motivate us to stay ahead of impending disasters. The fear of failure is like a shadow at our heels, threatening to overtake us. On the basis of our success in avoiding failures, we erroneously conclude that our worth or value is rooted solely in our performance.

The other path is the way of resignation or passivity. Comedian W. C. Fields once quipped, "If at first you don't succeed, then quit. There's no use in being a fool about it." The price of failure may be too high: disapproval, anger, imposed guilt, ridicule, and rejection. So we may avoid any unnecessary risks. A life with no risk *appears* to offer safety and security, but it *delivers* guilt, boredom, further apathy, and even lower feelings of self-esteem.

An Anatomy of Failure

We find an anatomy of failure in the life of Moses. Exodus 3 begins with Moses in exile. He had just murdered an Egyptian and, fearing for his life, had fled from Pharaoh into the wilderness.

For forty years, Moses lived in the desert, undoubtedly hounded by a host of condemning voices that reminded him he had been rejected by the Jewish nation as well as by his adopted Egyptian family. When God appeared to him in the burning bush, Moses was struggling with an identity problem—the result of failure and rejection. After forty years of exile in the desert, he was full of self-doubt.

God told Moses that He was going to send him to free the Israelites, to which Moses responded, "Who am I?"[1] God simply replied, "I will be with you."[2] Above all, Moses needed God's reassuring presence. Without Him, Moses could never stand before Pharaoh; the rejection would be too painful. Left alone, he would certainly fail.

Moses' next question was, in effect, "Who are you? What is the name of the One who sends me?"[3] God graciously responded. Even though He told Moses who He was (v. 14), Moses again resisted His command and listened to the nagging voices of self-doubt. Exodus 4:1 reveals Moses' feelings of uncertainty: "What if they will not believe me, or listen to what I say?"

God then gave Moses two signs of His divine presence. First, He transformed Moses' staff into a serpent. The second sign was the instant affliction of Moses' hand with leprosy and its equally instantaneous and miraculous restoration. These two visual aids were embedded in Moses' memory to remind him that God's presence was powerful and transforming. God would be with him.

In spite of these convincing and powerful displays of God's omnipotence, Moses' feelings of inadequacy resurfaced: "Please, Lord, I have never been eloquent, neither recently nor in time past, nor since Thou hast spoken to Thy servant; for I am slow of speech and slow of tongue."[4] God then reminded Moses who made his mouth and told Moses that He would teach him what to say (v. 11).

After all this dialogue with God, Moses dared to make one more response, the essence of which was, "I can't do what you've asked. Please choose someone else."[5] Rather than focusing on God, Moses focused on himself. He was like the little boy in the school play whose one line was, "It is I, be not afraid." But on the night of the play, the boy came out on stage and exclaimed, "It's me, and I'm scared!"

Only when Moses saw that there was no way out did he submit to God's call. He was so convinced of his own worthlessness that it took time for God to convince him otherwise.

Likewise, your mate also may have a difficult time believing God and you. He, too, may be plagued by failure. His failure may not have been murder, as Moses' was, but it may be one of dozens of experiences that can whisper "you're a failure" in his ear. These whispers of failure may include:

- a broken friendship
- a lost job
- personal rejection at work
- perpetual unemployment
- an idea that didn't work
- a bad investment
- a strained relationship
- accusations by a child
- a bad decision
- words spoken in anger that can't be taken back
- marital unfaithfulness
- a previous divorce
- having lashed out at a child in anger
- a foolish mistake or poor judgment

Note that in this chapter of Moses' life, part of God's solution to Moses' self-worth problem was a companion—Aaron. The two brothers became a team. Undoubtedly, Aaron frequently reminded Moses of the truth: he was God's man for the assignment, and God would be faithful to His promises. Just as Moses needed Aaron, your mate needs you.

Why We Fail

Failure comes from not reaching standards—God's, ours, and others'. We fail because we are human. Failure is a part of the flawed fabric of our humanity.

At our house, we have experienced plenty of failures, both great and small. For years, a meal without a spill was nothing short of miraculous. The milk may have gone shooting across the supper table or formed a lazy river that cascaded over the edge, splattering onto the floor. We've seen some classic spills: two simultaneously, four at one sitting, and one glass of chilled apple juice that spilled perfectly into Dennis's shoe (while he was wearing it). Our favorite phrase for the children became, "It's okay. Everybody makes mistakes."

One evening, I (Dennis) spilled my drink during dinner. A little hand patted my arm, and Rebecca (then a five-year-old) reassuringly said, "It's okay, Dad. Everybody makes mistakes."

It's comforting to know that we are not alone in our failures. Others, too, have needed and claimed God's forgiveness when they failed. King David failed through his adulterous relationship with Bathsheba and the murder of her husband. Peter failed by denying Christ. Thomas doubted. Saul (Paul) assisted in the murder of Stephen.

Yet none of these lives represented total failure. Each of these men sought forgiveness. They didn't give up. They kept on. They left a track record of faithfulness in spite of personal foul-ups.

Sometimes people "fail" because they set their expectations too high. At other times they allow the unrealistic expectations of others—including their mates—to become their standard.

Do you recall seeing, at the circus or on television, a performance featuring dogs who were trained to jump through hoops? The most unlikely dog—a tiny one—would jump through the hoop just when you knew there was no way the little fellow could possibly leap that high. But the trainer knew what to expect out of his performers, and, to the crowd's delight, the little dog always succeeded.

Unlike the circus trainer, some spouses haven't studied and worked with their mates enough to know their limits and potential abilities. Or, if they have determined their mates' capabilities, they don't like what they see. Perhaps others keep raising the "hoops" higher and higher. When their mates find the point they can't reach, the spouses react by saying, "I knew you couldn't do it!" or "I can't believe you can't do this; it's so easy." They conclude that their mates are failures in this area—and let them know it.

Have you held up hoops for your mate? Ask God to show you any areas in which you are contributing to your mate's feelings of failure or rejection. Be sure you're not part of the problem so you can be part of the solution.

The Antidote for Those Who Fail

What is the solution for the fear of failure? How do you encourage a partner whose feelings of failure are triggered by the most insignificant of circumstances? We have found that one of the most powerful principles in building one another's self-esteem is: *Give your mate the freedom to fail.*

When you give your mate the freedom to fail, you begin to remove the pressure to perform for acceptance. You free your mate to take risks and try again. You free him to excel. Failure then becomes a tutor, not a judge. In the presence of freedom, we learn from failures instead of being intimidated by them. In the absence of condemnation, confidence in how God can use you mounts.

For years, we talked about moving to the country. The thought of the children having room to roam sounded inviting, but moving a large family is a chore. More importantly, it was a risk. What if we didn't like driving back and forth to town? What if we didn't like being isolated from friends? So we put off the decision.

Then one day Barbara said, "So what if we decide we don't like it? We can sell and move back to town!" Her statement clicked; it gave me (Dennis) the freedom to make a decision—even a wrong one! We decided to try it, and we love it. But the decision came only after the fear of failure was removed.

If you would like to give your mate the freedom to fail, we recommend six gifts you can give that will begin to release him. Keep in mind that you, too, will possibly fail by taking back some of these gifts. That's okay. Failure is a part of learning for both of you.

1. The Gift of Compassion

In chapter 6, we discussed how the past holds a great power over a person's life. Perhaps your mate is overly cautious and has difficulty changing or making decisions. Most likely, most of this fearfulness has been ingrained in him for years. He needs your compassion and patience as he begins to take risks. Compassion says, "I share your feelings."

Every person's life has a context. During his childhood, your mate may not have experienced a relationship in which he had freedom to fail. Perhaps his "failures" taught him to expect rejection, disapproval, and anger from those in authority. He may have learned to feel that rejection is the natural consequence of failure.

Parents, coaches, teachers, peers, boyfriends, girlfriends, siblings, and other significant people gave him a personal heritage of either success or failure. The more you fully grasp the context of your mate's journey to adulthood and express compassion for where your mate has been, the more freedom your mate will feel to admit failures to you.

Whatever his background, your mate needs your compassionate, consistent, and tireless belief in him. Talk about the context of his life and together gain understanding of past mistakes as well as present ones. Don't leave your mate alone to deal with his failures. Tell him that you are unlike those who have rejected him; your commitment is unwavering and your love is consistent, despite his imperfections. In this climate of compassion and patience, he will begin to feel free to take risks and to fail without fear of rejection.

2. The Gift of Continual Affirmation

Years ago, I (Barbara) drove to the grocery store and accidentally backed our van into a couple's newly painted Camaro, denting it slightly. I felt so foolish, and my apologies didn't make the dent go away. Understandably, the car's owners were not happy and insisted on calling the county sheriff's office.

I called Dennis, and as I waited for him to arrive, I wondered what he would think and say. I was pretty sure he wouldn't be upset with me, but I speculated for a while.

When he joined me at the store, he assured me that everything would be fine—that in the end it didn't really matter. We both knew I had made a mistake, and it would have accomplished nothing for him to drive home a moral lesson or give me some driving tips. I needed to experience his approval, and I needed to know he wasn't angry with me. He affirmed me, and I felt like pieces of a puzzle coming together.

Henry Ward Beecher wrote, "Compassion will cure more sins than condemnation." One of our favorite verses, 1 Peter 4:8, says it best: "Love covers a multitude of sins." Continuous, ongoing, unbroken approval in the face of many mistakes and failures of life will build your mate's self-esteem.

3. The Gift of Perspective

Jesus said, "You shall know the truth, and the truth shall make you free."[6] As partners in the pilgrimage of life, we are responsible to speak the truth to one another in order to help balance our perspective of failure.

Understanding the truth of God's sovereign rule—that He is in control—brings an eternal view to your mate's mistakes. The promise of Romans 8:28—"God causes all things to work together for good"— beautifully illustrates His absolute supremacy. These words offer comfort, reminding us that nothing is wasted in His economy. God can use even our mistakes and failures. Encourage your mate to believe God and, as a couple, ask Him to use your failures for good.

Another view you can give your mate is that most failures are not as big as they appear in our minds. All of us need the help of others to see the overall picture. Momentary mistakes are not that monumental when seen against the backdrop of a person's entire life.

4. The Gift of Disassociation

Most people don't realize they can fail and not be a failure. They have not learned to separate their *worth* as persons from their *performance*. Many find it difficult to have their ideas, work, or accomplishments criticized. They feel that others are criticizing and rejecting who they are, not just what they have done.

A teacher told one mother that her son was not a good student. "He can't learn," said the teacher. "He'll never amount to much." But the mother chose to believe in her son rather than listening to the voice of this "authority." As a result, that young man grew up in a home of loving acceptance, secure in the knowledge that he was a person of value.

In spite of all this, he continued to fail. In fact, he failed ten thousand times on one project before he, Thomas Alva Edison, perfected the electric lightbulb. His close association with failure caused Edison to comment, "I failed my way to success." His mother's belief in him was the human fuel for his inventive spirit.

How can you help your mate learn to fail without feeling like a failure? Try not to discuss a problem in your marriage or family with accusing words such as, "You never . . ." or, "Your ideas are always . . ." Those kinds of extreme statements verbally link your mate with his performance, insinuating that he is a failure. Instead, use your words with discernment to help him see the distinction between his personhood and his performance.

When you discuss issues with your mate, begin by expressing your commitment and loyalty to him as a person. Then give your mate the benefit of the doubt. Remove the accusing edge by saying, "I may be wrong, but did you . . ." or "I feel that . . ." or "It would help me a lot if you would . . . (fill the car with gas, balance the checkbook, pick up your socks, etc.)."

You may discover that your mate struggles with admitting he has failed. Perhaps his self-worth is dependent upon his performance. By admitting failure, he would be admitting that he doesn't have it all together, and that's just too threatening. But don't give up. In time, he'll understand the difference between his worth as a person and the worth of his performance.

Tell him the truth: He is loved by you, esteemed and valued by God, gifted, and yet limited. Call to mind his past accomplishments. Most importantly, help your mate separate himself from his failures. Focus on him as a *person*, too, not just on his performance. When your mate knows how to handle failure without *being* a failure, he truly has the freedom to fail.

5. The Gift of Encouraging Decisive Living

Many times in life, we fail not because we make the wrong decision but because we make no decision at all. Seeking safety and security, we escape to the seemingly trouble-free world of procrastination and indecision. Never venturing out of our protective covering of indecision, we avoid risking a wrong decision that might end in failure. We decide *not* to decide.

You can strengthen your mate by helping him understand that a risk-free life is also a potentially boring and selfish life. By eliminating risk, we eliminate many pleasures, too. Security and safety are not found in hiding from reality and responsibility. In fact, the opposite is true. Failure ultimately looms on the horizon for the person who avoids the decision-making process. He is riding a fence with both feet firmly planted in midair—there is little stability.

If your mate tends to be overly dependent upon you in decision making, gently begin to send a few more decisions his way. Sometimes verbalizing "You decide, I trust you, and I'll back you in whatever you decide" can be very freeing. In this way, he learns that he can make good decisions. Your mate's good decisions spawn self-confidence and increased trust in his decision-making abilities.

6. The Gift of Forgiveness

The effects of failure can be disarmed through the miracle of forgiveness. Pure and free, forgiveness gives us something we often don't deserve. This is how God relates to us as His children. He gives us love when we deserve punishment. Forgiveness says, "I choose to accept you fully, just as you are, and I will neither reject you nor remind you of your failures."

Forgive your mate when his error has affected you. Urge him to receive God's forgiveness and to forgive himself, if necessary. The act of forgiveness opens the door to healing.

Paul has some good advice: "And be kind to one another, tenderhearted, forgiving each other, just as God in Christ also has forgiven you."[7] He also writes, "Bearing with one another, and forgiving each other, whoever has a complaint against any one, just as the Lord forgave you, so also should you."[8]

Whatever the situation, mistakes carry a price tag. The price can be extra work, suffering, financial expense—or all three. Perhaps your mate's failure caused you to be late, which you hate. Maybe his failure cost him a bonus, which you were counting on to buy a new loveseat. Because of your partnership in marriage, your mate's mistakes and failures will affect you to some degree. When you forgive your mate's failures, you give up your right to punish. Forgiveness is an act of the will—a deliberate choice that means you will not retaliate when you feel the other person has wronged you. True forgiveness doesn't throw your mate's failures up to him or use them to hurt him.

Beware, too, of rationalizing away your need to forgive. Don't say to yourself, *My wife is more at fault in this than I am, so I'm not going to give in and ask to be forgiven.* That's pride talking. Keep in mind that people seldom evaluate situations with an unbiased view. As the old adage says, "Rare is the person who can weigh the faults of others without putting his thumb on the scale."

The gift of forgiveness is not just in *giving* forgiveness, but in *asking*

151

for it when you're wrong. Whether you're 90 percent in the wrong, or only 10 percent, asking for forgiveness takes the logs out of the fire. Verbalize it. Be specific. And don't fudge. Some people try to weasel out of their responsibility so they won't have to admit they were wrong. But in doing so, they miss the benefits of forgiveness.

Forgiveness stands with the open arms of a loving relationship, ready to embrace. It is illogical for your mate to resist such an aggressive love. By removing the fear of rejection, you give your mate renewed hope to keep trying without fear of failure.

The Suspender Principle

The way to build your mate's self-esteem is not to seek to fill your lives with successes, nor is it just to avoid failures. That is impossible. Instead, give each other the freedom to fail, and support one another when you do.

Two people together can be like a pair of suspenders; when one falls, the other still holds on. You and your mate need each other. The need to be encouraged and believed in never changes. As we were working on the revision of this book, a classic illustration of failure occurred in my (Dennis's) life.

While we were out in the yard one day, Barbara pointed out a tree she wanted to have removed. There were several problems with this tree—and, actually, it was these problems, plus the risk of failure that had kept me from removing the tree years earlier. First, the tree was very near the house, enclosed within a white picket fence that also appeared to be in the path of the tree when it fell. Second, I'm no precision engineer when it comes to working with my hands.

But I screwed up my courage to tackle the project. The tree fell only partway—lodging itself precariously against another tree that stood perilously close to the house. So I tied one end of a rope to the stuck tree and wrapped the other end around the trailer hitch of my car. Barbara was standing by, watching my frustration mount. But she kept encouraging me, being very careful to keep her suggestions to a minimum.

When the rope snapped, so did my patience. I jumped into the car in a huff and drove thirty minutes to town to buy the biggest rope I could find! My afternoon was now shot, but I was determined to win the battle of the trees!

I finally succeeded in getting the rope around the tree after nearly accidentally hitting my teenage son in the head with a small brick that I had used to throw the rope. Then I attached the rope to the car and down came the tree—smashing in half a ten-year-old prized Japanese Maple, my favorite tree!

Barbara's response was to come over to me, wrap her arms around me, and tell me how proud she was that I had tried to cut down the tree. She didn't yell at me. She didn't jump on my case. In the midst of my feeling like an absolute klutz, she simply loved and affirmed me.

After soothing my ragged feelings, she then attempted to mend my favorite tree, while I calmly set out to finish cutting up the tree I had finally removed.

Her love and belief made my failure tolerable. And that's your assignment with your mate, too.

———————◄•►———————

ESTEEM BUILDER PROJECT

(Use a sheet of paper if necessary.)

1. Evaluate your mate's "fear factor." How fearful is he? A little? A lot? Only occasionally? Frequently?
2. In what ways have your words and actions increased or decreased your mate's fear of failure?
3. List, in order of priority, the two or three "gifts" from this chapter that you need to give to your mate. Beside each gift,

write how you will reinforce its truth practically in your mate's life.

4. Why not give your mate authorized freedom to fail? You can formally present him with a document to that effect—custom designed, signed by you, and "notarized" to make it official.

BUILDING BLOCK #6:
Pleasing Your Mate

*B*y focusing on pleasing your mate,
you communicate that he is valued,
cherished, and loved.

11

New Furnishings for an Empty Home

---◆---

- *Pleasing Your Mate Produces Value*
- *God Wants Us to Please Our Mates*
- *Pleasing Your Mate Provides Encouragement during Tough Times*
- *Why Don't We Please Our Mates?*
- *Neglect Leaves the Door Open*
- *Requirements of a Partner-Pleaser*
- *Ideas for Pleasing Your Partner*
- *Pleasing Your Wife*
- *Pleasing Your Husband*
- *Be a Grateful Receiver*
- *Esteem Builder Project*

---◆---

A *CLASSIFIED AD READS AS FOLLOWS:*

For Sale: One 52-year-old husband. Never remembers anniversaries, birthdays, or special days. Seldom holds hands, hugs, kisses, or says, "I love you." Rarely is kind or tender. Will sell cheap—two cents. Call 555-0366. Will negotiate.

That advertisement illustrates the end result of a hollow marriage. Undoubtedly, that woman's self-worth bears the mark of her husband's lack of attention. Had her husband made a conscious effort to strengthen her self-worth by pleasing her, that advertisement never would have appeared.

Did this husband begin their courtship and marriage with this list of "seldoms" and "nevers"? Probably not. Early in their relationship, this couple probably experienced the pleasure and delight of pleasing one another, because the desire to please is born out of love. But why is pleasing one another so bountiful during courtship, engagement, and the spring of marriage but often so scarce as a marriage moves into summer, fall, and winter?

Before we answer that question, let's explore how pleasing your mate builds his self-esteem and produces other worthwhile results.

Pleasing Your Mate Produces Value

To please means "to satisfy, make content, gratify, gladden, cheer, delight." When we are pleased, we smile. A smile indicates happiness and satisfaction. Just as new upholstery changes an old, worn chair into a piece of furniture that looks brand new, so can pleasing your mate refurbish his self-esteem.

When you pay attention to what pleases your mate, you validate his uniqueness as a person. Knowing his interests and acting to accommodate them lets him know you care. Whether it's fixing the screen door, spicing up your sex life, carrying out a promise, losing fifteen pounds, working more around the house, or being on time, your actions communicate, "You're number one in my life, and I want you to know it."

What could you do right now to please your mate? What would cause his face to beam with excitement? Do you know? Will you do it? When? If not, why not? If you really love him, why wouldn't you want to please him all the time?

God Wants Us to Please Our Mates

Pleasing your mate is a command of Scripture. Romans 15:1-3 reads: "Now we who are strong ought to bear the weaknesses of those without strength and not just please ourselves. Let each of us please his neighbor for his good, to his edification. For even Christ did not please Himself." There are three key phrases here.

First, we should "not just please ourselves." God has not put us here merely to satisfy our own wants and needs. But in narcissistic America, we're being bombarded daily with advertising that entices us to satisfy ourselves.

Second, "Let each of us please his neighbor for his good." Who is your closest neighbor? Your spouse. So you are to please your spouse for his particular good.

Finally, consider the phrase, "For even Christ did not please Himself." What did Christ seek to do? He gave Himself up and died so that we might live!

The purpose of Christ's giving Himself up is found in the little phrase, "to his edification." This is the concept of building another's self-esteem. Biblically speaking, edification means to build one another up, to let the Word of God dwell in another person's life so that he can become a complete person. Pleasing your mate defeats selfishness.

In Philippians 2:3-4, we read: "Do nothing from selfishness or empty conceit, but with humility of mind let each of you regard one another as more important than himself; do not merely look out for your own personal interests, but also for the interests of others."

I am convinced that great marriages and great families are rooted in self-denial. In a truly biblical, Christian marriage, both people are willing to give up their lives for one another in order to love their mate properly. What but the love of your mate would make you give up your favorite sport or recreation?

During the early years of marriage, I remember looking in the rearview mirror of the car as I pulled out to go fishing with several of our children one Saturday. Barbara was standing on the porch, left with a couple of kids in diapers while I went off to the lake with the older kids to have a good time.

While I was sitting out in that boat, not catching anything, I continued to think about Barbara. *You know, I am pleasing myself, but I have not done a good job of pleasing her.* I realized I needed to give up some of my hobbies for a while in order to please her and reduce her burden. But you know what happened? Once the youngest kids grew older and Barbara's burden began to lift, she began to encourage me to fish and hunt with the children. Now when I leave the house on one of these trips, I look in the rearview mirror and see her on that same porch, waving good-bye with a smile.

Pleasing Your Mate Provides Encouragement during Tough Times

Life is tough. If most of us would tell the truth, not many days are really "great days." Many more are tougher than we care to admit.

It's encouraging to know on those difficult days, however, that the person who knows you best is thinking about pleasing you and making your home a haven. To have one person thinking about me and my day is a great encouragement.

I (Dennis) will never forget one particularly hectic period when our garage began to resemble a junkyard. I couldn't get any free time to clean it up, and the kids kept bringing in treasures the neighbors were throwing away.

Then one day I came home and found the garage spic and span! I even checked the house number to make sure I had the right address. Barbara had waded into the mess with the kids and cleaned it out—a real sacrifice for her because she gets allergies and starts sneezing from the dust. But that clean-up job greatly encouraged me.

Why Don't We Please Our Mates?

Although God wants us to please our mates and doing so brings great blessing and encouragement into our lives, we don't often make an effort to do it. Why? Let us give you six reasons:

First, we believe the contest is over and the prize has been won. Isn't it fascinating that during the courtship phase, men and women compete vigorously for the prize of marriage and, when the "right person" is found, both members of the relationship go to great lengths to please each other? They jog and work out to maintain the best possible image. A young woman may dress with his favorite color or style in mind or attend some sports event she doesn't enjoy. As the popular song of the late '60s says:

> . . . *[they] do the things he likes to do,*
> *wear your hair just for him, 'cause*
> *you won't get him thinkin' and a-prayin'*
> *wishin' and a-hopin'.* . . . [1]

Men are no different. A young man will make time for picnics and walks in the park. He may save his meager earnings for flowers, cards, letters, and gifts. He's so thoughtful. He treats her to evenings out on the town. She feels like a queen, proud to be with such a considerate person. They talk for hours and dream of the future. Confidence grows that this blissful state will last forever.

Then the wedding ceremony comes and goes. Almost overnight, couples are transformed into tightwad pragmatists. They've "won the prize." But the desire to please, which so recently flowed instinctively, begins to recede like a desert stream in the heat of summer. What started as a dream fades away as disillusionment replaces romance.

Second, poison words overpower positive words. One of the most bitter, sarcastic relationships recorded in this generation was between two of Britain's finest individuals—Sir Winston Churchill and Lady

Astor. Although not married to each other, these two typify what happens to far too many husbands and wives.

On one occasion, Lady Astor made the insulting remark, "Mr. Churchill, if you were my husband, I'd give you poison to drink."

He shot back, "Lady, if you were my wife, I'd drink it!"

But Lady Astor didn't give up easily. On another occasion, she saw her golden opportunity when Churchill had been drinking liberally. Lady Astor, probably assuming that he would not have the presence of mind to retaliate, accused him indignantly, saying, "Mr. Prime Minister, I perceive that you are drunk."

A wry smile broke across Churchill's face as he retorted, "Yes, Lady, and I perceive that you are ugly. But tomorrow I shall be sober."

As in Churchill and Astor's relationship, many marriage partners today have traded *pleasing* one another for *poisoning* one another. They have swapped positive words for negative, piercing ones.

Third, reality overtakes romance. Who hasn't enjoyed being under the influence of romance's gravity—that "walking-on-air" feeling? But then the couple hits the ground. Suddenly, paying bills and saving for the future leaves little money for flowers and candy. Meals must be cooked, and babies must be held and fed. Couples become so busy surviving or striving for a particular lifestyle that they don't have the creative energy to consider how to please their mates. *Besides,* they tell themselves, *he knows I love him,* or *she knows I care.*

Fourth, familiarity breeds complacency. When a couple's romantic feelings wane, familiarity and complacency can move into a marriage. Each partner becomes content with the status quo. There does not seem to be much more to learn about the other person. Duty replaces desire as the motivational force in pleasing one's mate.

Fifth, tasks become more important than people. Some people tend to be indifferent to the needs of others. These are usually task-oriented, goal-oriented people, who say, "Bring on the task!" Then, in order to meet their objectives, they might run right over anyone who gets in the way—including their mates!

Task-oriented people need to slow down and realize that they can smell the roses and build relationships as they go about accomplishing their goals.

If you fit this description, you may need to refocus on your marriage relationship by reading a good book that spawns creativity and romance in your marriage.

Sixth, anger or bitterness takes root. People who are embittered against their partner often don't realize that they are harming themselves as much as (or more than) their mates. As someone has said, a marital conflict is like a shootout between Siamese twins!

Possibly you're bitter because you have tried to please your mate, only to find that you've fallen short of his expectations. You may have decided that pleasing your mate is an impossible task and you no longer want to try.

Why not seek counsel on how to get rid of your bitterness? Why not ask forgiveness for your bitterness and try to please your mate again, and again, and again . . . no matter how he responds?

Neglect Leaves the Door Open

Too often, people ignore those closest to them. With the "prize" secured, they don't feel it's necessary to maintain the relationship in order to keep the competition at bay. But if they do not focus on their mates, they leave the door wide open for others to come in and look around. "Noncompeting" mates lose by default.

When a spouse feels neglected and bored at home, he may seek excitement elsewhere. One of the chief ingredients in extramarital affairs is the fresh interest that two people express in each other.

Ladies, other women out there right now may be interested in competing for your man.

Men, have you ever thought about your wife not being there one evening when you come home?

In a healthy way, Barbara and I try to stay mindful that the competition is not over. Yes, we are secure in our marriage commitments. But, no, we are not lazy. We realize that men and women will not go shopping for pleasure, fulfillment, excitement, or companionship if they have all they can handle at home.

Have you neglected your mate? Why not start competing for him again? Done in a healthy manner, it's fun.

Requirements of a Partner-Pleaser

When someone loves another person, pleasing that person should be the most natural thing in the world. But there are several prerequisites for achieving this "natural" state.

1. A partner-pleaser knows his mate.

The best way to find out how to please your mate is to ask, "What could I do to please you? Which three things really please you? Which things, if I do them, will communicate love, worth, and value from me to you?"

As you seek to learn what pleases your mate, consider the following provided by Dr. Willard Harley, who has counseled more than two thousand clients in private practice.

A Husband's Five Most Basic Needs in Marriage

1. Sexual Fulfillment
2. Recreational companionship
3. An attractive spouse
4. Domestic support
5. Admiration

A Wife's Five Most Basic Needs in Marriage

1. Affection
2. Conversation
3. Honesty and openness
4. Financial support
5. Family commitment

Too often we fall into the trap of confusing what pleases our mate with what pleases us. Barbara once pointed this out to me (Dennis). As a sign of my affection, I was gently rubbing the back of her neck. She looked up at me, smiled, and said, "We've been married fourteen years. When do you think you'll remember that I don't like having my neck rubbed?" Since I like having my neck and back rubbed, I assumed Barbara did, too.

Another way to gather knowledge is through observing and listening. Has your mate ever said, "I really like . . ." or "I wish sometime you would . . ."? If so, that is the place to start. Observe him. Where does he experience repeated frustration? Can you help in that area? Are you willing?

To keep communication lines open and to remain informed about each other's lives, try to establish a regular time together for planning, talking, and dreaming. We try to set aside Sunday evenings as our time to talk and think through our calendars and schedules. When will we spend special time with the children? When will we spend special time together?

Planning communicates that we care enough to consult one another ahead of time. It instills value. Consistently spending time talking together also increases our knowledge of each other and provides opportunities to please.

2. A partner-pleaser is willing to sacrifice.

In our nation's economy, one usually determines the value of a piece of merchandise or a service by how much one has to give up, or sacrifice, to gain it. If my son wishes to buy a leather basketball, it will cost him three weekends of freedom in order to complete enough chores to earn the money to pay for it. Therefore, the value he places on the ball is three weekends.

In a similar fashion, your mate often interprets how much you love or value him by how much you are willing to sacrifice for him.

Some sacrifices are easily recognizable. These include special gifts on standard occasions or for no reason at all. These gifts do not need to be expensive, but don't fall into the rut of always giving inexpensive ones either. Remember, surprises are fun at any age. They bring pleasure and help your mate to feel special. That, in turn, helps build self-esteem.

As a man, I doubt if I will ever understand why women get so excited about flowers. But I don't need to understand; I just need to know that periodically I should give them to Barbara. In a survey of over eight hundred couples at one of our FamilyLife Marriage Conferences, flowers were ranked #1 in communicating love and romance in marriage. A bouquet of flowers carries a large value. It says, "I love you."

For the woman trying to please her husband, it has often been said that the way to a man's heart is through his stomach. Why not cook the foods he enjoys? Be careful not to become his mother, feeding him only what is "good for him." Spoil him a little. This communicates that you care enough to sacrifice your healthful standards to please him.

Another form of sacrifice in marriage comes when we show an interest in our mate's hobbies and pastimes. I (Barbara) have always had an interest in art and enjoy looking at paintings in art galleries and museums. When we married, Dennis had no such interest. He considered art museums to be great places in which to get bored quickly. But to please me, he has visited quite a few museums. He has also encouraged me to take watercolor lessons. He even asks questions to learn more about this side of my nature.

Once he sacrificed watching an evening newscast to look through an art catalog with me. It wasn't a big sacrifice, but it communicated a respect that made me feel valued. His involvement told me, "I care about the things you enjoy."

In contrast, although Dennis has always loved fishing, I had no appreciation for the sport when we married. I tended to agree with the person who said, "A fisherman is a jerk on one end waiting for a jerk on the other."

But to please Dennis, I did a lot of fishing during the early years of our marriage. Later, when our expanding population of children made it impossible for me to go with him, I encouraged him to go alone or with other men, and later, as our children grew up, to take them along.

In the process of pleasing one another, we have become richer. Our horizons have expanded. I have learned that there is skill, patience, perseverance, and reward in fishing. I no longer consider it to be a waste of time. Fishing has become important to me because it's part of what makes Dennis who he is. We have great vacation memories of fishing at night while our children were asleep.

The final form of sacrifice is probably the most important: time. You can make more money, and you can buy more flowers, but you can't make or buy more time. Each day is made up of twenty-four hours—nothing will change that. There are 86,400 seconds in a day. How will you spend them? If you sleep for eight hours and work for nine hours, you have only 25,200 seconds left. How can you use them best?

How often do you hear, "I'd love to, but I don't have enough time"; or "Sure, let's get together, *if* we can find the time"; and "What am I going to do—I'm running out of time"?

We're all running out of time. Psalm 90:12 admonishes us to "number our days." How many do you have left? How will you use them?

To give of your time requires the greatest sacrifice. Does your work deserve virtually all of it? Or your wife and family deserve a portion? Do you want to communicate your love to your wife? If so, give her your time—undivided and focused on her. Take time for a quiet walk or a scenic drive. Above all else, simply take time for each other. If blood is the gift of life, then time is the gift of love.

3. A partner-pleaser is romantic and adventuresome.

"Human nature," Oswald Chambers wrote, "if it is healthy, demands excitement, and if it does not obtain the thrilling excitement in the right way, it will seek it in the wrong. God never makes bloodless stoics. He makes passionate saints."

Isn't that a great statement? We're to live life as an exciting adventure! That adventuresome approach to life includes marriage. Marriage was never intended to become predictable or boring. One cynic said, "The period of engagement is like an exciting introduction to a dull book." But unless you work at adding adventure, your marriage can become dull, filled only with the daily routines of life.

Every marriage needs the pleasing feeling of romance—time to refresh the relationship, renew the friendship, and delight in one another. But some of us spend so much time meeting other people's needs and hammering out life's details that we have no time or no energy left for romance in our relationship with our mates.

Life is too short to waste. Why not be a bit unpredictable and add some sizzle to your mate and to your marriage? Think back to what created those sparks originally—the courtship, the fun you had together. Bring some of that fun back into your life. Your mate's self-image will grow as you become an adventuresome partner.

You don't have to spend a ton of money to have an adventure. It can be a weekend getaway. It can be anything that takes you away from the routines and refreshes and renews your relationship. Maybe it's just an evening set apart when you farm out the kids. Or you could simply go to bed early, light the candles, and talk and renew your relationship.

One area in most marriages that tends to become predictable is sex. Find out what specifically pleases your mate and continue to communicate and grow in this intimate area of your marriage relationship. Also, express what pleases you, not just what doesn't. Almost every person derives great satisfaction by pleasing someone he loves. But if the recipient does not express appreciation in return, then the giver is left wondering if he has pleased his mate.

Vonette Bright offers a healthy perspective on the sexual dimension of the marital relationship. In the area of pleasing her mate, she says, "If I can find a better way to bake a cake, then I want to know it."

A wife needs to dress to please her husband. She should remain attractive to him. She should be willing to splurge occasionally on lingerie and to put on a "little something special" without his having to ask. A husband, in turn, must provide plenty of romance and tenderness. He needs to continue to communicate love, affection, and caring.

During the ebb and flow of life, needs and emotions change, requiring continuing sensitivity on the part of both mates. You cannot please your mate physically without risk, without first learning and being sensitive to his needs.

Keep in touch, literally. When you were dating, touching was as automatic as pleasing one another. In fact, it was a part of the expression of romance. For many married couples, touching is a forgotten avenue of communicating worth.

Relearn the delights of touching one another. Hold hands, embrace, and stroll arm in arm, just as you did when you were dating. Share with one another where you like to be touched, and how. Nonsexual touching can be a small but important way to communicate, "I want to give you a little bit of pleasure."

As you consider areas that will please your mate, but that are difficult for you, stop and contemplate the alternative. Millions of marriages have died because both partners stopped trying to please one another. Tell your heavenly Father how you feel, and ask Him to give the strength to try again. Then stir the sparks of creativity to life. Give, without demanding a response or even expecting one.

Ideas for Pleasing Your Partner

For the creative person, pleasing your mate may be a natural part of your personality. But a less creative person may need some coaching in becoming a partner-pleaser. And all of us need an occasional cue card to remind us to reach out. We are including lists of common partner-pleasers. Pick out something you haven't tried before; don't give complacency a foothold in your marriage relationship.

Pleasing Your Wife

1. Take the children out for a few hours and encourage her to do something just for herself.
2. Take her on a picnic that you have planned.
3. Pray with her and read the Scripture to her.
4. Rake the yard and plant some bushes or flowers, etc.
5. Leave her a love note . . . under the pillow, in her purse, pocket, etc.
6. Make all the arrangements for an evening out—call the babysitter, make dinner reservations, and possibly stay overnight in a hotel.
7. Send her a card for no reason at all—maybe one that reminds you both of a special memory.
8. Organize a scavenger hunt, with the final reward being a special gift or a trip for two.
9. Use the phone. Call her just to say, "I love you and was thinking about you."
10. Do one thing you did when you first met your mate and were dating.
11. Take walks together.
12. Keep your stuff out of the kitchen.
13. Clean out the car for her and fill it with gas.
14. Shorten your work hours.
15. Allow time to do planning with her.

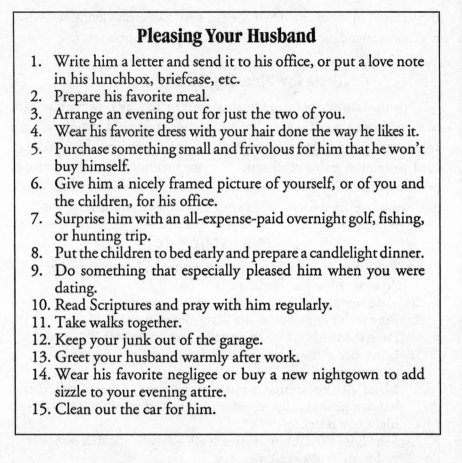

Pleasing Your Husband

1. Write him a letter and send it to his office, or put a love note in his lunchbox, briefcase, etc.
2. Prepare his favorite meal.
3. Arrange an evening out for just the two of you.
4. Wear his favorite dress with your hair done the way he likes it.
5. Purchase something small and frivolous for him that he won't buy himself.
6. Give him a nicely framed picture of yourself, or of you and the children, for his office.
7. Surprise him with an all-expense-paid overnight golf, fishing, or hunting trip.
8. Put the children to bed early and prepare a candlelight dinner.
9. Do something that especially pleased him when you were dating.
10. Read Scriptures and pray with him regularly.
11. Take walks together.
12. Keep your junk out of the garage.
13. Greet your husband warmly after work.
14. Wear his favorite negligee or buy a new nightgown to add sizzle to your evening attire.
15. Clean out the car for him.

As you read earlier, Romans 15:2-3 says, "Let each of us please his neighbor for his good, to his edification. For even Christ did not please Himself." How can you edify (build up) your mate and thereby enhance his self-worth? By discovering—and doing—what pleases him.

Just as salt adds flavor and acts as a preservative in food, pleasing your mate is a preservative in your marriage. It brings delight to your mate. His self-esteem is built because you make him feel valuable, special, and important. And the enchantment and thrill of first love will return to you, giving your own worth an extra boost.

Be a Grateful Receiver

If, as a result of reading this chapter, your mate begins to take risks and to do things that please you, be sure to be a grateful receiver. Being appreciative is the best way to ensure that the giving will continue.

Putting down or failing to notice the first steps of pleasing will quench the tiny flame of giving love. Express approval and gratitude. Praise your mate, even if his attempts to please you end in failure the first time around. Build him up, and he will be more likely to try again.

Remember, learning to please your mate requires time.

———————◄•►———————

ESTEEM BUILDER PROJECT

(Use a sheet of paper if necessary.)

1. What truly pleases your mate? List, in order of priority, five things you could do that would please him.
2. Reflect over your marriage and write down 3–5 things your mate has done that have truly pleased you.
   a.
   b.
   c.
   d.
   e.
3. List in order of priority five things he *could* do that would please you.
   a.
   b.

c.

d.

e.

4. Why not consider doing—today or this weekend—the one thing that would please your mate most? Set a time on your calendar to do it, and then follow through.

5. Exchange your lists with one another and plan when you are going to please him.

BUILDING BLOCK #7:
Doing What Is Right

Your genuine applause for right choices will motivate your mate toward a biblically obedient lifestyle.

12

Turning Cheap Imitations into Priceless Originals

───────◆◆◆───────

- *Are You Faking the Christian Life?*
- *Pleasing God Is Satisfying*
- *Eli's Sons Chose Disobedience*
- *Dennis Exposes His Own Charade*
- *Encouraging Obedient Living in Your Mate*
- *Tips for Encouraging Obedience*
- *God Is Bigger than Your Mate*
- *Confidence through Submission*
- *Esteem Builder Project*

───────◆◆◆───────

HAVE YOU EVER "FAKED" the Christian life? Or have you watched your mate act "religious" when you knew he was far from God? How do you feel when you disobey God and what must it be like for your mate to live with you when you are ignoring a command of Scripture?

At the heart of self-esteem is our relationship with God. Our obedience to Him secures a sense of well-being and contentment. He gives us peace when we are faithful, when we "hear" His Word and "do it."[1]

On the other hand, disobedience to God can result in a heavy yoke of guilt. Knowing that God's displeasure or anger is burning against us, we cannot experience positive self-worth.

Are You Faking the Christian Life?

Some people are excellent "fakes." Publicly, they may do an abundance of "Christian deeds" and use the right Christian clichés. But privately, their lives are a charade. They aren't listening to God. Their lives are a mockery.

A young man who had just graduated from law school set up an office, proudly displaying his shingle out front. On his first day at work, as he sat at his desk with his door open, he was wondering how he would get his first client. Then he heard footsteps coming down the long corridor toward his office.

Not wanting this potential client to think that he would be the first, the young lawyer quickly picked up the telephone and began to talk loudly to a make-believe caller. "Oh, yes sir!" he exclaimed into the phone. "I'm very experienced in corporate law. . . . Courtroom experience? Why, yes, I've had several cases."

The sounds of footsteps drew closer to his open door.

"I have broad experience in almost every category of legal work," he continued, loud enough for his impending visitor to hear.

Finally, with the steps right at his door, he replied, "Expensive? Oh, no sir, I'm very reasonable. I'm told my rates are among the lowest in town."

The young lawyer then excused himself from his "conversation" and covered the phone in order to respond to the prospective client who was now standing in the doorway. With his most confident voice, he said, "Yes, sir, may I help you?"

"Well, yes you can," the man said with a smirk. "I'm the telephone repairman, and I've come to hook up your phone!"

We sometimes fake the Christian life in the same way. Preoccupied with self and wanting our own way, we ignore God and pretend to be spiritual. Instead of having Christ's character imprinted on our lives, we go our own way, and our Christianity becomes a forgery.

Pleasing God Is Satisfying

The basis of obedience is faith. We please God when we walk by faith. "And without faith it is impossible to please Him, for he who comes to God must believe that He is, and that He is a rewarder of those who seek Him."[2] Living by faith is not passive—it requires action. We are to listen to God's Word and then obey, putting shoe leather to His commands.

Just as obedience is a choice, so is disobedience. Disobedience is a refusal to listen, a rejection of the truth. Our disobedient actions say that we don't believe that what God says is reliable or accurate.

When we willfully disobey God, we lose our peaceful feelings of value, and we do not experience His love and forgiveness. This does *not* mean we are worth any less in God's eyes. We only experience *feelings* of worthlessness. God's love for even the most rebellious Christian never diminishes.[3] But the inner sense of our priceless worth as Christians fades when we live in passive or willful disobedience before God.

Eli's Sons Chose Disobedience

The Scriptures include many stories of those who fell under God's disapproval because of their disobedience. One of the most tragic is the account of Eli's family, which is recorded in 1 Samuel. Eli and his two sons were part of the priesthood of the nation of Israel. Their inherited responsibility was to give spiritual leadership to the people. However, Eli's sons were not interested in serving God. "Now the sons of Eli were *worthless* men; they did not know the LORD" (italics added).[4]

Not only did they not know God, but also they didn't even care enough to observe the customs of the priesthood. These men abused their role as priests. "Thus the sin of the young men was very great before the Lord, for the men *despised* the offering of the LORD" (italics added).[5] The word *despise* means "to scorn, feel disgust toward, hate, loathe, abhor, laugh at." These strong words tell us how the sons of Eli felt about God and His prescribed plan for forgiveness (the offerings). The sons chose disobedience, and their lifestyle was flagrantly rebellious.

Notice what God said to Eli several verses later: "Those who honor [revere, respect, value, esteem] Me I will honor, and those who despise Me will be *lightly* esteemed" (italics added).[6]

This story shows that God is pleased with those who obey Him. And our experience is that a person walking closely with God *knows* and *feels* God's pleasure. After all, we were created to know God and to enjoy Him. When we experience Him, we experience life at its fullest; on the contrary, when we drift away from a close walk with Him, life becomes empty and worthless.

Dennis Exposes His Own Charade

For more than thirteen years, I (Dennis) faked it in church. Oh, I had my moments of feeling close to God—when I saw a beautiful sunset or did something good "for the Lord." I was a Christian, but for the most part I was "playing church." My Christian life consisted of little more than "fire insurance" and making a once-a-week trip to the "agent's office."

I was going my own way. I chose either to ignore God's prescribed path for my life or to flagrantly disobey it. I was going to run my own show and didn't see why God should have any meaningful part in it. My life was a living example of a statement made by the great Reformation leader John Calvin, who said, "The torture of a bad conscience is the hell of a living soul."

When I turned twenty, however, something happened. I had accomplished every goal I had set at that point in my life. I was prospering. Everything I touched seemed to turn to gold, yet I still didn't feel good about myself. I was empty and lacked self-respect and value. I knew that I was compromising what God had commanded, but I was doing my best to ignore Jesus Christ on a daily basis.

Ultimately, my emptiness drove me back to my Christian roots to find forgiveness and the God I needed. Through a friend's guidance, I began to study Paul's epistle to the Romans and found that God loved me and wanted His best for me. I discovered there was no comparison between God's best for my life and my own "best." I was living in a fuzzy, two-dimensional, black-and-white world while, by comparison, God had a crystal-clear, full-color, three-dimensional experience waiting for me . . . if only I would obey Him.

I concluded that I had been treating Jesus Christ like a spare tire. When I got into trouble, I'd pull Him out of the trunk for a couple of days, then stick Him back in the trunk until I had another flat. It dawned on me that the God of the universe who loved me had not come to be a spare tire, a hitchhiker, or my driving companion. He had come to be Lord of my life—the owner and driver of my life.

I recall being astonished that the God of creation valued me so highly that He still called me His "son" even though I had not called Him "Father" for years. His relentless love just kept coming after me.

Finally I gave in and gave up. I relinquished all rights to Him and, during a period of three months, placed my life back into His hands. I made Him full owner and let Him take over the steering wheel.

By submitting to His plan, I now live a life that is more valuable and exciting than anything I could possibly have had by going my own way. Walking with God and obeying Him on a daily basis provides a sense of worth and value that is beyond description. I have peace of mind because I seek to please the living Lord of the universe. I can't imagine living any other way.

Encouraging Obedient Living in Your Mate

Giving God the lordship—allowing God's daily control of my life—is fundamental to a self-image that is approved by God and is a prerequisite to obedience. Once a life is submitted to Christ, thousands of decisions lie ahead that will either validate this commitment or prove it wrong. But thankfully, the choices come one at a time. It is in these daily forks in the road that the Holy Spirit guides us in the way we should go. His sanctifying work in our lives produces a contentment and peace that is real and satisfying.

Once you are yielded to Jesus Christ by faith and allow His power to work in and through your life, you can spur your mate on to become an obedient Christian. Here are some ways God can use you to encourage your mate toward obedience.

1. Model obedience to Christ.

A model is an example. Models are used in many professions, including medicine and dentistry, and in most fields of art. In architecture and science, they are used as illustrations. They are also studied and observed carefully for the purpose of copying or gaining knowledge.

In the same way, you are a model to your mate. Your life is under observation by the one closest to you. It's unavoidable.

Does your life demonstrate obedience? Do you live what you believe or merely talk it? What knowledge does your mate gain about godliness, contentment, and prayer from your example (not your words)? Would your mate want to copy the model you exhibit?

Jesus referred to His disciples as the salt and light of the world.[7] Your assignment is to create an environment in which your mate can see (light) what the Christian life really is and can become thirsty (salt) for that lifestyle.

Become an example by walking with God (which is not to be confused with church "work"), and by yielding your life to him by faith. You will become salt and light to your mate as your life gives evidence of the peace and contentment God promises.

179

Modeling obedience to Christ is impossible unless you are filled with the Holy Spirit. As you surrender daily by faith to His power, you will grow and mature as a Christian. As you continue to submit to the Scriptures, and the Holy Spirit in you, you will become the model your mate needs to see.

2. Applaud right choices.

Your mate needs you to be a cheerleader, not a preacher. Praise and applaud your mate's right choices; don't just tell him what he does wrong. Most likely he already receives daily reminders of his failures from a host of other people.

One couple faced losing their home because of a mistake made in preparing their income tax return. The amount owed was sizable, and it seemed entirely possible that the only way they could pay the debt was by selling their home.

There was another option, however. As they discussed their situation during the next three days, they were given all sorts of advice from attorneys and tax consultants. Not all of the advice was ethical. They were told, for example, there was a strong possibility that the IRS would never detect the error. The couple was tempted to wait it out.

Yet, they knew what they had to do. The choice was clear, though not easy. The wife urged her husband to do the right thing. "I want you to do what's right," she told him, "even if it means selling the house."

And they did what was right. They decided to file an amended return and pay the balance owed, even if the house had to be sold. It was an agonizing decision because they had worked hard on their home to make it just the way they wanted it.

After making the decision, they looked at each other and swallowed hard. But inside, they had a firm assurance that their choice was pleasing to God. Their confidence seemed to grow with each passing moment.

Some days later, with smiles on their faces, they shared how they had worked through their temptation. Because of their right decision, they had peace with God, and another brick was laid firmly in place in their character and self-image. They learned the truth of what Francis Bacon said: "A good conscience is a continual feast." And, in the end, they didn't have to sell their home, after all.

We, too, have faced many temptations in our marriage. We have been tempted to be unfaithful, to take each other for granted, to say something that would wound deeply, or to become embittered toward one another when we disagree. But we have committed to verbalizing our temptations to each other. We tell each other how we feel. Then we talk about a solution.

Likewise, you can support your mate in doing what's right. Cheer his right choices. Affirm him. Tell your mate you admire him when he stands for what is right and that he inspires you to follow Christ, too.

Another way to encourage obedience in your mate is to express verbal appreciation for his convictions and character. Convictions and character are shaped when we cooperate with God's Spirit and obey His truth.

Tips for Encouraging Obedience

Here are some tips that we've found helpful in our marriage when one of us wants to do "his own thing."

1. Don't nag. Love him for who he is. Being nagged at is like being nibbled to death by a duck.
2. Don't plot. Instead, pray for him.
3. Don't look for him to obey God perfectly every time—give him grace and forgiveness.
4. Don't tear him down for who he isn't and what he doesn't do. Build him up, even when you think he doesn't deserve it.
5. Don't listen to ungodly counsel that tells you to quit. Surround yourself with Christians who will encourage you to fulfill your marriage vows.
6. Pray that your mate will be surrounded by godly Christians who will love him and share with him what he needs to hear. (Don't do it yourself. Let God do it.)

Do you frequently tell your mate you are proud of him? For what he stands for? For his good reputation in the community? For his consistency in making the right choices? For the example he is to your family? By praising and elevating your mate's character, you reinforce values that are close to God's heart.

3. Pray for obedience.

Building your mate's self-esteem requires a partnership between yourself and God. No one can do it alone. The importance of prayer for your mate cannot be underestimated.

James 5:16 says, "The effective prayer of a righteous man can accomplish much." Effective prayer is asking God to do what He already wants to do in your mate's life. God delights in answering such prayer because He wants you to know Him, to see Him work, and to continue to come to Him.

Praying for your mate during your lifetime is a privilege. The Scriptures tell us, "You do not have because you do not ask."[8] We need to go to God repeatedly with our needs and requests, expecting Him to act on our behalf. Paul admonishes us to "pray without ceasing."[9]

Be careful about praying negatively for that list of traits you don't like in your mate. Instead, pray positively. View your prayers as an opportunity to team up with God in building godly qualities into your mate.

Come before God's throne on your mate's behalf, requesting that he will know God's love more fully and that God will develop a teachable, pure heart within him. Pray for an increased desire to obey and follow Christ. Ask God to give your mate a growing awareness of the benefits of walking with Him. Ask, too, that faithfulness, contentment, patience, self-control, discipline, and other godly virtues will be developed in his life. Study the Scriptures (start with 1 Corinthians 13, Romans 12, and Galatians 5:22-23) and ask God what else to include in your prayers for your mate.

Years ago we received a phone call from a desperate woman. Her husband was not interested in spiritual things, and she had done everything she could think of to urge him to make a commitment. She left open Christian books by his side of the bed, with portions underlined in bright ink. She scattered tracts and pamphlets around the house. Her home probably resembled a well-stocked Christian bookstore!

She left tapes in the cassette player in his car, turned to just the right place. If he pulled out the cassette, guess what station she had the radio tuned to? The local Christian broadcast. That button on his radio was preset to get "the Word" to him.

After talking for some time, she finally listened as we gave her our advice: "Don't say another word to your husband about Christ—no books, tapes, notes, tracts, and no more setting up meetings in which other couples can corner him. Just live the Christian life and *pray*. If he asks a question about your faith, answer him. Just obey Christ and pray for your husband. But don't say another word about Christ—not even one!"

Up to that point, the woman had concluded that God couldn't do it without her. She felt that she was doing God a favor by keeping after her husband! Reluctantly, she agreed to follow our advice. She applied the principle found in 1 Peter 3:1-6 and began the process of winning her husband "without a word."

Not much happened during the first few months, yet she remained silent about her spiritual desires for him. Then God's Word and her "speechless" strategy began to work. Slowly her husband warmed up to spiritual things. A year or so later, he began attending a Bible study with a group of businessmen. A few months after that, he received Christ and became a growing Christian and witness for Him.

We wish we could promise you and every reader of this book that this woman's answered prayer would become a reality in your marriage. Unfortunately, there is no such promise, but don't give up. No matter what your situation, there is hope. *Your* life and *your* prayers may be used by God to get your spouse's attention.

God Is Bigger than Your Mate

Do you believe God is bigger than your mate? Do you believe God is fully capable of getting his attention? Do you feel God must use *you* to get your spouse's heart turned toward Him?

Sometimes we forget that God loves our mates more than we do, that He desires that they be totally yielded to Him. As Christians, we often have little understanding of God's ingenuity and power. We act as if He were some weak, senile old man who needs our help to do His work. This is especially true in our thinking about our mates. We feel that we alone can straighten out our spouses.

By thinking like this, we take on God's responsibility. Yet only the Good Shepherd knows and can employ the most effective methods for getting the attention of a wayward sheep. On the other hand, God may choose to use you to model the Christian life for your spouse and to pray for him.

Confidence through Submission

Unfortunately, at times, we all choose the wrong fork in the road. We don't do what is right. When this is true of your mate, don't be a "finger-pointer." Remember the lessons on failure and give your mate the space and freedom to fail.

Abraham knew the satisfaction of a life lived in obedience before God. It's recorded in Genesis 25:8: "And Abraham breathed his last and died . . . satisfied with life." He didn't die full of regrets. He died with the peace that can come only to a person who—as God's child—obediently walks in the power of God's Spirit.

Because God made us in His image, it stands to reason that when we fully submit our lives to His control, we begin to recapture the identity and confidence that was intended for us in the beginning, before the Fall.

In his book, *Beyond Personality*, C. S. Lewis writes about the identity that is found in self-denial and surrender to Christ:

> The more we get what we call "ourselves" out of the way and let Him take over, the more truly ourselves we become. . . . In that sense our real selves are all waiting for us in Him. It is no good trying to "be myself" without Him. . . . The more I resist Him and try to live on my own, the more I become dominated by my own heredity and upbringing and surroundings and natural desires. . . . I am not, in my natural state, nearly so much of a person as I like to believe: Most of what I call "me" can be very easily explained. It is when I turn to Christ, when I give myself up to His Personality, that I first begin to have a real personality of my own. . . .
>
> But there must be real giving up of the self. You must throw it away "blindly" so to speak. Christ will indeed give you a real personality; but you must not go to Him for the sake of that. As long as your own personality is what you are bothering about, you are not going to Him at all. The very first step is to try to forget about the self altogether. . . . Lose your life and you will save it. Submit to death, death of your ambitions and favorite wishes every day and death of your body—in the end: Submit with every fibre of your being, and you will find eternal life. Keep back nothing. . . . Nothing in you that has not died will ever be raised from the dead. Look for yourself, and you will find in the long run only hatred, loneliness, despair, rage, ruin, and decay. But look for Christ and you will find Him, and with Him everything else thrown in.[10]

ESTEEM BUILDER PROJECT

(Use a sheet of paper if necessary.)

1. After reading the following box, write out your own contract with God as a couple.
2. (Optional) List areas in which you need to model the Christian life for your mate, and ask God to help you be an excellent model.

Our Contract with God

After we were married, we wanted to symbolize together what both of us already had done separately. So our first Christmas together, we made up a "Title Deed to Dennis and Barbara Rainey's Life."

That Christmas, before giving gifts to each other, we signed our contract with God, granting Him complete ownership of our lives, marriage, and family. Both of us felt great satisfaction that what we had done was pleasing to God and was right. We have never regretted our decision.

That document is filed safely in our safe-deposit box with all of our other valuable papers as a reminder of who has ultimate ownership and authority over our lives. It is a reminder that our lives are not our own.

If you haven't already done this, study Luke 14:25-35 together and write your own contractual document. Together, give God total rights to your lives, family, and possessions.

If your mate isn't ready to sign, then why not make an individual contract with God? You can sign it yourself. Put it in a safe place with your other valuable documents.

BUILDING BLOCK #8:
Helping Your Mate Develop Friends

By encouraging your mate to develop close friendships, you enable others to affirm his value and significance.

13

Friends: Reflectors that Magnify

———◆———

- *A Friend: Someone Who Chooses to Like You*
- *Friendship: Spokes on the Wheel*
- *Good Friends Reinforce Your Efforts*
- *Best Friends Help Us Weather the Storms*
- *Obstacles to Building Strong Friendships*
- *Tips on Building a Close Same-Sex Friendship*
- *A Word to Husbands*
- *A Word to Wives*
- *Every Couple Needs a "Couple Friend"*
- *Good Friends Help Build Self-Esteem*
- *Esteem Builder Project*

———◆———

I T WAS CHRISTMAS DAY, 1984. The home video equipment and the 35mm camera were busy from early morning until nearly noon. The living room was littered with tissue, ribbon, and dozens of foil wrappers from Hershey's Kisses that had met their intended destination. Five children filled the room with delighted squeals and constant motion, as if they were battery-charged toys. Dennis and I sat and watched, enjoyed and directed . . . and yawned.

No extended family came to help us celebrate that year because I was pregnant and due in two weeks. I was too tired to prepare a big Christmas dinner, so we had an ordinary lunch and some cookies. Then we cleaned up our mess, and the two youngest children and I retreated upstairs for an afternoon nap.

By evening, we all felt a little lonely. We had enjoyed our day as a family, but we wanted to share the holiday with someone else. Fortunately, some friends invited us to drop in. So after an early dinner, we gathered the children and some diapers and new toys, and drove to town.

We were a motley crew. Our four-year-old, Rebecca, wore the pajamas from her grandma and grandpa that she had unwrapped early that morning. The others had on assorted collections of old and new clothing. I was wearing what had become my daily maternity uniform—jeans and a red flannel shirt, one of only two or three garments that still fit. I had decided to wear no makeup that day. Dennis, also choosing to go grubby, was unshaven.

Our friends, who had visited with family members and feasted all day, greeted us at the door, and our kids disappeared with theirs for a time of show and tell. We four adults, accompanied by their two-year-old and our Deborah (then almost twenty months), made our way to the dining room. After sampling some delicious Christmas sweets, we had a wonderful time of fellowship and conversation.

We were with friends. The fact that our dress and appearance didn't match theirs was irrelevant. We felt accepted for who we were. We felt valued without having to perform, and we left their home that night feeling happy and content.

George Santayana said, "One's friends are that part of the human race with which one can be human." That's how we felt that December 25th. We came as we were, without pretense, and received the love of friends.

A Friend: Someone Who Chooses to Like You

A friendship, like marriage, is a chosen relationship. A friend is someone who admires you, believes you are worth the investment of time and energy, and has singled you out—from among the throngs of other people—to get to know.

One of our children's books says simply, "A friend is someone who likes you." You can count on a committed friend to overlook the petty things others use to pick us apart. Yet a good friend will confront us with painful truths, too, when we most need to hear them.

This is the kind of friendship that counts, the kind of friendship the Christian community was meant to provide. Close, Christian friends love each other and seek to know each other in an increasingly intimate fashion. Within such a friendship, two people can be real and, in spite of their realness and the reality of their selfishness, can accept each other.

As I (Dennis) understand the Bible, it is a book that tells us about relationships—how to establish our vertical relationship with God and how to demonstrate His love in our horizontal relationships with people.

In Genesis 2:18, we read: "Then the LORD God said, 'It is not good for the man to be alone; I will make him a helper suitable for him.'" In effect, God was saying, "I have chosen to make man with a unique need that cannot be met with my personal presence as God. I'm going to make him with needs that must be met by his fellowman."

Initially, I believe God intended for Eve to perfectly and completely meet Adam's need for intimate friendship. But after the Fall, I think only a part of our deepest relational needs can be met within marriage. We also need close friends to fulfill our deep need to be known, accepted, and loved.

Friendship: Spokes on the Wheel

Marriage is like the hub of a wheel. It is the point of strength and as such should provide the assurance of total acceptance. In marriage, we find a haven from others' rejection and disapproval.

But no marriage was meant to bear the total responsibility for building self-esteem in another person. That would be an enormous weight for one person to carry alone. Instead, both partners need to reach out from the hub and extend the spokes of friendship that strengthen each of them and expand their horizons. They need others outside the marriage who affirm them. These spokes, or close friends, do not threaten the security and strength of the hub. Instead, the marriage is actually enhanced and strengthened by the presence of a few stout and loyal friends.

You may be thinking, *My mate and I like each other—we don't need anyone else.* No matter how good a marriage relationship you have, you still need friends. A married couple with no friends outside the marriage will be unable to achieve a healthy, balanced self-esteem.

In a mature marriage relationship, a man and a woman can acknowledge their deep needs to each other without insisting that those needs be met only in the marriage. They recognize their need for friends—close confidants with whom one can be real, unaffected, and natural.

Without friends, a marriage can become ingrown. We've seen some couples become so concerned about their own desires, needs, and wants that they become too inwardly focused. Preoccupied with their own narrow world, they seldom reach out to others and thus have a very poor perspective of themselves.

Good Friends Reinforce Your Efforts

Do you want your mate's perspective of himself to improve? Encourage him to spend time cultivating friendships. A friend helps your mate to see his good qualities and to better understand his weaknesses. He reflects your mate's true value and worth, his significance and importance. He gives your mate a correct perspective of himself and keeps him headed in the right direction. Like a triple mirror in a dress shop, you and your mate's friends *combined* present many positive reflections. Different perspectives reflected by different people can build your mate's self-esteem.

Good friendships reinforce the worth-building that takes place in your marriage. Having a friend communicates to your mate that someone else likes him for his ideas, thoughts, and character qualities. At times, your mate may feel that you are committed to him only because you have to be, or that you are prejudiced toward him in a positive sort of way. But a friend—an objective third party—can encourage your mate by echoing the very things you've said. Your mate will begin to believe your affirming comments because another person has said them too.

Best Friends Help Us Weather the Storms of Life

Job changes, failures, and unexpected circumstances can all shake an otherwise settled self-image from its moorings. Life's ups and downs can spawn questions about one's self-worth and confidence. Self-doubt can spread quickly, almost overnight.

All of life's changing circumstances are handled better with more than one person alongside. Your mate especially needs a friend who will be willing to go with him through the difficult seasons of life, such as menopause, the birth of a child, the empty nest, a lost job, a midlife crisis, or difficulty with a teenager.

I (Dennis) believe the best kind of friendships are formed in a bunker—during the battles of life. A friend who came out of World War II said, "You know, I have some people with whom I have shared instant camaraderie, instant deep friendship because I went through World War II with them during some very trying circumstances." He then added that it's those moments of trial, of testing, of difficulty, of some kind of "battlefield" experience, that meld people together.

Likewise, Christianity takes the motif of the battlefield, applies it to real life, and says, "Hey, our marriage is not taking place on a romantic balcony. Our marriage is taking place on a spiritual battlefield, where we are called to regain spiritual turf for Jesus Christ." We, too, need friends who stand by us in the bunker.

Author Laurence Peter said, "You can always tell a real friend. When you've made a fool of yourself, he doesn't feel you've done a permanent job." A true friend is one of a few who can bring value and perspective when your mate has "blown it." Like you, a good friend will "hang in there" when it seems the whole world has walked out. He will exhibit the unconditional love of God.

Obstacles to Building Strong Friendships

Despite all the blessings a close friend can bring, it isn't easy to establish such a friendship. It takes time. It takes work. And our lives provide many obstacles to building intimate friendships.

One reason many of us are lonely is because of the culture in which we live. We have many acquaintances but few intimate friends. Dr. Roberta Hestenes, president of Eastern College in St. Davids, Pennsylvania, calls this condition "crowded loneliness." "We are," she believes, "seeing the breakdown of the natural community network group in neighborhoods."

One reason is that a large number of Americans move each year. If people think they will be moving, they won't put down roots. In addition, people don't know how to reach out and touch people. This combination produces crowded loneliness, and it affects all of us.

Other obstacles to building friendships include:

- Busyness—full schedules that leave little room for the commitment of friendship.
- Lack of knowledge of how to establish friendships. If parents didn't model the value of having friends, we may not know what friendship is all about.
- Unwillingness to admit our need for friendship—being used to "comfortable," superficial relationships.
- Fear of vulnerability and intimacy—suspicion that others may hurt us or use our weaknesses against us.

- Disappointment with past friendships in which friends have betrayed us or let us down.

Tips on Building a Close Same-Sex Friendship

The first step toward friendship is to admit your need for a close friend. There are few encounters as intimidating as facing another person and saying, "I want you to know I love you, and I need you as a friend."

Now, I (Dennis) have trouble even admitting that to Barbara! For me to admit that need to another man—a peer, someone I want to cultivate as a friend—is risky.

But some time ago, I went to a fellow and bared my soul. "I want you to know that you're a close friend of mine," I told him, "and I need your friendship."

His mouth dropped open. "Really?"

As I began to explain, a look of shock spread over his face. I remember going home after that lunch and panicking. *I've bared my soul here. I've become too real. I blew it! I scared this guy off. He's going to bolt.*

I experienced all the feelings that come when you risk letting another person into the interior of your life and admitted your need. Yet, as a result of my sharing and my friend's response to it, our friendship deepened and moved to new levels.

I don't believe that my experience with friendship is all that unique. In fact, I think my feelings point out several facts about friendships.

First, we often assume that someone else knows how we feel; therefore, we never mention it. But it's better to take a risk than to play it safe and make the assumption that another person knows you need him.

Second, after you admit your need for friendship, it's time to take practical steps to make that relationship a priority. Friendships deepen when they are cultivated. This means putting that person into your schedule. It means making time for him, even if you have to turn down other things.

I can't say enough about the importance of planning to make friendships a reality. This is especially important in the area of couple relationships, where you and your mate are good friends with another couple. As couples, it's easy to neglect the relationship and make contact only occasionally. Decide to make it a priority this year to solidify and strengthen your friendship with at least one other couple.

A Word to Husbands

Here's a tip for building your wife's self-esteem that will please her immensely. Give your wife a weekend off to get away for a friendship-building retreat. Encourage her to invite a female friend she wants to get to know better. Make sure she has an "expense account" for the weekend, to use as needed. On Sunday evening, your wife will return with a better perspective of herself. She'll be encouraged and built up in ways that you, as a man, could never accomplish.

This retreat is especially needed if your marriage is in its early years and/or if you have moved and uprooted many of your wife's established friendships. It is also important if she is occupied with young children or works outside the home, thus leaving little time to develop friendships.

In my relationship with Dennis, I (Barbara) am confident of his understanding of me, my role, and my struggles. We have spent endless hours talking together to create this rapport. He has been with me through many difficult times. He has been a "substitute" mother to the children when I've been out of the house, so he knows a great deal about that role and its responsibilities.

But there is a point beyond which he cannot go. Only another wife and mother can really share the pain I felt in childbirth, as well as my struggles with submission, and can join with me in prayer about these issues. Other mothers can provide the support and motivation I need to carry the daily weight of bringing up children. No husband or father is able to give that same type of support.

I need a deep affinity with two or three women, and I have it. It's wonderful. I am affirmed every time we talk by phone, get together, or correspond. And when I feel good about myself, Dennis benefits, too. He feels less pressure to try to meet all of my needs.

A wife needs at least one other woman with whom she can identify. This woman, who is not to take the husband's place as the primary source of approval, should supplement the self-image you are helping your wife build. Your wife's friend will take your place only if you are not doing your job by loving your wife as Christ intended.

We would encourage you to resist the tendency to be threatened by your wife's outside friendships with women. Give her time and encouragement to develop these friendships. You'll never regret it.

A Word to Wives

Most men don't have in-depth relationships with other men. Does your husband? If he doesn't, do you know why? Do you understand your man's needs? Most likely he struggles with his time, his macho image, and his inability to know how to relate to another man.

Most men carry images of manhood they've picked up from the media, books and movies, and from men they have observed in their families. Generally, the "strong" men they've seen were not portrayed as being emotionally vulnerable. As a result, most men don't have friendships that go deeper than a surface level. Worse, they don't know how to deepen their existing friendships. Therefore, your mate will need your encouragement to develop a close friendship with at least one other man.

Because women naturally tend to be more transparent, they form friendships more easily than men. Men are more inclined to find the added significance a friend provides in such pursuits as business, politics, or sports. They speak of having many "friends," while women use the term more selectively.

Your husband is more vulnerable to self-doubt if his only close friend is you. That doesn't mean your role is not crucial; it means that he needs the accountability another man will provide, just as you need another woman with whom to relate. Encourage him to share his job, relationship struggles, and questions about life's issues with another man he respects. If he is struggling over a particular decision or issue, suggest that he discuss the problem over breakfast with a Christian man he respects. You can remind him that he, like you, needs to be real and authentic with a friend. Encourage him to let others into his life.

"Iron sharpens iron," wrote Solomon, "so one man sharpens another."[1] A good friend will "sharpen" your husband, influence his spiritual growth, and counsel him along the way. The friend will hold your mate accountable for what he says he'll do, and also will be loyal when others are not.

Every Couple Needs "Couple Friends"

As a couple, you need "couple friends"—a relationship in which both the husbands and wives have a special affinity for each other. We prayed for such friends and, for years, tried to find the right "mix." We are thankful that now we share that affinity with four or five special couples. Some we see frequently, others only occasionally, but the friendships remain solid.

One summer we spent a portion of our vacation with one such couple. Our friendship had evolved over several years while teaching a graduate-level course with them every summer. We honestly didn't begin this relationship with the goal of becoming intimate friends, but through the years we've seen God knit our hearts together in a special way.

We cherish fond memories of the four of us hiking around a lake, riding horseback through aspen groves and knee-deep flowers, and spending casual times sharing dreams, ideas, questions, and concerns. With those pleasant memories comes an occasional phone call or gift—reminders of our value in their lives and their value in ours. It's hard not to feel good about ourselves when a few choice people know us well and still like us.

Several years ago, we had dinner with a pastor and his wife who are contributing significantly to the Christian community. As we talked, the subject of friends came up. They shared that they maintain an intimate fellowship with three to five couples. These people are committed to a lifetime friendship. They don't all live in the same town or go to the same church, but they know they can count on their friends to be there when the going gets tough; they have a mutual understanding.

Good Friends Help Build Self-Esteem

Do you have couple friends? Individual friends? Ask God to direct you in developing both types of essential relationships. Spend time with the people to whom He leads you. Get to know them and share yourself openly and honestly. Communicate your love for them and your commitment to them as your friends. The blessing will be mutual.

I (Dennis) remember two very dark days when I really questioned my worth as a man. Both resulted from problems at work that caused me to wonder about my effectiveness as a leader. These were times of self-doubt, discouragement, and emotional turmoil.

Fortunately, I had two very godly friends with whom I had been developing a relationship. I had helped them during their points of crisis, and now I needed them. It was difficult to admit my need, but thanks to Barbara's encouragement I opened myself up and asked for their advice, counsel, and help.

These two men stood by me and, along with Barbara, reminded me of the truth about myself. It was difficult to believe at first, but slowly, over a period of time, what they said and how they reacted made a difference in my life. Their acceptance, counsel, and wisdom were invaluable. Their gifts of time communicated to me that I had value. Their belief in me as a man told me that I was okay, even during the difficult situations.

That's friendship. It's a joy, a risk, and a responsibility. It's also a comfort to know that people want to be with you, whether you are rich or poor, sloppy or immaculate, famous or unknown. Friends support your self-esteem.

So do yourself and your mate a giant favor. Develop some lasting friendships and watch how these allies assist you in building your mate's self-esteem—and at the same time, your own.

ESTEEM BUILDER PROJECT

(Use a sheet of paper if necessary.)

1. Inventory all of your mate's friendships. Who is his best friend of the same sex?
2. Give your mate and his best friend a weekend retreat, during which they can talk, shop, hunt, etc.
3. As a couple, during the next six to twelve months, pray and ask God to direct you to one or two couples with whom you would like to pursue a friendship. Then begin to cultivate those relationships by spending time with each couple.
4. One great way of solidifying friendships is through a small group study that we've published called the HomeBuilders Couples Series. There are nine books in this series; one is a companion study guide to this book. These helpful resources

have been used by couples to enhance communication in their marriage. Excellent for small groups, the HomeBuilders Couples Series is great for neighborhood studies or Sunday school. Call 1-800-999-8663 for information.

BUILDING BLOCK #9:
Keeping Life Manageable

Completing the construction of your mate's self-image requires making tough decisions, knowing your values, thinking prayerfully, and keeping life simple.

CHAPTER

14

Getting the Ice Off Your Balloon

————————◆————————

————————◆————————

DO YOU SOMETIMES FEEL STRAPPED into some kind of schedule that has jerked you off the ground and has caused you to soar to heights you never dared before? Some of us are living at our limits. We're hanging on and getting numb.

In conversation with friends, have you noticed recurring statements (said with a sigh) such as, "We are just so busy these days" or "As soon as this month is over, our schedule will lighten up, and then we'll get together"? As a culture, we are forever in a hurry—rushing, pushing, frantically cramming more into an already swollen schedule.

All of us live under pressure. We hide it, we're driven by it, we work under it, and we're squeezed by it. We're overcommitted, overextended, and overloaded. Pressure is a normal part of life.

The problem is, many of us do not know how to handle these pressures. Millions of Americans suffer physical problems because of stress: ulcers, sleeplessness, hypertension, weight problems, and allergies.

It seems as though most people want to get off the pressure merry-go-round, but few are willing to throw the switch and make some hard decisions. As a result, many people are burned-out, strung-out, and wrung-out by their drive for significance. Instead of getting somewhere or anywhere, they simply get exhausted. They discover, as Samuel Butler said, "Life is one long process of getting tired."

What about your mate? Does his lifestyle contribute to his self-esteem or merely to his fatigue? Perhaps, as you build him up, you will need to aid him in eliminating nonessentials from his schedule.

A good friend confided in us recently, "Life used to be so simple. Now, it seems so complex. There are the children, work demands and pressures, bills, home maintenance, friendships, church responsibilities, social obligations, long-term financial planning, and . . . well, the list seems to go on forever. We can't win for losing. I feel like I'm drowning, and my mate doesn't seem to be helping. Instead of keeping me afloat, she's sinking too. In fact, my mate keeps pulling me down."

Going Up or Going Down?

Maybe you've felt like our friend—emotionally sinking under the weight of it all. His sinking feeling reminds us of the story of "Double Eagle II," the first balloon to cross the Atlantic Ocean.

Three thousand forbidding miles stood between three men in a balloon called Double Eagle II and Europe. Presque Isle, Maine, was covered with darkness as a handful of hopefuls huddled around the helium-filled balloon. Silently, the Double Eagle II inched its way upward. Men and nature would battle again in the attempt to cross the Atlantic.

The men waved good-bye as they started their journey. Two previous attempts had failed; miraculously, all had survived.

Soaring by day and drifting downward at night, the crew masterfully rode the winds like an imaginary angel for three nights and two days. Then, a few hundred miles off the coast of Ireland, the weather changed as ominous, gray clouds surrounded them. Ice crystals, twinkling with deceptive beauty, began to form on the balloon, which rose five stories above them. Soon, sheets of ice weighing thousands of pounds forced the giant balloon downward.

Panic replaced peace as the crew watched the altimeter tell the story ... 24,000 feet ... 20,000 ... 16,000 ... 12,000. ... With no solar rays to melt the ice, the crew believed they were headed for an unwelcome baptism. All excess weight had to be eliminated. Frantically, the ballast was dumped. Books, canned foods, and other equipment were shoved overboard. The ice pushed them down still farther ... to 8,000 ... 6,000 .... "Mayday! Mayday! Mayday!" they radioed the distress signal, along with their position. Then they tossed over a video camera they'd hoped to use to record their landing. Finally, they reluctantly jettisoned their marine radio as they fought to remain airborne.

Three frightened men watched helplessly as the rolling angry Atlantic came up to meet them ... 4,000 ... then suddenly—eureka! They leveled off and broke through the gray mist into sunshine. The balloon soared as the warm rays melted the sheets of ice.

Crossing the jagged coast of Ireland, they floated above rolling green hills and then reached the English Channel. Thousands of cars lined the rural roads of France as the Double Eagle II came to rest in a cornfield a few miles from Paris and the airport where Lindbergh had landed a half-century before them. They had made it.

Which way is your mate's balloon headed? Is it soaring smoothly aloft? Or is it dipping toward the sea? Can you spot ice crystals forming? If so, what's causing them?

If your mate's balloon is making a rapid descent, will you help him remove those burdens, or will you add more weight? Most likely, you are strategic to the solution. Will you offer lift or letdown?

Self-Image and Simple Living

If your mate is personally insecure, he may be attempting to fill that vacuum of insecurity in his self-image by crowding his life with activity. Busyness boosts his self-importance by making him feel needed. Discontentment and comparison drive him to add more activities to his already overcrowded schedule.

Blurred by a life that is often out of control, he loses his focus and sense of priorities. Ultimately, he experiences failure, which further damages his self-image.

Here are some suggestions we have found to be beneficial in keeping life manageable for the Rainey household:

- Determine your family's core values—the things in life you feel are most important. Many are driven today because they have never sat down as a couple and hammered out the areas where they are unwilling to fail.
- You can't always please everyone, but you should please those you value the most. Determine whom you wish to please and live accordingly. You can't meet everyone's expectations.
- Pressure and stress can be a result of responsibility. By discarding a responsibility or two, you can lighten your load and reduce some pressure. Ridding ourselves of all responsibility is not an alternative. Doing what He has called you to do, however, and depending on Him in the process, will put pressure in perspective.

- At all costs, avoid comparison. It only breeds discontent, envy, and drivenness.
- Consider what's at the root of your busyness. Do you stay busy because you have a need to feel important? If you free up your schedule, you might be forced to face who you are . . . or aren't.
- Practice saying, "No, I'm sorry, I can't do that" at least once a day until it's easier to say no when people ask you to do things. The word *no* can be a powerful crowbar in dislodging other people's control over your life and schedule. (By the way, you don't owe people an excuse!)
- Learn to settle for limited, achievable objectives. We have learned that we usually expect too much from ourselves in any given twenty-four-hour day. *Remember: You have all the time you need to do everything God wants you to do!*

Get Rid of the Excess Baggage

Unfortunately, we are not exempt from the temptation to overextend ourselves. We struggle with schedules, goals, and expectations about life and priorities. Like yours, our days are full from the first ring of the alarm to the last light out at night. With our children in different stages of development, it gets pretty crazy at times. But we work together to avoid living under the peril of the urgent. We have determined to win where it counts the most—at home.

Because we have six children, we repeatedly are asked, "How do you do it all?" Our answer is simple: "We do *not* do it *all*." That six-word sentence has been a boxcar full of help to us. Admitting the obvious is liberating. It may help you and your mate too.

Guess what? No one else does it all either. Because a person does one or two things well does not automatically mean that he does everything well. No one can, so why should *you* try? Your phantom may give you the idea that you have to have your life perfectly together, but don't believe it. Relax and repeat with us, "We do not do it all." It may be hard, though, because we are a society of overachievers.

As individuals and as a couple, we have areas in which we continue to fall short. At times we feel like social nerds. We don't go out with friends or invite people into our home as much as we'd like. The flower beds are filled with an odd assortment of weeds; rooms are unpainted; chairs are in need of repair. This "season" in our marriage will pass, however, and someday these two social nerds will come out of the closet and make their debut.

Just as the crew of the Double Eagle II had to dump much of its excess baggage to survive, you may have to lighten your load. You and your mate probably have so many activities and responsibilities going simultaneously that your marriage, like the helium balloon, may be falling. We recommend that you join us in periodically checking your marriage altimeter.

Early in our marriage, we drove together to Cincinnati on a business trip. Barbara was distressed because she was not accomplishing all that she did when she was single. I asked her to go over her "to do" list with me as we made the two-hour journey.

I'll never forget that list. It was overwhelming. I felt distressed for her. She had more to do than three people could have accomplished. Cooking, sewing, quilting, cleaning, watercolor painting, laundry, reading, grocery shopping, writing letters, entertaining, Bible study, doing things with me—all added to an already crowded schedule. And she was pregnant—totally drained by the first trimester of pregnancy.

None of her objectives were being reached, and she was feeling like a failure. Together we prioritized her list and began to eliminate nonessentials. Afterward, Barbara was just as busy as ever, but she was relieved to know that she didn't have to do everything.

That was the first of many similar discussions in our marriage relationship. We both tend to expect too much of ourselves, and as a result we sometimes consider that we have failed. Usually the impression of failing is from within and is simply not true. It results from holding to a standard that couldn't be achieved by Superman or Superwoman.

We've found it is tough to maintain a proper perspective on scheduling and realistic expectations about what can be accomplished. Life can get out of control, and like a runaway train, it can be very destructive. So periodically we get away and check our expectations about life. It is very beneficial to sit together and analyze all that we expect of ourselves and of each other, as well as what others expect of us.

Likewise, you can help your mate scale down his expectations to reasonable standards. Take time out to help align your mate's schedule, overhaul his goals, and establish his priorities *before* the ride gets rough.

Be Careful How You Walk

We need to be wise about what we take with us on our journey through life. Paul writes, "Therefore be careful how you walk, not as unwise men, but as wise, making the most of your time, because the days are evil. So then do not be foolish, but understand what the will of the Lord is."[1]

Wisdom evaluates life by God's standards. It looks at life through God's eyes. Wisdom frequently examines the circumstances of life and then consults God and His Word for the right response.

Evaluate your life and marriage with prudence. Is your mate's altimeter rising or falling? Is there a break coming in your mate's schedule, or is his pace nonstop? Check your own altitude too. Wisdom may tell you that it's time to throw some excess baggage overboard in both your lives.

I (Dennis) face a constant struggle in this area. A chorus of voices calls out to me at every turn and places high expectations on me. My dentist wants me to floss between meals. My doctor wants to know how much I weigh, what I eat, and how much I'm exercising. My accountant wants me to keep better records and stay within my budget.

The police expect me to drive within the speed limit. Advertisers pressure me to buy more. Hollywood entices me to compromise my morals. My employer demands that I do things quicker, better, cheaper, faster, and with the right attitude. My neighbor's lawn lays a guilt trip on me because it is always perfectly manicured and weed free. My peers insinuate that I should be well-read by bringing up the latest ten books they've read during the past two days. The mailman delivers all kinds of response pieces—bills, forms, surveys, catalogs, and fund-raising appeals from Christian organizations and the church.

Barbara wants me to meet her needs, to fix things, to help direct our family. The children want me to spend time with them. Then there are the unpredictable interruptions of life—brown recluse spiders in the house, termites, auto accidents, surgery, a job change.

At the end of all this, there's God. He wants us to obey Him and to witness to others.

Most likely you face these types of expectations—and more. So make your choices carefully (another expectation!) and wisely.

We have several suggestions for evaluating your lifestyle:

First, determine your values. Mentally zoom ahead fifteen or twenty-five years into the future. Will you regret not having done something twenty-five years from today? How do you want to characterize your relationships? In the book of James, we read, "If any of you lack wisdom, let him ask of God, who gives to all men generously. . . . But let him ask in faith."[2]

If you need wisdom to determine your priorities and values as a couple, ask God for it. Then expect Him to give it and begin to act.

The first time we listed and compared our top five values, we were quite surprised. One of mine was "developing relationships"; one of Barbara's was "hard work." Interestingly, neither of us listed the other's values on our respective lists. It wasn't that I didn't believe in hard work or that Barbara didn't think relationships were important. We just believed other things were more important to each of us at that time in our lives.

Since then, we have spent many hours discussing our individual values—those things we hold very dear to our hearts. As we have matured, many of them have changed in importance.

Values Inventory and Analysis

Determine your mate's values by following these steps:

1. Pick an evening with at least one hour of guaranteed quiet time. (Put your answering machine on and turn off the front porch light.)
2. Spend five to ten minutes individually listing the top five values you believe are most important.
3. Compare lists.
4. Ask your mate "Why?" for each item he listed. Find out his reasons for his choices. Discuss your differences.
5. Date and keep both lists.
6. Watch his schedule, activities, and free time to see if they "match" his list. Does his expenditure of time match his top five values? How can you help him live according to his values?
7. Schedule another values analysis in a year.

Now when we set our goals, which are a reflection of our values, we understand what is important to one another. As a result, our objectives and priorities have begun to demonstrate principles that both of us have brought to our marriage.

Second, evaluate your goals and priorities. Take time with your mate to be alone, think, and listen to God. Give your mate time to do this alone also. Ideally, the two of you should get away together for a long weekend at least once a year, with no business agenda on the side. With some unstructured time, you can think clearly. Take a nap. Go for a walk together. Talk about your life and contemplate the direction it's going. Do you like where you are headed? What do you want life to look like in a few years?

Planning will bring security, purpose, and stability into your lives. When you anticipate what's going to happen during the coming weeks and months, you will be much better prepared to handle any eventuality.

You can't accurately plan or set goals and priorities, however, without first taking time to think and pray. Start by setting aside Sunday as a day of rest. Within the Ten Commandments, God has provided a longstanding truth that our modern culture is ignoring, to its detriment. The Sabbath is to be a day set apart unto God—a day of rest in which to refuel our perspective and refresh our communion with Him.

God knows that after working hard for six days, we all need some time off. The problem is, we ignore His command and race through life. But our need for rest can't be denied. Exodus 34:21 restates God's command to rest in this way: "You shall work six days, but on the seventh day you shall rest; even during plowing time and harvest you shall rest."

It's important to step out of the mainstream of life. That is the purpose of the Sabbath—to give us time to think, to reflect, to think critically about life and where it's taking us.

As a result of our decision to try to rest on Sundays, we have begun to reap the enriching qualities of clear minds, relaxed spirits, and the knowledge that our life is well-pleasing to God. (Gordon MacDonald, in his book, *Ordering Your Private World*, has an entire chapter on this subject that we highly recommend.)

Third, expect difficulties to come your way. We don't anticipate interruptions, crises, trials, and difficulties, so we're not prepared for them. C. S. Lewis wrote, "What we must do is stop regarding unpleasant or unexpected things as interruptions of real life. The truth is that interruptions *are* real life. The real life that God sends us day by day. What we call our real life is but a phantom of our imagination."[3]

When we realize that the unexpected is what real life is all about, we'll quit being so disappointed. We'll not feel quite as much pressure to try to live a perfect life. Interruptions come in all sizes, don't they? There are small ones, medium-sized ones, and large ones.

Responding to Unplanned Difficulties

A few years ago, I (Barbara) was sitting in a Bible study at a friend's home when a phone call came for me. Our daughter, Ashley, told me that Rebecca, then six years old, had just fallen off our twelve-foot-high deck onto hard, rocky ground, and landed on her head! Rebecca, it turned out, was fine. But nonetheless it was a big interruption, an unplanned difficulty in our lives.

We know you could tell some war stories of interruptions in your life. Those interruptions cause pressure. They force us to evaluate our lives and to think through what's really important.

Author Max Lucado wrote, "When a potter bakes a pot, he checks its solidity by pulling it out of the oven and thumping it, like that. If it sings, it's ready. If it thuds, it's placed back in the oven. The character of a person is also checked by thumping. Have you been thumped lately?

"How do I respond?" he then asks. "Do I sing, or do I thud?"

Jesus said that out of the nature of the heart a person speaks. There is nothing like a good thump to reveal what is inside. The true character of a person is seen not in momentary heroics but during the thumping humdrum of day-to-day living.

Pressure can be good. Someone has said, "A diamond is a lump of coal that made good under pressure." God calls us to allow pressure to press us together with our mates and to press us toward Christ until we become godly diamonds. Then God can cut away and sharpen us so that we will reflect His image to our mates and others around us.

Fourth, allow God's Spirit to control your life. Jane Ann Smith, mother of six and a good friend of mine (Barbara), wrote a poem I would like to share with you. It reminds us of who is in control as we live our lives:

> *Who is controlling you?*
> *It's what makes the difference in everything.*
> *When I get angry and yell at my children,*
>   *they are controlling me.*
> *When I get angry at my husband and say unkind words,*
>   *he is controlling me.*
> *When I share gossip with friends,*
>   *they are controlling me.*
> *When I cuss at the driver in the next lane,*
>   *he is controlling me.*
> *When my thoughts hover over unclean things,*
>   *my thoughts are controlling me.*
> *When I become depressed about my situation,*
>   *my situation is controlling me.*
> *When I become jealous of the success of a friend,*
>   *my ego is controlling me.*
> *When I camp on my own success,*
>   *my pride is controlling me.*
> *When I want what my friend has,*
>   *my lust is controlling me.*
> *And when I hate someone,*
>   *Satan is controlling me.*

My friend goes on to say, "God paid a high price for the right to control us." And it's true—He did. God wants to control us, to fill us with His Spirit, to guide us in making right choices.

You and your mate will strike the proper balance in your lives and be able to face the pressures pushing in on you when you're filled with the Spirit—being subject to Christ, daily yielding your lives to Him.

Prayer is absolutely essential to being filled with the Spirit and having God control your lives. Dennis and I have made it a habit to pray at night, but recently we've been challenged to increase our praying. The more we pray, we find, the more in tune we are with God's Spirit in our lives.

In order to be filled with the Holy Spirit, it's also critical to spend time in God's Word. As Robert Lewis, our pastor in Little Rock, wrote, "The Holy Spirit will be faithful to remind us of God's Word if we are faithful in learning it."

The Holy Spirit speaks the truth to you and me, but He can't speak to us much if we don't know much about God and His Word. Storing up rich passages that have meant a lot to you will guarantee recall when you need them most, through the power of God's Spirit. God wants you to be dependent on Him.

As you are filled with His Spirit daily, you will learn to be content. First Timothy 6:6 reads: "Godliness actually is a means of great gain, when accompanied by contentment." You see, sometimes the pressures that you and I consider to be burdensome are the very things God has placed on us to cause us to rely on Him.

It is important to learn to be content with what God has given you, with where God has placed you, and with the people God has given you to influence. As Helen Keller said, "So much has been given to me I have no time to ponder that which has been denied."

Fifth, practice good decision making. Sometimes pressure can come from procrastination and indecisiveness. Procrastination can create pressure in your relationship with your mate. To conquer the pressure of procrastination, obtain the facts, take time to reflect, get your mate's advice, seek wise counsel, and then make the decision together prayerfully.

Many young people today do not know the art of good, biblical decision making. As parents we need to teach our kids good decision-making skills because the culture they're going to be living in will be more intense than the one in which we live.

Sixth, be accountable to your mate. Accountability—giving your mate access to your life and being vulnerable enough to admit you need help—is another key to handling life's pressures. Accountability is also a willingness to hear the truth from your mate.

Accountability is a warning system. It pulls you back and keeps you honest. Barbara, for example, sees me more clearly than I see myself. She sometimes warns me when I'm tempted to overcrowd my schedule or when I'm about to mishandle some problem with the children. Then she steps in and either makes some adjustments or helps me make them so that the stress I'm feeling is reduced, and I avoid making major mistakes.

Have you permitted your mate enough access to your life that he or she is able to say anything you need to hear? Or have you walled off certain areas, with "off limits" signs posted outside?

Pride keeps many spouses from ever letting their mates in. But one of the keys to partnership and building your mate's self-esteem is to begin to open your closets and say, "Come on in. It's not very clean. But I need you to help me, to love me, and to accept me . . . just as I am."

Also at the heart of accountability is teachability and honesty. In order to be accountable, you've got to be willing to hear, and you've got to be willing to be truthful.

Accountability means becoming accountable in an area of struggle or repeated failure. For example, I (Dennis) don't accept speaking engagements without first consulting Barbara. She serves as my balance wheel, helping me not to overbook or to take on some assignment that would put our family last in order of priority. She's my partner, and in a partnership, each is accountable to the other. Accountability mutually protects and strengthens the partners.

Life and its pressures are best handled in a partnership. Two people see things more clearly than one. You and your mate need to agree on what you will accept and what you will turn down.

Keep Life Balanced

Just as high-wire artists must maintain a precarious balance, so Christians must balance their spiritual walk and daily life. Living a balanced life requires concentration, observation, and corrections along the way—some minute, others more drastic.

You and your mate may be too reclusive, too cautious. You may need to step out onto the wire and take some risks. God did not give us life to bore us, but to provide opportunities to trust Him and to grow in faith.

It may be that you and your mate continue to live an unreasonable lifestyle because you never get off the merry-go-round to evaluate all that you're doing. Like us, you may need to assess your life regularly to keep it on target. When you keep life balanced, however, you give your mate the benefit of self-control. Over the long haul, you will see your mate's load lightened and his productivity increased. His self-image will be enhanced if you help him keep a reasonably simple and manageable schedule.

ESTEEM BUILDER PROJECT

(Use separate sheets of paper as necessary.)

1. As a couple, list all your activities under one of the two areas shown, then evaluate each one.

   Those We Can Control *Those We Cannot Control*
   a.   a.
   b.   b.
   c.   c.
   d.   d.
   e.   e.

2. Go back through your lists and highlight the activities that tend to pull you and your mate down. Discuss your solution. Can you or should you help by taking responsibility? Should your lists be scaled down or modified? How do your lists affect one another?

3. List the top five values you hold as important. (A value is something that you esteem, cherish or treasure, such as your job, your achievements, your family, your marriage, your relationship with God.)

   a.

   b.

   c.

   d.

   e.

4. Compare your "values" lists with your "activities" lists. Do your activities match your top five values? If not, why?

5. Prioritize your activities list in a way that more clearly reflects your values. Write out what you have decided.

6. Together, decide on specific ways each of you can help the other to maintain a balanced lifestyle.

BUILDING BLOCK #10:
Discovering Dignity through Destiny

*True significance is found as we invest
in a cause that will outlive us.*

chapter 15

What Is Your Destiny?

———◆◆———

———◆◆———

HELEN KELLER WAS ONCE ASKED, "Is there anything worse than being blind?"

"Yes," she replied, "the most pathetic person in the whole world is someone who has sight but no vision."

Vision. What is it? Vision is possessing a sense of purpose in life. It's seeing ahead into the uncharted future and knowing where you're going. Vision is leaving a mark on the present by visualizing the future. Jonathan Swift said in 1699, "Vision is the art of seeing the invisible."

Vision doesn't come easily. Your mate needs you to help bring a sense of vision, direction, and purpose to his life.

We believe mankind's purpose is found in the Scriptures. God has a plan for each believer's life,[1] and it is our responsibility to walk by faith, totally dependent upon Him to fulfill His purpose in and through us. When your mate's purpose is elevated above the temporal, his personal dignity and esteem receive a promotion.

Feelings of significance, one of the pillars of a positive self-esteem, are seldom found in a wanderer, a nomad who drifts through life. But a person with a sense of personal destiny—confidence that God is at work in His life—knows that he has been chosen, handpicked and set apart from the rest of humanity for a divine purpose.

God has chosen you and your mate to fulfill His customized plan in your marriage, family, and world. Have you caught that vision? Has your mate?

Ask Yourself Some Tough Questions

The American culture of the late twentieth century has been defined as narcissistic, selfish, and short-sighted. We are a people who live for the moment, unmindful of the future. We want satisfaction now. We don't want to plant seeds that grow oak trees; we want to plant seeds today and harvest the trees tomorrow!

Rather than seeing our children as ambassadors to the future, we view them as impositions who get in the way of what we have to do here and now.

Many individuals, and most couples, are not asking enough questions about life. Caught up in the rush of living, they seldom take time to step out of the mainstream long enough to take a look at where they are going. Seneca said, "You must know for which harbor you are headed if you are to catch the right wind to take you there."

Do you and your mate know where you are going? Ask yourself:

- What is my vision, direction, purpose, and pursuit in life?
- What is my mate's vision, direction, and purpose?

221

- What is God's ordained destiny for my mate? For me? For our marriage? For our family?

Can you answer these questions? Are you confident of your answers? Perhaps you and your mate are searching for your purpose, direction, and vision in life. Perhaps you have never given much thought to your destiny.

Step Out in the Right Direction

In her book, *Gift from the Sea*, Anne Morrow Lindbergh quotes St. Exupere: "Love does not consist in gazing at each other, but in looking outward together in the same direction." Love doesn't turn us inward toward one another; love exists so that we can build each other's self-esteem, face outward together, and impact our society.

Many Christian families today lack a sense of unified purpose and, instead of turning outward, are turning inward—not toward one another, but toward self. Instead of having an impact on the world, they blend in. Instead of cutting across the grain of the culture, they go with the flow.

Conformity leads to compromise. Compromise leads to mediocrity. Mediocrity leads to sin and a wasted life. Finally, a wasted life leads to a lost legacy.

Furthermore, aimlessness is not the only obstacle to the fulfillment of your purpose in life. You must also take action. Will Rogers warned, "Even if you're on the right track, you'll get run over if you just sit there!"

You and your mate may be Christians who are "on the right track," but you also have to be moving toward something—deciding on a daily basis how to use the life God has granted you. Why not gain God's vision for your life? Why not determine His "call," individually and as a couple?

Your vision, or call, probably will include accomplishments and relationships. Whatever that vision, dream, or goal encompasses, it will give context and meaning to minor decisions as well as to major ones.

Determining your direction is like developing a sixth sense: the sense of faith. Through it you first begin to grasp the unseen. You and your mate will develop self-esteem as you fulfill God's unique plan for your lives. You will both begin to see and feel your importance in God's eyes as you discover your importance in His plan. You will feel valued and needed by the One whose opinion counts most.

You and Your Mate Are God's Workmanship

Paul spoke of direction and vision: "For we are His workmanship, created in Christ Jesus for good works, which God prepared beforehand, that we should walk in them."[1] Is Paul speaking of a definite plan by God for an individual's life? We believe so. Look again at the verse:

For we are His workmanship,	*God made us*
created in Christ Jesus	*He redeemed us*
for good works,	*our purpose*
which God prepared beforehand	*God's plan*
that we should walk in them.	*our responsibility*

This is all part of the divine master plan for humanity. God is accomplishing His perfect work and perfect plan through imperfect people. He wants to use you and your mate to accomplish His plan. In return, your life will reflect great value, worth, significance, and dignity as you yield to God and participate with Him in His "good works."

Can you think of anything more satisfying than fulfilling the Creator's design for your life? To fulfill the purpose for which you and your mate were created and brought together will bring ultimate dignity to your lives.

A Man with a Destiny

A man who lived in England during the second half of the eighteenth century illustrates the principle of destiny. At the age of twenty-one, William Wilberforce was elected to Parliament. He was a small man, barely five feet tall, but his natural ability as an orator made him a giant among men.

In the fall of 1785, Wilberforce made a decision to receive Christ as his Savior and Lord. As a young Christian, Wilberforce observed the injustice of a trade that depended on the sale of human beings. He wondered if God had saved him only to take him to heaven, or if God had more in mind. Did God have a plan for his life, a place for him to serve?

His conscience was pricked. Wilberforce wrote in his diary: "Almighty God has set before me two great objectives: the abolition of the slave trade, and the reformation of manners."[2]

Wilberforce set out to use his political position to remove the blight of slavery from his homeland. He knew it would be a bitter battle in Parliament against the wealthy businessmen whose fortunes were built on slave trading. It's doubtful, however, that he could have foreseen the long years of repeated defeat and discouragement ahead of him. He and his compatriots were ridiculed and derided, but they remained faithful to the cause that burned in their hearts.

After twenty years of repeatedly introducing a bill to abolish slavery, Wilberforce saw the House of Commons and the House of Lords pass the bill in 1807. But the effects of his efforts reached even further. A great spiritual movement spread across England. Many members of Parliament had become committed Christians during those twenty years, and other reforms to aid the oppressed began to grow.

In 1797, Wilberforce wrote about his views of Christianity: "I must confess equally boldly that my own solid hopes for the well-being of my country depend, not so much on her navies and armies, nor on the wisdom of her rulers, nor on the spirit of her people, as on the persuasion that she still contains many who love and obey the Gospel of Christ."[3]

Wilberforce had a mandate from God and a vision for his country. He was not content just to wear the title of Christian; he felt he must *live* it.

In your life as a couple, as in Wilberforce's life, long-range goals can keep the fires of perseverance burning during the downpours of short-term disappointments. A dream—a vision—can help to keep hope alive, even after repeated failures.

Helping Your Mate Gain a Sense of Destiny

Before you embark on this quest, you must understand and carry with you a couple of perspectives. Without them, you would be like an old-time miner going into a gold or silver mine to search for precious metals with no hard hat, pick, or flashlight.

First, God is intricately and ingeniously involved in creation. He knows the grains of sand in the ocean,[4] the names of all the stars,[5] the number of hairs on your head, and the very instant every little sparrow dies.[6] If He knows the tiny details from the bottom of the ocean to the ends of the universe, then we can correctly assume that He knows everything that is going on in our lives as well.

Second, God is sovereign. He is fully in charge. He has a divine design for each individual life.

What is the purpose of His reign? Which goals are He accomplishing? Clearly, God's overall plan is to redeem humanity to Himself. Incredibly, He has chosen to use men and women like you and like us to execute His plan of influencing eternity.

As you discuss the greatness of God and the unspeakable privilege of being chosen by Him, your mate's self-esteem will quietly grow in strength. Just as the reward of gold and silver may await the miner who perseveres, God is building and storing a lasting reward in heaven for those who find and obey His call and plan for their lives.

Discovering Your Mate's Destiny

Take the challenge of eternal reward to heart. Arm yourself with the right perspective of God and His sovereignty and begin to search for your mate's destiny and your own.

1. Look to the past.

Watch for qualities that God has built into your mate's life to prepare him uniquely for a particular task. What causes or ideas continue to surface in your mate's thinking and conversation? What injustice makes him angry? What burdens his heart about your town, your state, or your world? What are his bedrock convictions that God has built into his life?

We, for example, did not arrive at our present field of ministry overnight. Initially, we worked with high school students, helping win them to Christ and beginning the process of discipleship in their lives through Bible studies.

During those years we made some interesting observations. Often a student would express an interest in spiritual things, only to go home and face discouragement from his parents. At other times, a student's spiritual growth would be negatively affected by a divorced mother or father. We began to see the need to help marriages so the children would not suffer.

We also saw the need to do everything we could to strengthen our own marriage. As a result, we ended up moving to Little Rock to help start what is now the FamilyLife ministry.

In 1776, during the Revolutionary War, a young man was captured for spying on the British. His response to his captors has never been forgotten in our land, for Nathan Hale said, "I only regret that I have but one life to give for my country." If your mate had a choice, for what cause would he be willing to give his life?

2. Help your mate inventory his talents.

In Matthew 25, Jesus told His disciples the parable of the talents.

A master gave each of his three servants a certain sum of money. The master rewarded the servants who faithfully used and invested the talents they were given, but he took the talent away from the one who buried it and did not use it.

By observing your mate, you can help him discover his abilities and gifts (those unique areas of spiritual capability listed in Romans 12 and 1 Corinthians 12). With increased confidence, he can be a more faithful servant and use the talents that God has given him to further His kingdom.

As you assess your mate's talents, both of you will probably feel the need for outside help. Ask friends who know your mate well to give their opinions. Ask your pastor or another mature Christian for ideas.

Encourage your mate to be faithful in what you both already know he does well. Beware of adding too many expectations or building them too high. Your mate doesn't have to do everything all at once. He can spend a lifetime investing those talents for the good of mankind and for heavenly reward.

3. Help your mate to focus on faith in God.

Your mate's destiny unfolds in the future, but it is shaped and fulfilled by daily choices. This is illustrated in the biblical account of Israel's history.

God constantly told the Israelites that they were a special people. The Jews knew that God had set them apart to make a unique, significant contribution to mankind. That helped to build national unity; they were excited about who they were and where they were headed. But what they chose to believe individually about themselves and their relationship with God made a big difference in their personal participation in God's plan.

One thing we most remember about the Israelites is that they "grumbled in their tents."[7] They fussed, complained, and generally felt sorry for themselves. Through their negative self-talk, they convinced themselves that God had forgotten them, and they lost their sense of destiny as a nation.

Negative "self-talk" (unbelief) can do the same to us today. If we tell ourselves that God has forgotten us, or that He doesn't know what He's doing, we, too, are "grumbling in our tents." Even our internal conversations can express discontent and dissatisfaction with the present. Although God has chosen us, we can convince ourselves that our destiny is no different from the average person's.

Negative self-talk says such things as, "I don't have any talents God could use," "My life won't amount to much," or "I'm just one person in five million." Some of the people of Israel convinced themselves through negative self-talk that God had deserted them in the wilderness. They liberally spread around their germs of grumbling until the whole nation became infected.

Self-talk can be positive too. For example, when our children are afraid, we ask them to tell us what the truth is: that Daddy and Mommy love them and will protect them and that Jesus loves them and will protect them. Then we remind them of a song or a verse in the Bible, or we pray with them. We encourage them to *believe* the truth.

I (Barbara) used similar self-talk several years ago when I went through a time of being fearful whenever Dennis was out of town. At night I went to sleep, repeating a couple of verses from Proverbs that reminded me of the truth: God is in control, and He cares for me. That's the essence of faith—it takes God at His word and believes Him.

As your "divine destiny" begins to emerge, it will demand action. Action demands risk. And risk demands faith—your faith and your mate's faith. Resolve together to fulfill your God-given call to the best of your ability. Find a place to serve:

- Is it through a community service project?
- Is it in the local church?

- Is it at home with the children?
- Is there a ministry for which you can volunteer to help?
- Do you need to make a vocational/career change?

God usually doesn't reveal His whole plan at once. When we make a commitment, He gives us light, a little at a time, to encourage us to walk by faith. Then, when we have walked that far, He gives us more light.

Leaving a Legacy

A husband and wife who walked by faith and, consequently, left a legacy far beyond anything they could have imagined, lived in the early 1700s in colonial America. Their names were Jonathan and Sarah Edwards.

Jonathan Edwards felt God's call to become a minister. He and his young bride began a pastorate in a small congregation. During the years that followed, he wrote many sermons, prayers, and books, and was influential in beginning the Great Awakening. Together they produced eleven children who grew into adulthood. Sarah was a partner in her husband's ministry, and he sought her advice regarding sermons and church matters. They spent time talking about these things together, and, when their children were old enough, the parents included them in the discussions.

The effects of the Edwards's lives have been far-reaching, but the most measurable results of their faithfulness to God's call is found through their descendants. Elizabeth Dodds records a study done by A. E. Winship in 1900 in which he lists a few of the accomplishments of the 1,400 Edwards descendants he was able to find:[8]

- 100 lawyers and a dean of a law school
- 80 holders of public office
- 66 physicians and a dean of a medical school

- 65 professors of colleges and universities
- 30 judges
- 13 college presidents
- 3 mayors of large cities
- 3 governors of states
- 3 United States senators
- 1 controller of the United States Treasury
- 1 Vice President of the United States

What kind of legacy will you and your mate leave? Will it be lasting? Will it be imperishable and eternal? Or will you leave behind only tangible items—buildings, money, and/or possessions?

The apostle Paul instructed Timothy to invest his life in *faithful* men who would be able to pass God's truth on to the next generation.[9] Where does God want you and your mate to invest the time you have been given?

Five Essentials in Leaving a Legacy that Will Outlive You

1. Fear the Lord and obey Him.

Your legacy begins in your heart, in your relationship with God. Psalm 112:1-2 reads: "How blessed is the man who fears the LORD, / Who greatly delights in His commandments. / His descendants will be mighty on earth; / The generation of the upright will be blessed."

On our first Christmas together (see page 188), Barbara and I gave a gift to God first. These sheets of paper became title deeds to our lives—to our marriage, to our hopes of having children, to our family, to our relationships, to our rights to our lives, to whatever ministry God gave us—we gave everything to Him.

2. Recognize the world's needs and respond with compassion and action.

In Matthew 9:36 we read: "And seeing the multitudes, He [Jesus] felt compassion for them." You and your mate need to leave a legacy by being committed to doing something about our world. Many Christians today are walking in the middle of the road; they're so focused on what other people think that they are unwilling to take any risks in order to make an impact for Christ. In light of this, Jamie Buckingham wrote, "The problem with Christians today is that no one wants to kill them anymore."

When you fly over rows of houses, do you wonder how many people in those homes know Jesus? This year thirty million people will die without hearing the name of Christ. Hundreds of millions will pray to idols. Someone needs to reach these people with the Good News.

John F. Kennedy, in *Profiles in Courage*, described the need for courageous people: "Some men show courage throughout the whole of their lives. Others sail with the wind until the decisive moment when their conscience and events propel them into the center of the storm." If you want to leave a lasting legacy, you need to act with courage to reach out to those in need.

3. Pray as a couple that God will use you to accomplish His purposes.

As recorded in 1 Chronicles 4:10, Jabez prayed, "Oh that Thou wouldst bless me indeed, and enlarge my border, and that Thy hand might be with me, and that Thou wouldst keep me from harm."

What did Jabez ask God to do? Bless him. Give him new turf and enlarge his sphere of influence. Keep him from temptation. Stay with him. Pray this prayer with your mate, and at the end of the year, see how different your lives will be.

4. Help your mate be a better steward of his gifts and abilities.

Help him recognize how God has used his gifts and abilities in the past. Serving others? Teaching the Scripture? Advising a Christian ministry?

Help him plug into the local church, which needs committed

laymen and women who have strong, godly character and a vision for their communities.

Help him recognize his convictions. Thomas Carlyle says, "Conviction is worthless until it can convert itself into daily conduct." Help your mate determine what he is willing to die for so he can ultimately determine what he can live for.

5. Ask God to give your children a sense of purpose, direction, and mission.

The challenge here is to leave your children a heritage, not just an inheritance. As someone once said, "Our children are messengers we send to a time we will not see."

Dignity through Destiny

David Livingstone, the missionary to Africa, said, "I will go anywhere, as long as it is forward." And by moving forward and advancing God's kingdom, he undoubtedly also advanced his sense of dignity.

Gaining a vision and a direction in life will yield significance to your mate's life as well, especially if the omnipotent God of the universe has set that heading and direction. In fact, true vision, direction, and destiny can come only from the One who controls not only the present but also the future. By discovering your eternal destiny, you will begin to build lasting dignity in your lives. The internal awareness of that God-ordained dignity will enhance the self-esteem of every member of your family.

The challenge is the same for all of us. Will we follow Christ and fulfill His call and vision for our lives? Just as we found spiritual life in no other Person than Jesus Christ, so we find a dignity like no other in the destiny He provides.

ESTEEM BUILDER PROJECT

(Use a sheet of paper if necessary.)

1. Begin to discover your destiny as a couple by talking and dreaming together about what you wish you could do with your lives. Which areas, issues, and needs of people would you like to affect? Take notes of your conversations. Pray that during the weeks and months to come, God will guide your conversations and begin to reveal His leading to you.

2. If you already have a sense of vision and destiny, write out your vision for *your* life (be specific). Ask your mate to do the same for *himself.*

3. Review each other's statements and respond to what each of you has written.

4. Describe the legacy you would leave if you were to die today.

5. How would you like your legacy to be different from what you have described?

6. Discuss with your mate what steps you need to take to make your desired legacy a reality.

16

Five Investment Tips
that Will Yield a Great Return

———————◆◆◆———————

———————◆◆◆———————

MAN TO MAN: FROM DENNIS

TOM PETERS, AUTHOR of the bestselling book, *In Search of Excellence*, was once exhorting a group of corporate officers. After speaking to these leaders for several hours, he challenged them to raise their standards.

Finally, a top executive interrupted him to voice dissatisfaction. "Peters, I'm tired of hearing all this stuff on excellence! We don't need this! Our company is *no worse than anyone else's.*"

Outwardly, Peters passively listened to the corporate leader's tirade. But inwardly, his mind was racing: *Now wouldn't that statement make a great byline right under the company logo—"International Widgets . . . We're no worse than anyone else."*[1]

As men, our attitude can be very similar to that corporate leader's. Exasperated with all the areas in which we have to provide leadership, we might exclaim, "I'm tired of hearing what I need to be doing, where I'm failing as a husband, and everything that's wrong in our marriage. After all, *our* marriage is no worse than anyone else's!"

Although you may have felt that way on occasion, as I have, I'm confident that you wouldn't want to proudly display a sign in your front yard declaring that motto. And, as the head of your family and your mate's leader, you recognize that you (along with the rest of us) can use some advice or counsel in knowing exactly what to do next. You need a few, solid "investment tips" so that the stock of your wife's self-image will soar in value.

When I was twenty and a sophomore in college, I received a hot investment tip from a stockbroker. I'll never forget Dashew Business Machines (no relation to International Business Machines, I can assure you). Without getting my dad's advice, I invested five hundred dollars in four hundred shares. After all, it was coming out of bankruptcy, so it had no place to go but up. It couldn't go lower than $1.25 per share . . . or so I thought.

My baptism into Wall Street was a harsh one. Dashew went from $1.25 to $.87, to $.50, to $.12, and finally out of sight and back into bankruptcy court. Sometime later my dad found out and suggested that I use the stock to wallpaper my room! It would serve as a reminder to invest in stocks that are proven and to get my investment advice from a trustworthy authority.

The Wise Investment

The Scriptures are the best, most proven, and most authoritative "Investment Tip Sheet" you'll ever read. Like having a copy today of the *Wall Street Journal* that will be published forty years from now, the

Bible tells you how to invest in your wife's life *today* if you want to experience a fabulous return in forty years. And, by the way, as her stock goes up, you will share in the profits!

Your wife needs your creative investment energies if she is to become all that God created her to be. To help you in this area, here are some of the best investment tips I know for giving both of you a rich return on your investment.

Investment Tip 1: Treat her as a fully participating partner.

Today the business world has all kinds of partnerships: silent partners, financial partners, equal partners, controlling partners, minority partners, and more. But in marriage, God intended for us to have only one kind: a fully participating partnership.

The apostle Peter sets forth the concept of mutual partnership as he instructs a man to treat his wife as "a fellow heir of the grace of life."[2] Although her function and role as a woman differs from yours as a man, she has an equal inheritance as a child of God.

When you recognize your wife as a fully participating partner in your life and marriage, you build her esteem. If you exclude her from your life, you devalue her worth as a person and her identity suffers. Without realizing it, you send your wife an unmistakably clear signal that says: "I don't need you. I can live my life without you."

Some husbands believe that the most difficult words to say are: "I love you" or "Will you forgive me?" But the three-word admission that seems the most threatening of all is: "I need you."

That *is* hard to admit, isn't it? When is the last time you told your wife you needed her? No, not just for this duty or that errand, but you really needed her full participation in your life. When you express that need, she *feels* needed because you become vulnerable and dependent upon her. She *experiences* her importance in your life.

Something in my male ego grabs hold of my tongue and keeps me from saying that to Barbara as often as I should. Pride? Yes. A false concept of manhood? Undoubtedly. But most assuredly, at the heart of the matter is foolishness. I really *do* need my wife! She is God's personally hand-selected provision for me.

A man may fear he will lose his wife's respect if he admits his need, but I've experienced quite the opposite. When I express my absolute need for Barbara, she is so built up and encouraged that she is free to respect me even more. I do not lose my identity as a man by expressing my dependence on her.

You will make your wife a participating partner in your life when you tenderly look her in the eyes and say, "I need you." Why not make this an experiential reality in your marriage by frequently saying:

- "I need you to listen as I talk about what's troubling me. And I need your perspective on my problems and your belief in me as a person."
- "I need you to help me become the man God created me to be."
- "I want you to have total access into my life. I need you to keep me honest in areas of my life in which I could stray from Christ. You may question me or confront me on any issue."
- "You are the person I most trust with my life."
- "I need you for your advice, judgments, and wise counsel on decisions I face, especially at work."
- "I need your prayers for a temptation I am facing."

When I become the sole proprietor in our marriage and treat Barbara as a silent partner, we both lose. She loses the opportunities I can give to include her, develop her, and make her feel important. I lose because I tend to make poor decisions when I am isolated from her.

I want to encourage you to let your wife into the interior of your life. Are you keeping her out of some area of your life? Do you tend to act independently of her in any area, including career or business? She may be more interested than you think. What about financial matters? She most likely will offer a perspective that you need to hear. A difficult office relationship? Her advice might solve the problem.

Investment Tip 2: Protect her.

The apostle Peter also exhorts husbands, "You husbands likewise, live with your wives in an understanding way, as with a weaker vessel, since she is a woman."[3] Peter's emphasis here is on "understanding" because she is a "weaker vessel." Your wife wants a man who understands her and her needs.

Your wife needs to feel safe, secure, and protected. As her husband, it's up to you to provide that security. I was reminded of a woman's need for protection years ago when I attended a couples conference. During the conference, a young woman was raped in her room. As the speaker told the other conferees a man had forced his way into this young woman's room, I noticed an interesting phenomenon. Instinctively, and in unison, as though led by an orchestra conductor, nearly every husband in the audience tenderly slid his arm around his wife. Likewise, almost every wife slipped closer into his protective embrace. It was a physical gesture of a woman's need for safekeeping and a man's natural desire to protect his wife.

People use locks, burglar and fire alarms, and lighting systems to protect their most valuable possessions. When we invest in protecting our wives, we also are making a statement about their value to us, thus building their worth even more.

Certainly you already protect your wife physically. You wouldn't think of having it any other way. You discourage her going out at night if it is dangerous. You protect her by encouraging her to lock the car when she goes shopping. You talk about what to do if a stranger forces his way into the house. And you provide the kind of security she needs at home for the times you are away. All these statements and actions demonstrate that she indeed is valued and that you care about what happens to her.

But are you protecting her from other muggers in her life, such as:

- Overscheduling, letting her life get out of balance, and becoming driven?
- Others' manipulation of her emotions and time?
- Her own unrealistic goals or expectations, which set her up for failure?
- Her tendency to compare herself with others—where she repeatedly comes up short in her own eyes?
- Burnout at work? At home?
- The children, who would take advantage of her weaknesses that they know so well?
- People who repeatedly discourage her?

Obviously, you can't protect your wife from every pressure, worry, fear, or loss. But you can do your best to anticipate many of these problems before they occur and to establish a solid security system for her protection.

As I protect Barbara, I experience the satisfaction of knowing I am fulfilling my God-appointed privilege. Being firm and helping her say no causes me to feel that I'm really helping this woman be successful by protecting her from negative outside forces. In fact, I think protecting her helps *my* self-image as a man as much as it does hers, because I feel needed and important.

One additional thought: Your wife will need different types of protection at different times and at various stages in her life. Be prepared to adjust accordingly.

Wife-Builder's Inventory

The following questions help me "inventory" Barbara's life and needs. By answering these questions periodically, I maintain my protection of her and thus help to build her self-esteem.

- What is the pace of our life? Sometimes my schedule causes more problems for her than it does for me. Are there any breathers for her? For us?
- What kind of pace can she keep? For how long? What does she need after an intense period of activity or involvement?
- What tends to crush her? What pops her balloon? What causes her to feel that she's failing? What can I do about it?
- Which decisions do I need to make that will reduce pressure or break loose a logjam? Am I putting off some things that, if I went ahead and did them, would facilitate her daily routine and thereby help her in the long run? (I've seen my procrastination cost Barbara a lot emotionally.)
- Does she need to be rescued for an evening? A weekend? An extended period? When can I carry her off for a romantic retreat—for just the two of us?
- What direction can I give her to protect her as she moves through a difficult period of time?

Investment Tip 3: Honor her.

When God established marriage, He knew that one of the greatest components for building worth into another person would be honor. We see this in His command to each husband: "Grant her honor as a fellow heir of the grace of life."[4] Webster defines honor as "high regard or great respect given; especially glory, fame; distinction."

It is no wonder so many wives are flooding the workplace today. Some have to work; they need the income. But some wives don't have to work; they do it because they are seeking the honor, fulfillment, and significance they are not receiving from their husbands.

After watching the marriages of numerous Christian leaders disintegrate, I have come to some conclusions. One is that there is no such thing as a marriage blowout—only slow, small leaks. Like a tire that gradually loses air without the driver noticing, many marriages have slowly gone flat.

Every marriage is susceptible to leaks, and ours is no exception. The world lures my wife with glittery, false promises of fulfillment and true significance. If I fail to honor her and esteem her as a woman of distinction, then I ignore the reality of her need and the deceptive power of the world's promises. It's just a matter of time before she will begin to wear down and look elsewhere for worth.

Following are a few techniques to honor your wife that can give you a competitive edge while also building your wife's self-esteem:

First, honor your wife by learning the art of putting her on a pedestal. If you focus on honoring her and caring for her needs, and on nurturing her as your most valued relationship, then you can truly make a difference in how she feels about herself. Capture your wife's heart by treating her with respect, tenderness, and the highest esteem.

Second, honor your wife by recognizing her accomplishments. Frequently I look into Barbara's eyes and verbally express my wonder at all she does. She wears many hats and is an amazingly hard worker. At other times, I stand back in awe of the woman of character she has become. Her steady walk with God is a constant stream of ministry to me.

Third, honor your wife by speaking to her with respect. Without careful attention, your tongue can become caustic, searing, and accusing. Washington Irving once said, "The tongue is the only tool that gets sharper with use."

My tongue can be fueled by a disrespectful attitude. I work hard in this area. I'm not always as successful as I'd like to be, but I know that honor begins with an attitude. Also, if any of the children ever talk back to Barbara or show disrespect, they know they have to deal with me when I get home. Our children are great, but they will mug her if I let them. She's outnumbered! So I encourage our children to respect her too.

If your wife works outside the home, she has some unique needs for honor. She may need the practical honor of a free evening once or twice a week when you volunteer to do it all: put the children to bed, clean the kitchen, do the laundry, etc.

Fourth, honor your wife by extending common courtesies. You may think that these little amenities were worthwhile only during court-ship, but actually they are a great way to demonstrate respect and distinction over the long haul. Common courtesy is at the heart of servanthood; it says, "my life for yours." It bows before another to show esteem and dignity.

Hats a Wife Wears

Listed below are just a few of the hats some women wear today:

For the family:
- Meal planner
- Nurse
- Counselor/comforter
- Policeman and judge (to settle internal disputes)
- Clothier/wardrobe consultant
- Budget and financial planner/penny pincher
- Teacher/tutor
- Cheerleader
- Career woman
- Spiritual advisor
- Nursery worker
- Seamstress
- Cook
- Maid
- Linguistics specialist (in the dialect of two-year-olds)
- Resident "Emily Post"

- Administrator/schedule planner
- Interior decorator
- Chauffeur
- Environmentalist (maintaining a proper home environment)
- Family traditionalist
- Preserver of family history

For her husband:
- Confidante
- Companion
- Lover
- Advisor
- Encourager
- Partner
- Comforter
- Hostess and entertainer

For the community:
- Caring neighbor
- Gracious entertainer
- Volunteer
- Counselor
- Friend
- Church member

A woman is the crown jewel of God's creative handiwork. We should be careful not to treat her like one of the guys—slapping her on the back, for instance. The majesty of God is displayed in your wife. Why not exalt her by demonstrating courtesy? (Warning: If you suddenly begin a rash of "old courtesies," you may need to alert the emergency medics to get some smelling salts ready!)

The thought of demonstrating courtesy reminds me of a story my friend and FamilyLife Marriage Conference colleague Bob Horner told me:

> After noticing her neighbor bringing home flowers for his wife five nights in a row and passionately embracing her each time, Mrs. Richards brought

this to her husband's attention. "You know, I've observed the strangest thing. Every evening this week our neighbor has walked to his door with a gift and a bundle of flowers and has given them to his wife as he kissed her and entered his home. Isn't that romantic? Why can't you do that?"

Mr. Richards replied, "I couldn't do that. I hardly know her!"

But as time passed, he began to think, *That must be what really excites women.* So he went out and bought a big box of candy and a bundle of his wife's favorite flowers. Arriving home a little early that afternoon, he rang the doorbell, and when his wife appeared, he passionately embraced her. As she fell in a heap on the floor, he exclaimed, "My gosh, what happened?"

She answered, "Oh, this has been the worst day. Our son received a terrible report card, Mom was admitted to the hospital, the roast burned, the washing machine broke, and now to top it all off, you come home drunk!"

Sometimes our courtesy doesn't elicit the reaction we expect, but it's worth it!

I have found I can bring great dignity to Barbara by doing the following:

- Buying her a new dress which *wasn't* on sale.
- Validating her emotions by listening before I answer.
- Appreciating her sexuality rather than making fun of her with comments such as, "Oh, you're just a woman!"
- Shopping with her and picking out something that I think she looks regal in.
- Giving her a free weekend while I stay home with the kids, so she can go antique shopping with friends.
- Going on a walk together so she can share with me what's on her mind.

When you honor your wife, she'll become even more honorable. You both win!

Investment Tip 4: Develop her gifts and horizons as a woman.

Barbara's life is filled with battling the tyranny of the urgent: meeting needs, negotiating sibling rivalry disputes, and juggling busy schedules. Most of her day is spent giving to others, and she generally ends it by dropping into bed, exhausted.

For years I watched her go through this daily ritual of giving her life away. Being the perceptive man that I am, it finally dawned on me that I should help my favorite lady express some of her creativity in other ways. It occurred to me that while I'm taking management classes and reading professional journals, books, and magazines, Barbara is occupied continually with the needs of our family. She needs me to look out for her and to encourage her to grow and develop also.

The Scriptures mandate that I do this. Consider the familiar passage in Ephesians 5:25–29, especially verses 28 and 29: "He who loves his own wife loves himself; for no one ever hated his own flesh, but nourishes and cherishes it, just as Christ also does the church."

Notice the words describing what we are to do for our wives: *love*, *nourish*, and *cherish*. All these are part of building into your wife's life and developing her self-esteem.

First, help her grow as a Christian. Your wife is your number one disciple. Do you encourage spiritual growth in your wife? It's the smartest thing you could possibly do. When your wife grows in this area, not only does she triumph at life, but *you* benefit as well. Help her to grow spiritually by praying regularly for her and with her—at bedtime, in the morning before leaving for work, at mealtimes. It *will* encourage her.

Interact together over God's Word and its application to your individual lives, as well as to your family. Encourage your wife to employ her spiritual gifts in service to others outside your home if she has time.

Second, develop her talents. Take part in her life by nurturing the development of her dormant talents. Like fruit seeds that never have been planted in fertile soil and watered, your wife's gifts may need your care in order to germinate.

If you already have done this, you know that she responds to this personalized focus. She feels that you value her and are helping her to expand her life and utilize her gifts so that she might be even more productive. Perhaps your wife already has influence. Can you supply additional resources so that she can become even more effective?

Third, help her develop new horizons. Most of us fail to anticipate major change points in the lives of our wives, such as the birth of a child, children's teen years, menopause, and the empty nest. When your children leave home, your wife will suddenly have enormous chunks of time and attention to devote to another worthwhile cause. Are you developing her today so that she will be ready to take some risks later?

Barbara is continuing to fashion a vision for her life that we both believe will be very satisfying to her. Why not assist your wife in uncovering a vision that will be meaningful to her? By helping her to keep her horizons clear and focused, you will encourage her growth and development. And after years of helping her broaden her life, you will enjoy watching as your wife gains a new sphere of influence.

Investment Tip 5: Assist in problem solving.

Isn't it interesting that, for most men, work gobbles up most of our most creative problem-solving energies, our best leadership, and our most noble attitudes? Home usually gets the leftovers. One of my friends has on his office desk a plaque that reads, "Save a little for home."

Your wife would benefit if you saved a little more for home too. Start by considering this question: What one problem in your wife's life, if solved, would truly strengthen her? Is there a complete roadblock in the way or just a small boulder? How could you remove it?

If you are to see your wife win, you must be intimately involved in solving the problems that surround her. If she is discouraged continually in certain situations, then put all your creative leadership ability behind her and gently give suggestions toward solving that problem. Here are some ideas:

- Watch your wife carefully. Observing her life may turn up problems that can be isolated and solved quickly.
- Get the facts. What exactly is the problem? Whose responsibility is it? What is the cause of the problem?
- Discuss your alternatives together. Be sure to find out what your wife really feels is best in the situation. She may be too close to the problem, or she may know what needs to be done and simply need your leadership and backing to take action.
- Go to God in prayer. Ask Him for the wisdom and resources to solve the problem. Be careful of procrastination; make a decision under God's leadership and then help your wife to implement it.
- Evaluate the results. Inspect what happens. Refine the decision and its implementation through thorough analysis of how things are working out.

A manager comes alongside his associates and applies resources to shore them up at their points of weakness. You can, and should, do the same for your wife. It might mean that you have to assume some of her responsibilities.

Does your wife have an area or two in which she consistently fails? Time management? Budgeting? Meal planning? Problem solving at work or at home? You can help. By choosing to develop her in these areas, you encourage her growth so she can better handle the pressure. But you have a choice. Either develop her to handle the responsibilities or come alongside her to help accomplish the tasks. She needs you to help her become all God created her to be.

Persevere in Your Investment

You may be married to an insecure woman with low self-esteem. You may have tried already for a week or two to help her become more confident and self-assured but, because you haven't seen immediate results, you may be discouraged. Please don't give up. It may take years before you begin to see your wife blossom, but it will be worth the effort and the wait.

One word of caution: You will be tempted to take the path of least resistance; that path will be crowded with other husbands. But you'll have a far greater reward if you truly persist at investing your life in your wife.

King David understood the benefits of perseverance. When he first began to assemble and organize a group of men in the desert, he attracted "everyone who was in distress, and everyone who was in debt, and everyone who was discontented."[5] About four hundred of these vagabonds, social misfits, and outcasts answered David's call for military training.

I'm realistic enough about leadership to know that David must have swallowed hard as he looked over his ragtag band. Undoubtedly he was tempted to put another advertisement in the paper and draft another group. But these were the men God had given him, so he accepted them and began to invest his life in theirs. He immediately started a program that would turn them into a band of trained soldiers.

For more than seven years, David personally guided their development. Undoubtedly, progress was slow, setbacks were routine, and improvement was, at times, unnoticeable. Finally, after years of perseverance, there emerged a crack fighting unit of men who were experts with sword, sling, spear, and bow and arrow. In 1 Chronicles 11, we read of the incredible feats these men achieved. Using them as the core of his militia, David drove all alien invaders out of Israel. That group of misfits became known as David's "mighty men."[6]

Your wife couldn't possibly be described in such ragged terms, but her life and her self-esteem can become a trophy of the grace of God. If you invest the time, energy, and prayerful leadership needed to build into her life, she can become a more confident wife and woman—a "mighty" woman of God.

Barbara's Tips to Men

Barbara's tips on how to minister to a wife are also helpful:

- Seek to understand her role and her struggle. (If she works outside the home, understand her job and the pressures it places on her, especially regarding her role at home.)
- Verbalize often, especially during her times of failure and discouragement, your complete acceptance of her. (Be sure that you really *do* accept her.) Liberally verbalize belief in her as a person and in her ability and worth.
- Verbalize your need for her and back it up by sharing with her your fears, failures, needs, dreams, hopes, and discouragements. Do it cautiously if this is new to you.
- Share at times when she can listen attentively and appreciate your transparency. (Don't share something serious when she's preoccupied with the kids or dinner.)
- Notice and praise her for the things she does for you (meals, laundry, etc.).
- Be willing to help her work through difficulties in her life: discipline, problems with the children, relationships with friends and parents, fears, resentment, etc.
- Be patient and realize that building or rebuilding her self-esteem is a lifetime process. It is not static. Territory can be lost by giving up too soon.

In many ways, I am a different woman from the one Dennis married. One of the most significant changes has been in my self-image. Dennis's willingness to listen and change his schedule, and his consistent expression of praise for me, belief in me, and commitment to me have literally changed my life. There is hope.

ESTEEM BUILDER PROJECT

(Use a sheet of paper if necessary.)

1 Which one of the following "investments" in your wife's life do you need to make a priority during the coming month?
   a. Treat her as a fully participating partner.
   b. Protect her.
   c. Honor her
   d. Develop her gifts and horizons as a woman.
   e. Assist in problem solving.
2. Review the section in this chapter that best applies to your wife. Next to the investment you choose, list which action points you need to take. Write out your investment strategy and set your goals.
3. Ask her to read this chapter and underline sections she'd like to discuss with you. Ask her to put a check by questions that would be great points of discussion. Then schedule a two-night getaway for the two of you to work your way through this chapter.

Imagine you have just received the following letter from your wife. How would you respond in writing? Be specific, and express how you feel.

My dearest husband . . .

Thank you for choosing me to share your life with you. Thank you for your honesty and transparency. I know it can be painful at times.

Deep down inside, I really know that you love me. But I'm a woman, and I need tangible reminders of your love. There is very little in this life of greater value to me than your love. I need it. I need you.

Could I ask a favor? I love to receive letters from you, but I don't ever want to ask for them—it takes all the fun out of receiving them if it's my idea. But would you write me a letter? I need to know:

- how you appreciate me
- what I've done to show that I respect you
- how I've been an encouragement to you
- how you appreciate the "little things" I do every week for you
- your unconditional acceptance, just as I am
- how I am a partner to you
- why you enjoy me . . .
- what you like about me
- how I've changed for good, or ways that you've seen me grow (I forget sometimes)
- that you want to lead me and do what is best for me
- that you want to meet my needs
- and that your love *will* persevere

You can write it any way you'd like, but please tell me. I really do respect you.

I love you,
Your wife

P. S. I'm not perfect either, but I'm glad we're in this thing together.

CHAPTER

17

Securing Your Man

———————◆————————

- *Understand His Manhood*
- *Respect His Person*
- *Adapt to Him and Share His Dream*
- *Character Inventory*
- *It Takes Years for Him to Become a Man*
- *Esteem Builder Project*

———————◆————————

WOMAN TO WOMAN: FROM BARBARA

OUR CHILDREN AND I ONCE WATCHED a new shopping center go up near our home. Initially, progress was rapid; the lot was cleared and the concrete pads were poured in one week. Then the walls went up, quickly followed by the framing for the roof.

But one day, we turned the corner and slowed our van in disbelief. The entire structure had collapsed! The wooden roof trusses lay flat in neat rows, surrounded by the remains of the crumbled brick walls. It appeared that there had been an explosion.

Puzzled, we asked what had happened and learned that the carpenters had failed to secure and brace the new structure properly. The building's roof, held in place only by two boards, had collapsed under the weight of two carpenters.

As I reflected with amazement on the need for support in the building's structure, I saw a parallel in our marriage. The roof is like my husband's self-esteem.

Ephesians 5:23 teaches that the husband is "the head of the wife, as Christ also is the head of the church." When we first married, I committed to being under the roof of Dennis's protection. He had all the structural basics, but he was brand-new at being my protector. Like that roof, he appeared to be solidly in place, but he needed me to help *secure* him—to *brace* him by believing in him.

Fortunately, I did come alongside him. Through the years, the weight of life's pressures has sometimes shaken him, but he has remained solidly over me as my roof, my protector. Today, although still not perfectly secure, my husband's structural integrity is much more stable. He tells me that I have had a major part in helping him to feel more sure of himself as a man and as a husband.

Likewise, you can strengthen your husband's self-esteem. But first you must recognize where he needs bolstering. Many women today are so caught up in finding their own identity that they, like the carpenters who were building the shopping center, make assumptions about their husband's self-confidence and security. Your mate may be full-grown on the outside, but inside he undoubtedly feels some insecurity. He's not so sure how to be a man in this world where women have growing independence and society is changing the traditional rules of relationships.

How does a wife build her husband's self-esteem? Basically, by making her responsibility as wife her number-one focus. By developing the right attitudes, a wife can meet some of her husband's needs— needs to be believed in, supported, and encouraged.

It has been said, "Behind every great man is a great woman." One woman believed that literally. She and her husband, the mayor of a large city, were walking down a city street one day when a construction worker on a nearby scaffolding leaned over and shouted, "Hello, Peggy." She turned to look and recognized the carpenter as an old boyfriend from high school. She returned his greeting, and they had a brief conversation before she and her husband continued their walk.

The mayor chuckled and said to his wife, "See there, if you had married him, you'd be the wife of a construction worker."

She looked at him and said, "No, dear, if I'd married him, *he* would be mayor of this city."

No matter what type of man you are married to, God wants you to set your sights on building his self-esteem. To help you begin, I recommend that you do three things: (1) gain an understanding of his manhood; (2) learn the secret of respecting his person; and (3) adapt to him and his dreams.

Understand His Manhood

The book of Proverbs is probably my favorite in the Bible because it contains such practical wisdom about everyday life. One of its main themes is the value of developing understanding. Consider each of these verses on understanding:

Incline your heart to understanding. (2:2)
Understanding will watch over you. (2:11)
Call understanding your intimate friend. (7:4)
A man [or woman] of understanding walks straight. (15:21)
Understanding is a fountain of life to him [or her] who has it. (16:22)

Notice that understanding is not an end in itself; it is a vehicle to wisdom, direction, and even to life. A person of understanding views life and people with God's perspective. It enables you to feel for another person, to identify with his struggles and difficulties, and to know what to say and what not to say. In the husband-wife relationship, your level of understanding often determines your level of acceptance. However, total understanding is not necessary in order to demonstrate the total acceptance that is crucial in building your husband's self-esteem.

At a FamilyLife Marriage Conference I talked to more than a dozen women who were experiencing problems in their marriages. One woman resented her husband's schedule. Another disagreed with her husband regarding how to discipline their children. A third was a young woman whose mate was jealous of the time she spent with her sister.

My advice to these women was basically the same: Seek to understand *why* your husband is feeling or acting this way. Focus on *him*, not on the negative circumstances and how *you* are affected. Is he communicating by his actions some deep needs for affirmation, commitment, or loyalty?

Also, give him your complete acceptance, even if you don't totally understand him. It may be necessary to ask God to help you accept your husband, for it may not be easy to live with your situation.

Why is acceptance so important to a man? Because without it, he will feel that you are pressuring him to become something he's not. With it, he will sense that you love him for who he is today and not for what you hope he will become.

Understand Male and Female Differences

There are three areas in which most wives have difficulty understanding their husbands. These three are foundational to all men, and having knowledge of them is essential if a wife is to help build her husband's self-esteem.

The first is understanding male and female differences. We are often taught today that men and women are just two sexually interchangeable units. To aid women's quest for political and economic equality with men, many experts have sought to explain away all social, emotional, and intellectual differences. These educators, sociologists, and psychologists imply that there are no differences between men and women other than the obvious biological ones.

As a result, we wives have been deceived into thinking that our husbands are basically like us. Men, as well as women, have lost their sense of wonder and appreciation for our God-given maleness and femaleness. This tainted perspective clouds our perceptions of our husbands.

Without a true understanding of how God has made our husbands different, we will be tempted to resent them for being the way they are. If we resent our husbands, we are ultimately resenting God, who designed their manhood.

I have found that as my understanding of my husband's distinctions as a man increases, I am less likely to be critical of potential irritants. My understanding quotient took a giant stride forward when I read Dr. Joyce Brothers' book, *What Every Woman Should Know about Men*. In her book, Dr. Brothers confessed that she was astounded to find the differences between men and women to be so vast.

She devotes an entire chapter to the differences between men's and women's brains. She cites evidence to prove that, although male and female brains are made up of two basic parts—a left and a right hemisphere—the function for each sex is quite different. Simply put, a man's brain operates specifically and compartmentally, and a women's operates holistically.

The right hemisphere of a man's brain can and does operate without the left hemisphere being involved, and vice versa. A woman's brain uses and integrates both hemispheres simultaneously. Thus, a man can give more focused attention to his work, while his wife can be tuned in to everything around her. This makes her more perceptive of people and their feelings and enables her, especially if she is a mother, to know what is going on in every part of the house at one time.[1]

I now understand why Dennis can be reading the paper and not know that the children, a few feet away, are terrorizing one another.

Rather than get angry with him for his apparent noninvolvement, I realize that one side of his brain is "off" and that he's just being himself—a man.

Also, when he comes home from work, the children sometimes scream for his attention, yet he doesn't seem to hear them. I tell them, "Relax, kids, your daddy's not home yet!"

Exasperated, they reply, "Yes he is, Mom. He's standing right there."

But I tell them, "*We* know he's home, but *he* doesn't know it yet!"

Dennis needs me to help him tune in at home. We both know it. In the first incident above, I may go into the living room, tap him on the shoulder, and ask him to solve the problem. Or I may do it myself. But because of this new understanding of his masculinity, I'm better able to accept him and his differences. Because he feels accepted, he has a greater freedom to be himself and a growing resolve to learn and change.

The beauty of understanding male and female differences is in seeing more clearly God's detailed design of the two sexes. He did not create man to be more important than woman. He values them equally. But in order to reflect the Trinity more accurately to the unbelieving world, God wisely designed us each—man and woman—with built-in distinctions. These are for the purpose of fulfilling different responsibilities in marriage. In living out these biblical patterns, we not only reflect God's image, but both partners experience the contentment intended in marriage.

Understanding His Need for Work

A second area of struggle for many wives is her husband's job and the pressures it imposes on him and everyone around him.

The past three decades of new ideologies about women's rights have left Christian women swimming in a wake of confusion. We have been told to seek personal fulfillment at the expense of our husbands and children, if necessary. Family, we hear, should not stand in the way of self.

Consequently, many Christian wives have lost sight of our husbands' needs because we have focused intently on our own. Even though more than 50 percent of you reading this book work outside the home, I'd like to explain briefly the importance of work in your husband's life.

Man was given the responsibility by God to toil, sweat, and gain from the labor of his hands. A man's work is part of the ruling and managing purpose that God spoke of in Genesis 1:26: "Let them rule over the fish of the sea and over the birds of the sky and over the cattle and over all the earth." Thus, your husband needs work in order to realize the satisfaction inherent in executing God's stated purpose for his life. His work gives him a sense of significance and importance in the world as he sees his efforts affecting life for good in the present and the future.

But this drive for significance sometimes pushes a man to extremes. In his effort to gain a sense of well-being and significance, he often becomes enslaved to his job. Attempting to gain importance through wealth or position, he makes his work his god. For hundreds of years, men have confused their net worth with their self-worth.

On the other hand, a man who is out of work lacks true self-respect. In this age of workaholism, losing a job is a traumatic blow to a man's esteem. It strikes at the core of his dignity. A man who doesn't work can't enjoy the satisfaction of a solid day's productivity.

Your husband needs you to help him keep these two extremes in balance. He needs you to praise him for his work, but not to push him to gain too much too quickly. When a man loses or quits his job, his self-esteem can sink. During these times, he needs you to stand beside him and encourage his efforts at finding employment. Men need to work.

Offer to type his resumé, and make it first class. With his permission, call a few friends in your church who might know of jobs. Pray that God will lead him to a job where he can utilize his strengths and make his own contribution.

What if your husband is employed, but you don't like his job? What if you think he spends too much time there? Do you still support him? Won't that only encourage him to work more?

Ann Landers once received a letter from a woman who was lonely and jealous of the time her husband spent at a local diner. She printed the letter with this response: "When you begin to offer the same thing on the menu at home, he may spend more time there."

The point of Ann's response was to make yourself more attractive to your husband than his acquaintances and job. Nagging won't bring him home. But understanding your husband's need for work and genuinely praising him will make you more attractive to him. He may find that he wants to spend more time with you and less at work because his work can't fulfill his need for companionship.

Understanding His Sexual Needs

The third sphere in which we wives, for the most part, do not really understand our husbands is in how his self-image is vitally linked to his sexuality. Sometimes we women judge our husbands' sexual needs by our own.

Many wives express that they are offended because their husbands are such sexual creatures. This attitude communicates rejection to a man. To ignore his sexual needs, to resist his initiation of sex, or merely to tolerate his advances is to tear at the heart of his self-esteem.

Jill Renich points this out in her book, *To Have and to Hold*. She states that for a man, "Sex is the most meaningful demonstration of love and self-worth. It is a part of his own deepest person."[2]

Dr. Joyce Brothers sheds further light on men and their need for sex when she writes, "By and large, men are far more apprehensive when it comes to sex than a woman might believe."[3] Those statements seem contrary to popular belief, don't they? Modern men are portrayed via the media as always being confident and assertive sexually.

The truth is, the typical man worries a lot. He worries about his sexual performance, his wife's enjoyment, and his ability to satisfy her. He worries about the future and all those tales he has heard about losing his ability to make love. These worries are signs of a low self-confidence. Thus, a man who feels like a failure in the marriage bed will seldom have the deep, abiding self-respect for which he longs.

But, as Jill Renich writes, "To receive him with joy, and to share sexual pleasure builds into him a sense of being worthy, desirable and acceptable."[4]

What if, on the other hand, your husband expresses little sexual need? Are you naively content because that means less risk for you? Or are you accepting or even resentful of his indifference without seeking to understand why?

Dr. Brothers addresses this issue as well. She calls it sexual boredom—complacency in the bedroom. She writes:

> Sexual boredom is a major element in the "twenty-year fractures," those divorces that occur after the children are grown and husband and wife find themselves alone for the first time in years. If sex gets lost in the shuffle of child-rearing and career-building, and if a man meets a younger woman who finds him attractive, he is extremely vulnerable. Not only because of his boredom and the difficulty of adjusting to life as a twosome again, but also because he is in the time in his life when change for change's sake looks good to him anyway. Too many women accept their husband's decreasing interest in sex without stopping to think what might be causing it.[5]

Your husband may lack interest in his sexual relationship with you for one of several reasons:

- He may be too busy. Many workaholics have nothing left over for home.
- He may be burying his sex drive, along with many other emotions. You or a good Christian counselor need to begin to help him open up.
- He may be experiencing depression, which takes away other basic drives as well.
- He may be deeply afraid of further rejection if you have in any way communicated rejection in the past.
- Unfortunately, he may be involved with another woman.

Women are generally security-minded, but too often a woman's need for security leads her into a sexual rut. Her husband may not say much, so she assumes that he is satisfied too. But he may not be. Beware of complacency. Be willing to make some personal sacrifices to protect your marriage from sexual boredom.

Great sacrifice communicates great love. Freely giving of yourself to your mate will make you a magnet to him, drawing him home, keeping him safe. The wife who really loves her husband will choose to take risks to please her man.

As you spend time together physically, be sure to reassure your husband verbally of your unconditional acceptance of him, especially if he is insecure in this area. Tell him that you like his body and that his imperfections and mistakes don't matter to you. His confidence will grow if you allow him the freedom to be himself and to be imperfect.

To please your husband sexually is to build his sense of value as a man. He will feel needed, fulfilled, and confident. He will experience the protection that marriage was intended to provide from the temptations of the world.

Benefits of Understanding

Understanding your husband and his differences, his need for work, and his sexuality will enable you to accept him more readily. The more you understand him, the more you will be able to:

- help him to put life into its proper context when he is down on himself
- help him comprehend his own humanity, failures, and frailties
- help him to open up (by creating an environment that enables him to be real with you)
- help him to learn to laugh at his weaknesses and at the aging process (by laughing with him, but never at him)
- help him to see his positive progress by reminding him how far he has already come

Understanding Him Makes You Valuable

As you gain understanding and give acceptance, your mate will develop the confidence to be vulnerable emotionally. He will feel freer to express fear, sadness, anger, and affection. You will become his most valuable asset, and he will treasure you, trust you, and depend on you. You will experience the truth of Proverbs 14:1: "The wise woman builds her house, but the foolish tears it down with her own hands."

Respect His Person

Part of God's specific instruction to wives is found in Ephesians 5:33: "Let the wife see to it that she respect her husband." In the *Amplified Bible*, this verse reads, "And let the wife see that she respects and reverences her husband—that she notices him, regards him, honors him, prefers him, venerates and esteems him; and that she defers to him, praises him, and loves and admires him exceedingly."

Why does God focus on this quality of respect? Why didn't He select other positive and necessary traits, such as kindness, sympathy, and forgiveness? Why didn't he emphasize love?

I believe that God, as the designer of men, knew that they would be built up as they are respected by their wives. When a wife respects her husband, he feels it, is supported by it, and is strengthened from it. A man needs respect like a woman needs love.

Your husband wants and needs to make a contribution in life that is worthy of another's respect. He needs to know that you feel he is important. Without your respect, he can't respect himself. You are his mirror. When you express your respect, he feels valuable and esteemed.

Meet a Worthy Queen

The Old Testament contains a wonderful story about a marriage that demonstrates great respect. It's like a fairy tale come true.

The book of Esther tells of a celebration given by King Ahasuerus (or Xerxes), ruler of the Persian empire. As a grand finale to the rejoicing, the king gave a lavish banquet for all the people in the capital city of Susa. He called for his queen, Vashti, to come "with her royal crown in order to display her beauty to the people and the princes, for she was beautiful."[6] But Queen Vashti refused.

Instead of honoring his request, Queen Vashti acted with "contempt."[7] She embarrassed her husband publicly before the entire population of the capital city. So, according to the custom of the times, the king removed her from her position of honor. The search began for a new queen, one who would be more worthy.

Esther was selected from among the most beautiful women of the kingdom to be the new queen. As the story continues, we discover that Esther was more than a beautiful young woman. Her worthy character is revealed as the romantic tale suddenly changes to a drama.

The uncle of Queen Esther informs her of a plot to destroy all the Jews living in the kingdom. Uncle Mordecai urges Esther to go to the king and plead with him on behalf of her people. The young queen is faced with a tough decision. She knows that the rules and laws of the palace dictate that no one can approach the king without being summoned; she knows what happened to the queen before her. But she was willing to risk her position for a higher good.[8]

In her decision to approach the king, several things are apparent about Esther's relationship with him. *First, she was not presumptuous.* She came before him as his queen, wearing her royal robes, but she came humbly, standing and waiting for him to notice her.[9] She didn't barge into the throne room. Even though she had a relationship with the king, she didn't abuse that privilege. God, in turn, honored her. When the king saw her standing in the entrance, he called her in and willingly received her. Esther was wise in her timing and respectful in her attitude.

Second, Esther respected her husband and his position as king. As she reached the throne, she touched his golden scepter, demonstrating that she recognized his authority and power. Esther never let her respect for him slip. She didn't dump all the facts on him the moment she entered his presence. She exhibited her high regard for her husband twice before she ever said a word.

Third, Esther began her reply to her husband, "If it please the king . . ."[10] In the other two recorded conversations between this king and queen, the same statement prefaces her remarks. This was *not* just an official formality, but a genuine expression to Ahasuerus of her overall commitment, respect, and submission to him as her husband and her authority.

Through the years of our marriage, I've felt that many difficult subjects needed to be brought to Dennis's attention. I wasn't sure exactly what to say. At times, I was fearful of his response But somewhere along the way, I learned what Queen Esther knew about broaching hot topics in marriage.

I learned, for example, to wait patiently for an appropriate time to talk with him. I also discovered the importance of prefacing my comments with statements like these:

- "I have something I need to talk to you about; would this be a good time?"
- "I want you to know that I love you, and I'm committed to you, and I believe in you."

- "I may be wrong, and if I am, I want you to tell me, but I feel . . ." or "I sense that . . ."

What I try to do, as Esther did so well, is to assure Dennis of my respectful loyalty to him as my partner and authority before I present my case. There are times when I speak frankly about his weaknesses and how I'm affected, but he is much more able to hear because of my loyalty and frequent verbal reassurances. He knows that even if nothing changes, I will still remain committed to him.

From the Palace of Persia to the Present

As wives, we do not need to attain royalty to become like Queen Esther. A jeweled crown and a royal robe did not make her a true queen; her attitude did. Esther shows us the importance of being perceptive students of our husbands. She knew hers well. She acknowledged his position and authority and chose to give him honor, praise, and esteem. I like what an older woman once shared, "I sought to treat my husband like a king. I realized if I wanted to be treated like a queen, then I needed to crown him king!"

Life has changed since Esther's day, but a wife's respect for her husband is still essential. God has given authority to every husband. Whether your mate's realm is a tiny one or a large one, he desperately needs your respect for who he is and what he does. By freely giving him this respect, you affirm him at the very core of his being. He feels proud to be a man. His self-esteem becomes more firmly established.

Perhaps you are thinking, *But I see little, if anything, to respect.* Perhaps you are like the young mother I know whose husband drank heavily and spent little time with the children. She had a difficult time viewing him with respect and honor. A deliberate change of focus from his weaknesses to his few strengths enabled her to begin to see her mate in a positive light. Gaining a better perspective may aid you in esteeming your husband too.

When photographing an extensive landscape, it's impossible to focus simultaneously on the flowers in the foreground and the mountains in the background. So the photographer adjusts the camera lens to bring his chosen subject into focus. When the photograph is developed, even the weeds in the field look good within the context of the overall picture.

Similarly, in viewing your husband, you must choose your focus. Continually concentrating on his flaws will negatively affect your overall perception of him. Yet, you can blur the image of those weaknesses so that you hardly notice them at all, and you can focus sharply on the positive qualities, causing genuine respect to develop.

Philippians 4:8 tells us: "Whatever is true, whatever is honorable, whatever is right, whatever is pure, whatever is lovely, whatever is of good repute, if there is any excellence and if anything worthy of praise, let your mind dwell on these things." Pay attention to your husband's admirable qualities rather than the negative ones. You can then offer him the respect that will build his self-esteem.

Adapt to Him and Share His Dream

The chameleon is noted for its ability to change color to blend in with its environment. This is the creature's primary means of protection. A chameleon can be viewed in two ways. First, we might despise it for its lack of character. After all, anyone who changes that readily must not know what he wants to be in the first place! To change constantly to match one's environment could be seen as being wishy-washy and spineless, reflecting no constant identity of one's own.

Or, we could view this four-footed creature as being very clever. He doesn't lose his identity as a chameleon when he switches from green to brown. He is only protecting himself from potential danger and harm. Viewed positively, this lowly reptile then becomes creative and competent.

Of course, the chameleon doesn't have the choice women do regarding adaptation. He has no free will; he is simply instinctively doing what he was created to do. He also illustrates that adapting to our husbands is more than a "how-to" question—it's a matter of perspective as well.

Character Inventory

What are your husband's positive character qualities? Is he compassionate, kind, and sensitive toward people? Is he disciplined and dedicated? Is he faithful and loyal, persevering during difficulties? Do the words *truthful, honest,* or *decisive* describe your mate? What are his talents and strengths? Make a list. Refresh your memory. Refurbish your respect.

List at least five positive character qualities that you respect and admire in your husband. Why not consider composing an encouraging note on five cards, highlighting each of these character qualities.
1.
2.
3.
4.
5.

Leonard Bernstein, the famous orchestra conductor, was once asked, "What is the most difficult instrument to play?"

He replied, "Second fiddle. I can get plenty of first violinists, but to find one who plays second violin with as much enthusiasm, or second French horn, or second flute, that's a problem. And yet if no one plays second, we have no *harmony.*"

Creating harmony in your marriage necessitates adaptation. To adapt means to acclimate, naturalize, become accustomed to, or become familiar with. When a woman adapts to her husband, she does not lose her identity, as some would say. Instead, she broadens it. In giving, she isn't depleted but *expanded,* just as the second violin enriches the music of the first violin.

Adapting is being a helpmate, not a help-maid. It's being a complement to your husband, not a competitor. God didn't design your position as a helper to be an inferior one. Have you noticed that, in the New Testament, Jesus refers to the Holy Spirit as the "Helper"? That title doesn't make Him a lesser member of the Trinity. God also refers to Himself as a helper in other passages (Psalms 54:4; 30:10; and 33:20). The term "helper" identifies His role; it describes His relationship with man.

Likewise, the role of the wife is no less significant than that of her husband. The terms used to describe our function merely tell us *how* we should relate to our mates. They have nothing to do with our value as women.

It is a special calling to come alongside a man, to adapt to him, and to help him become all God intended. It is a privilege that should not be demeaned. Be an involved partner in your marriage. Speak your convictions, opinions, and ideas. In order to lead your family intelligently, your husband needs your input. But maintain the delicate balance of being a helpmate without usurping his leadership. When you adapt to your husband, you grant him the freedom to lead you and your family and make it easier for him to follow God.

Through the years, as I have tried to fulfill my role as wife, I have struggled at times with the feeling that my desires and dreams were getting lost in the shuffle. Adapting to, respecting, and even understanding my husband has been difficult on many occasions. Sometimes the sacrifice seemed too great. In these instances, I felt as if God were leading me where I hadn't chosen to go and where I was not skilled.

During those times, the following beliefs have enabled me to maintain a positive perspective and to see my situation more clearly:

1. I believe firmly in God's sovereignty and am sure of His loving direction for my life.
2. I believe that God sovereignly led me to marriage. As a result,

I have chosen to submit my life, not only to God's authority but to my husband's as well.

3. I am convinced that God is still sovereignly leading me through my marriage, just as much as He did when I was single. God's will for me is not hampered by my married state.

4. Although much of God's will for me is a consequence of His will for Dennis, I believe I'm not a tag-along or an appendage. We are partners; we are one. God's will for *him* is God's will for *me*.

Maybe your husband has dreamed of other ways in which he would like to use his life and abilities. Do you know what they are? Does he feel free to talk to you about new ideas? Or do you ignore or discount his thoughts because you don't like them or because they are impossible anyway? Perhaps you are afraid of what it will cost you for him to accomplish his dream (a move, your career, loss of friends, further financial risk, time pressures, etc.).

Proverbs 20:5 reads: "A plan in the heart of a man is like deep water, but a man [woman] of understanding draws it out." Do you know what plans, dreams, and/or visions lie in the heart of your husband? A man who feels free to share the depths of his heart with his wife, knowing that she will listen without criticizing him and that she is willing to adapt to whatever he wants to do with his life, is a man who is free to become all that God intended and to do all that God has planned.

It Takes Years for Him to Become a Man

Months after that small shopping center near our home collapsed, it was finally completed. The builders made changes and structural modifications. Some were external, obvious to us as we passed by, while others were internal and couldn't be seen.

Your husband, like that shopping center, is still under construction. His self-esteem will take time, modifications, and improvements. Internally, your attitude of acceptance, respect, and adaptation are all essential to his structural integrity. Your external behavior matters, too, because your words and actions *can* help to construct a secure man.

Remember, it takes years for a man to become a strong husband. Be patient with him. Put aside your high expectations of how the phantom husband would lead his family spiritually, or behave socially, or perform intellectually. Keep your hope in God, not in your man. Then you will not be disappointed.

ESTEEM BUILDER PROJECT

(Use a sheet of paper if necessary.)

1. Which of these attitudes are most difficult for you to express toward your husband? Put a "??" by those that are a challenge and a "+" by those that are a strength.
   a. Understanding his manhood
   b. Understanding his need for work
   c. Understanding his sexual need
   d. Giving him respect
   e. Adapting to him
   f. Sharing his dreams
2. List three reasons why they are difficult.
3. What specific steps can you take in order to face the problem areas? Pray? Change your focus? Other?
4. What are your husband's dreams and goals? List as many as you can think of. Then ask him one evening to look at your list and see how on target you are.
5. Ask yourself, *Am I really willing to help him become and do all that God has planned? What do I fear most?* (A move to a new

home? A change in finances? The position I would be expected to fill as a result of my husband's position?) Am I willing to sacrifice my desires so that I can help my husband win? In prayer, give that area of fear and insecurity to God. Ask Him to free you from that personal concern so you will not hinder God's plans for your husband's life. Pray that you will be a truly biblical helper.

CHAPTER

18

Keep Your Torch Burning

———◆———

- Perseverance and Change
- Perseverance and Progress
- Perseverance and Purpose

———◆———

OUR GOOD FRIEND, Mary Graham, told us a stirring story that she watched unfold during the 1984 Olympics in Los Angeles.

With the Coliseum filled to the brim and the world looking on, the twenty-kilometer walk began. Hardly comparing with Edwin Moses' efforts to remain undefeated and Carl Lewis's four gold medals, the event began with about fifty entrants. They were to take seven laps inside the Coliseum, then exit the quarter-mile track and walk their race on the streets of Los Angeles for the next two-and-one-half hours.

With only three laps completed, a walker from El Salvador began to trail the other entrants by a great distance. During the fourth lap, all the other participants in the race passed him. As the other entrants exited the stadium en masse after completing their seventh lap, the bronzed young man still had two laps to go. The crowd cheered him on, however, and as he passed each section in the stands, they chanted, "El Salvador! El Salvador!" Finally, he exited the Coliseum.

Two-and-one-half hours later, the pack of walkers reentered the Coliseum, and of course, one emerged as the victor. He was given his gold medal and crowned with a sombrero as the crowd warmly applauded his achievement.

The crowd then settled back to watch a ten-thousand-meter run. Twenty minutes into that race, the twenty contestants were joined on the track by another man—the walker from El Salvador. The crowd roared with approval as he walked around the oval track, avoiding the runners of the race in progress.

Then the crowd rose to its feet when another walker entered the stadium. The determined walker from Central America—two laps behind when he had left the Coliseum—had passed this other walker on the course! In unison, ninety thousand people chanted "El Salvador! El Salvador!" as the young man finished the race—and collapsed.

The trauma wagon rushed to his side, but instead of taking the young walker directly through the exit where it had taken other exhausted athletes, the driver took a "victory lap" for that young Olympian. The crowd went wild. They cheered and applauded the courageous man whose name they didn't even know. It didn't matter. The young man from El Salvador had persisted and finished.

In a similar way, God has given each of us a course in life. We must run in such a way that we are able to endure, that we are able to finish the race that is set before us.

The book of Hebrews gives us a sober challenge: "Therefore, since we have so great a cloud of witnesses surrounding us, let us also lay aside every encumbrance, and the sin which so easily entangles us, and let us run with endurance the race that is set before us, fixing our eyes on Jesus, the author and perfecter of faith, who for the joy set before Him endured the cross, despising the shame, and has sat down at the right hand of the throne of God. For consider Him who has endured such hostility by sinners against Himself, so that you may not grow weary and lose heart."[1]

When attempting to build self-esteem into your mate, look to Christ. He will not disappoint you. He *does* answer prayer. He *is* at work in your mate. He *does* know what He is doing. Trust Him and keep growing strong in Him. Without Jesus Christ, no one can persevere in running the race. He is our hope.

Perseverance and Change

As you tenaciously work to elevate your mate's self-esteem, don't expect change to occur overnight. A Chinese proverb states, "A journey of a thousand miles begins with a single step." Lasting change rarely occurs immediately, but it can occur when you faithfully do what is right.

Be careful not to set your expectations for your mate too high. Circumstances change, as do people. The process may be like climbing in the Rockies—you climb one foothill only to find another mountain staring you in the face. That's the nature of life. But you will make little progress in your marriage apart from total commitment to your mate. We encourage you to keep climbing.

At our FamilyLife Marriage Conferences, we like to ask people, "If you have five frogs on a log and three of them decided to jump, how many frogs would you have left on the log?"

The answer is five.

There are five frogs on the log because there is a difference between *deciding to jump* and *jumping*. Commitment was never meant to be separated from action.

As you've read these pages, you may have seen a couple of strategies you should have implemented but haven't. They may seem too risky to attempt. But commitment demands risk, and risk builds trust and faith in your relationship with God. Why not exercise your trust muscle and "jump"?

Perseverance and Progress

Your mate's self-image, as well as yours, is progressive. That means you both are in process. It takes time—a lifetime. Paul writes, "But we all, with unveiled face beholding as in a mirror the glory of the Lord, *are being transformed* into the same image" (italics added).[2]

God is at work. We won't see the finished product until we stand before Him and see Him face to face, but we are being transformed into the likeness of His image. And that process benefits others, as well as ourselves.

Children need to see a harmonious marriage modeled by their parents. They need to see two imperfect people, who are vessels of God's perfect love, keep going after they fail. They need to learn from their parents' example. As your children see you and your mate growing in your self-esteem, they will experience more security and will develop in their self-esteem too.

The world, which is in the process of perishing, also will benefit from your example. You are the salt and light of the world of your next-door neighbors, associates at work, family members, and friends.[3] For them, your marriage may be the brightest reflection of what God is like. In fact, as we move into the twenty-first century, your marriage could become one of the greatest witnessing tools in our society.

Perseverance and Purpose

As you run the race, keep your direction and vision clear. Since you are partners for life, moving together toward a common goal, you can endure the race. As a couple, lose yourself in the infectious person of Jesus Christ and your love for Him. Cut yourself loose from the world and all of its alluring trappings. Grab hold of the imperishable will of God.

Also, as a couple, invest your lives in others. Teach them how to build up their mates' self-esteem. Instruct them in how to leave a heritage that will outlive them.

The Great Commission of Jesus Christ is still the greatest challenge that has ever been presented to the world. Go. Preach. Teach. Share Christ with everyone who will listen.[3]

Who knows . . . when you are whisked away to heaven, you may meet a throng of angels, saints, and friends who were cheering you on as you ran the race with your mate here on earth. Their applause, along with the beaming approval of Him who knows all, will tell you that your faithfulness was not in vain.

If you would like information on our FamilyLife Marriage Conferences, *HomeBuilders Couples Series*, or other books and tapes we have produced, please write to us:

Dennis and Barbara Rainey
P. O. Box 23840
Little Rock, AR 72221

How to Know God

The tragic 1985 earthquake in Mexico City took hundreds of lives, but in the midst of the rubble and ruin there were countless stories of how people had been miraculously rescued. One such rescue was that of Ruben Vera Rodriguez, a thirty-eight-year-old filing clerk who was buried beneath four floors of debris for almost four days.

His ordeal began at 7:18 A.M. on Thursday, when the first shock wave washed across the city. He was working on the third floor of one of the Labor and Social Welfare Ministry buildings.

The walls buckled, the pillars dissolved, and the four floors above him crashed down. He fell to the floor. The ceiling came to a halt eighteen inches above the inclined floor. He had landed with his head down, his feet up. "I couldn't move one foot," he says. "I couldn't raise my arm. I was buried alive."

Vera Rodriguez heard other office workers crying for help and the sound of rubble being moved. He felt he would be rescued quickly, but two days passed with no help. The voices of his colleagues fell silent.

From the first day of the entrapment, he had seen light from above reflected in front of him. So, gashing his flesh, he wriggled his way backward toward the light. Steadily, painfully, he crawled up toward the roof. Every so often he stopped and tried to gather his energy for another effort.

When the light would dim, he knew that it was getting dark. But he continued to crawl. He was about ten feet from the opening when his progress was blocked by a concrete slab and a steel bar. He yelled, "Here, up here! Help me! Please!"

"The rescuers were stunned. I was alive. . . ." After about an hour of digging, he was freed. "I felt I had emerged from the womb. The workers joked about how I was born once again, given new life. And it was true."[1]

Like Vera Rodriguez, you may feel trapped. Trapped under the rubble of a life that has ignored what God and His Word have to say about how to live.

You may have lived a religious life, but somehow your religion has not provided the fulfillment and satisfaction you feel it should—something is missing and you feel trapped.

Or maybe you find yourself trapped in a marriage that is less than the best, and you have turned to this book for solutions, thinking, "God may have some solutions for my life after all."

Perhaps you've seen everything you touch "turn to gold" and yet you still feel trapped by material possessions that just haven't satisfied as you had hoped they would.

Or perhaps you compare yourself with a friend who calls himself a "Christian." Your friend is different. Life doesn't box him in; he isn't under the pile; and he seems able to deal with life's difficulties with a perspective that is not the same as yours.

No matter what makes you feel trapped, you must be seeking to be who God created you to be as a person or you wouldn't be reading this book. And maybe in the process of reading our book, you've become aware that in order to build into your mate's life, you need to be closer to God personally.

If you've come to this conclusion, then you are very close to being "rescued" and truly "born again," but in a way much different from that of Vera Rodriguez. Let us explain how that can happen.

The Reality

One of the greatest realities the Scriptures teach is that of God's love for each person. Look at these statements:

You are honored and I love you. (Isa. 43:4)

I have loved you with an everlasting love;
therefore I have drawn you with loving-
kindness. (Jer. 31:3)

"I have loved you," says the LORD. (Mal. 1:2)

God's love for us is made obvious throughout the Bible, and it is also apparent that He desires us to live a significant and rewarding life. Jesus said, "I came that they might have life, and might have it abundantly" (John 10:10).

Since it is true that God loves us and that He desires for us to experience His ultimate purpose for our lives, why is it that many today do not experience God's love and the life He offers? And since God *wants* a relationship with every individual, why doesn't everyone automatically have it?

What separates people from the love of God today?

The Rubble

In the first moments after the walls had crumbled and the dust had settled, Vera Rodriguez did not fully understand the seriousness of his predicament. He didn't immediately realize he was helplessly trapped under four stories of twisted steel and concrete. After waiting for two days for help to come to him, he began to labor tirelessly for two more days trying to save himself. Though he had moved closer and closer to the light, he eventually discovered an insurmountable obstacle between himself and freedom, barring the path to life and trapping him in certain death.

Similarly, man finds himself helplessly trapped beneath the rubble of a life lived for himself. Isaiah wrote of this self-centered attitude: "All of us like sheep have gone astray, each of us has turned to his own way" (53:6).

Ignoring God, either by outright rejection of God and His ways or by simply never bothering to pay attention to what He has to say, we choose to go our "own way." The result of both attitudes is the same: separation from God. Consider the following:

For all have sinned and fall short of the glory of God. (Rom. 3:23)

The word *sin* may bring to your mind lists of rules that prohibit. But the word actually comes from a Greek archery term used to measure the distance between the bull's eye and where the archer's arrow hit. That distance was called the "sin." It was literally a measurement of how far the archer had missed the mark.

The "bull's eye" for humanity is God's perfect character. The Bible speaks of His character as holy, blameless, and righteous. He is the One in whom there is no flaw or imperfection. Against this perfect standard, exemplified by Christ's life, each person must measure his or her own life. As each person measures himself against God's perfect ideal, he realizes he misses the mark. Not just once, but repeatedly, man falls short.

Realizing their imperfection, many begin to labor tirelessly to make themselves acceptable to God. Yet their efforts are futile. Sin's barrier creates a humanly insurmountable obstacle between them and God. Just as Vera Rodriguez found a slab of concrete and steel blocking his escape route, so we, too, find that our sin and imperfect nature form an impenetrable blockade between us and God. No amount of human good works or religious efforts can remove the consequences of sin.

The result of sin is seen in Romans 6:23: "For the wages of sin is death." *Death* here refers to a spiritual separation from God.

If our sins have created a humanly insurmountable obstacle, then who can remove sin's barrier and rescue us?

The Rescuer

Christianity is the true account of God's personal rescue of man. What man couldn't do for himself, God did for him. Through the person of Jesus Christ, God has provided the way of escape:

But God demonstrates His own love toward us, in that while we were yet sinners, Christ died for us. (Rom. 5:8)

He made Him who knew no sin to be sin on our behalf, that we might become the righteousness of God in Him. (2 Cor. 5:21)

Jesus said to him, "I am the way, and the truth, and the life; no one comes to the Father, but through Me." (John 14:6)

And there is salvation in no one else; for there is no other name under heaven that has been given among men, by which we must be saved. (Acts 4:12)

As seen earlier, the consequence of sin is death. Sin demands a payment. These verses tell us that Christ became our personal payment for our sin. Jesus Christ is God's only provision for man's sin. He died in our place on the cross to tear down the barrier which separated us from God. And He rose again from the grave after three days to defeat death and offer eternal life to all who will believe in Him.

Jesus Christ, God's Son, came to earth to deliver God's message of love and salvation for mankind. Christ said, "I am the door; if anyone enters through Me, he shall be saved" (John 10:9).

Christ has provided each of us a way of escape. But just knowing that Christ offers us the route of escape from sin and death is not enough. It is more than just an intellectual acknowledgment of His teaching, life, death, and resurrection.

So what is required? What should your response be?

Your Response

Vera Rodriguez's only possible response to the insurmountable barrier was to cry for help. He realized he couldn't save himself. Likewise, you must come to the conclusion that you are helpless to remove sin's barrier—your cry to God must be one of dependence on God's trustworthiness to save you. He will hear your cry of faith. He will remove the obstruction of sin. But *you* must believe. Christ said:

Truly, truly, I say to you, he who hears My word, and believes Him who sent Me, has eternal life, and does not come into judgment, but has passed out of death into life. (John 5:24)

Here Christ promises to remove us from the position of separation from God (death), and place us in a new relationship with God by giving us eternal life. But belief here is more than just a mere intellectual assent; it is a commitment of trust and belief that Christ actually did pay for our sins on the cross to bring us out of death into life (a personal relationship with God).

Your faith does not mean that you are working your way to heaven and a relationship with God. It is not our human efforts or goodness that bring us into a right relationship with God, but our faith in His promise to save us. The Scripture is clear: "For by grace you have been saved through faith; and that not of yourselves, it is the gift of God; not as a result of works, that no one should boast" (Eph. 2:8-9). And again in John 1:12: "But as many as received Him, to them He gave the right to become children of God, even to those who believe in His name."

Receiving Christ means turning to God from self and sin (repenting) and placing faith in Christ for the forgiveness of your sins.

Perhaps at this point you may be saying, "I know all of that. I've heard it before." But have you ever made your own individual commitment to the person of Jesus Christ?

Just as a marriage begins when two people make a personal commitment, so it is with our relationship with God. No amount of knowledge about your fiancé will make him your mate. It is only when two individuals make that personal pledge of commitment to one another that they become husband and wife.

The following six questions may help you clarify what your need is at this moment:

1. Do you wish to know God in a personal way?
2. Do you understand that you are helpless to establish a righteous relationship with God yourself?
3. Are you willing to turn from your sin (repent) and turn to Christ to follow Him?
4. Do you see that you *need* Christ's provision for your sin?
5. Are you uncertain of where you would spend eternity if you died at this very moment?
6. Would you like to call God your "heavenly Father"?

If you answered yes to the questions above, you can truly "be rescued" right now by faith. One of the ways God has given us to express our faith and trust in Him is prayer. Prayer is simply talking with God, and is a way to place our faith and complete dependence on the fact that what God said is true. Why not express your need of God to save you right now by placing your faith in His Son Jesus Christ?

The following is a suggested prayer (your faith in God's promise is essential):

Lord Jesus, help. I need You to save me from my sins. Thank You for dying on the cross for all my sins. I now place my complete faith and dependence upon You to forgive those sins and give me eternal life. Live in me now, and begin to make me into the person You want me to be. Thank You for hearing and answering this prayer.

If you prayed that prayer and placed your faith in Jesus Christ as your Lord and Savior, then we have some information we would like to send you. Written by Bill Bright, the president and founder of Campus Crusade for Christ, it explains more fully how you can grow as a Christian. Please write us:

Dennis and Barbara Rainey
Campus Crusade for Christ
P. O. Box 23840
Little Rock, AR 72221

When you placed your faith in Christ to save you, you received the gift of eternal life. Look at the following promise of Scripture:

And the witness is this, that God has given us eternal life, and this life is in His Son. He who has the Son has the life; he who does not have the Son of God does not have the life. These things I have written to you who believe in the name of the Son of God, in order that you may know that you have eternal life. (1 John 5:11-13)

Look at the verses again. What do you have as a result of believing in Christ?

How *certain* can you be that you have eternal life? Answer: You can *know* you have eternal life on the basis of God's promise. Jesus Christ now lives in you.

One last word: Why not tell your mate today of your decision to trust Christ? In Romans 10:9, Paul encourages us to "confess with [our] mouth Jesus as Lord." Sharing with another your commitment to Christ will affirm your decision.

Like Vera Rodriguez who was rescued from a grave of physical rubble, we who have placed our trust in Christ have been rescued from the rubble of sin and have truly been "born again." We have experienced Christ's freeing power over sin and selfishness in our lives.

We hope you have too.

I am the light of the world; he who follows Me shall not walk in the darkness, but shall have the light of life. (John 8:12)

NOTES

Introduction
1. James Dobson, "Dr. Dobson Answers Your Questions," *Focus on the Family*, April 1986, 5.

Chapter One
1. Maurice Wagner, *The Sensation of Being Somebody* (Grand Rapids, MI: Zondervan Publishing House, 1975), 67.
2. Dr. Paul Brand and Philip Yancey, *In His Image* (Grand Rapids, MI: Zondervan Publishing House, 1984), 25–29.
3. Gloria Steinem, speech at International Women's Year Conference, Houston, 1977, in *To Manipulate a Woman* (pamphlet) (San Diego: Concerned Women for America).
4. Luke 1:37.

Chapter Two
1. Edwards Park, "A Phantom Division Played a Role in Germany's Defeat," *Smithsonian*, April 1985, 138.
2. Dorothy Corkille Briggs, *Your Child's Self-Esteem* (Garden City, NJ: Doubleday, 1975), 49.
3. H. Norman Wright, *Improving Your Self-Image* (Eugene, OR: Harvest House Publishers, 1983), 7–8.
4. Ibid, 8.

Chapter Three
1. Ovid Demaris, "The Other Side of Laughter," *Parade,* 5 May 1985, 4–9.

Chapter Four
1. John 8:32.
2. Luke 6:38.
3. Galatians 6:9.
4. Mary Mapes Dodge, *Hans Brinker* (New York: Grosset & Dunlap, 1984), 154–57.
5. 2 Corinthians 3:18.
6. Galatians 6:7.
7. 2 Corinthians 3:5.
8. 2 Corinthians 12:9–10.

Chapter Five
1. This concept was first taught us by Don and Sally Meredith. Don is the president and founder of Christian Family Life.

2. Genesis 2:24.
3. Genesis 3:10.
4. Charlie and Lucy Wedemeyer, *Charlie's Victory* (Grand Rapids, MI: Zondervan, 1993), 174–175, 176.

Chapter Six

1. Larry Crabb, quoted in an interview with *Tabletalk* magazine, portions of which appeared in Vol 13, No. 9, October 1989.
2. John Wesley Brown, "Good News for Parents," *Christian Century*, 1 May 1981, 513.
3. Ephesians 4:32.

Chapter Seven

1. Romans 12:1–2.
2. Ephesians 4:32.
3. Philippians 3:13–14.
4. 1 Peter 5:8.
5. Ephesians 6:10–11.
6. Revelation 12:10

Chapter Eight

1. Psalm 33:6, 9.
2. "Seeds," © 1981, Fair Hill Music. All rights reserved. Used by permission.
3. Ibid.

Chapter Nine

1. Philippians 4:8.
2. Ecclesiastes 3:1–2, 4.
3. James 1:2–8.
4. John 15:1–17
5. Job 42:2–6

Chapter Ten

1. Exodus 3:11.
2. Exodus 3:12.
3. Exodus 3:13.
4. Exodus 4:10.
5. Exodus 4:13.
6. John 8:32.
7. Ephesians 4:32.
8. Colossians 3:13.

Chapter Eleven
1. "Wishin' and Hopin'," Burt Bacharach and Hal David. Reprinted by permission. Blue Seas Music, Inc., NY, 1969, Jonathan Music Co., Inc. Assigned to Blue Seas Music, Inc., and JAC Music Co.

Chapter Twelve
1. James 1:22–24.
2. Hebrews 11:6.
3. Take a look at the promise of Romans 8:31-39 and the story of the prodigal son in Luke 15:11–32.
4. 1 Samuel 2:12.
5. 1 Samuel 2:17.
6. 1 Samuel 2:30.
7. Matthew 5:13–16.
8. James 4:2.
9. 1 Thessalonians 5:17.
10. C. S. Lewis, *Beyond Personality*, reprinted in *Mere Christianity* (New York: MacMillan, 1952), 189–90.

Chapter Thirteen
1. Proverbs 27:17.

Chapter Fourteen
1. Ephesians 5:15–17.
2. James 1: 5, 6.
3. Warren Martindale and Jerry Root, Eds, *The Quotable Lewis* (Wheaton, IL, 1990), 335.

Chapter Fifteen
1. Ephesians 2:10.
2. Charles Colson, "Standing Tough Against All Odds," *Christianity Today*, 6 September 1985, 25–33.
3. Ibid.
4. Genesis 22:17.
5. Psalm 147:4.
6. Matthew 10:29–30.
7. Psalm 106:25.
8. Elizabeth D. Dodds, *Marriage to a Difficult Man* in *Where Have All the Mothers Gone?*, Brenda Hunter (Grand Rapids, MI: Zondervan, 1982), 109.
9. 2 Timothy 2:2.

Chapter Sixteen

1. Adapted from Tom Peters, *The Excellence Challenge* tape series (Waltham, MA: EXCEL/MEDIA, INC., 1984).
2. 1 Peter 3:7.
3. 1 Peter 3:7.
4. 1 Peter 3:7.
5. 1 Samuel 22:2.
6. 1 Chronicles 12:21.

Chapter Seventeen

1. Adapted from Joyce Brothers, *What Every Woman Should Know about Men* (New York: Ballantine, 1981), 29–34.
2. Jill Renich, *To Have and to Hold* (Grand Rapids, MI: Zondervan, 1972), 55.
3. Brothers, 147.
4. Renich, 55.
5. Brothers, 154.
6. Esther 1:11
7. Esther 1:17–18
8. Esther 4:11, 14–16
9. Ester 5:1
10. Esther 5:4

Chapter Eighteen

1. Hebrews 12:1–3.
2. 2 Corinthians 3:18.
3. Matthew 5:13–16.

Appendix

1. "El Temblor! Tragedy in Mexico City," (UPI) *Reader's Digest*, January 1986, 63–64.

ABOUT THE AUTHORS

Dennis Rainey, author of *The Tribute*, co-founded FamilyLife in 1976 and now serves as its executive director. He is the daily host of the nationally syndicated radio program "FamilyLife Today," and is the recipient of the National Religious Broadcasters Radio Program Producer of the Year Award for 1995.

Barbara Rainey has faithfully served alongside her husband, Dennis, in ministry and at home. She is also a speaker and author.

The Raineys live near Little Rock, Arkansas, and have six children.

FamilyLife Conferences

A Weekend That Will Make a Difference.

For Your Marriage . . . For Your Children . . . For Yourself . . . For A Lifetime.

FamilyLife Conferences are bringing meaningful, positive change to thousands of couples and families every year. The conferences, offered in 75 cities throughout the country, are based on solid biblical principles and are designed to provide couples and parents—in just one weekend—with the practical skills to build and enhance their marriages and families. And not just for a week . . . or a month . . . or a year . . . but for a lifetime!

The FamilyLife Marriage Conference helps meet couples' unique needs by equipping them with proven solutions that address practically every component of "How to Build a Better Marriage." This conference gives you the opportunity to slow down and focus on your spouse and your relationship. You will spend an insightful weekend together, doing fun couples' projects and hearing from dynamic speakers on real-life solutions for building and enhancing oneness in your marriage.

Alumni of the marriage conference also have the opportunity to further build on that foundation of principles and application in the alumni session, Building Your Mate's Self-Esteem. This session is an important "next step" in creating a stronger marriage.

The FamilyLife Parenting Conference will equip you with the principles and tools you need to be more effective parents for a lifetime. Whether you're just getting started or in the turbulent years of adolescence, you'll learn biblical blueprints for raising your children. You'll receive proven, effective principles from parents—just like you— who have dedicated their lives to helping families.

For More Information

For more information, to register or to receive a free brochure and schedule on any of the FamilyLife Conferences, call FamilyLife at 1-800-333-1433. And do it today. For your marriage . . . for your children . . . for yourself . . . for a lifetime.

FAMILYLIFE™

Bringing Timeless Principles Home

P. O. Box 23840 · Little Rock, AR 72221-3840 · (501) 223-8663 · 1-800-999-8663
A ministry of Campus Crusade for Christ

The HomeBuilders Couples Series®

The HomeBuilders Couples Series® are the fastest growing small-group studies in the country. This series is designed to help your relationship build and grow on the solid, biblical principles found in God's Word.

Building Your Marriage
by Dennis Rainey

Here's help for discovering and applying God's blueprints for a strong, healthy marriage that will last a lifetime. Grow together as one by accepting your mate as God's perfect provision for your needs.

Building Teamwork in Your Marriage
by Robert Lewis

It's no secret that men and women are created very different. This book can help you learn how to understand, appreciate, and respect the differences you and your spouse will confront as husband and wife.

Building Your Mate's Self-Esteem
by Dennis and Barbara Rainey

Improve your marriage and experience new levels of love and fulfillment by learning how to build up and encourage each other in this eight-session study.

Mastering Money in Your Marriage
by Ron Blue

Managing money is a challenge for any couple, regardless of income level. Discover how you can make money matters a tool for growth instead of a bone of contention in your marriage through this study.

Resolving Conflict in Your Marriage
by Bob and Jan Horner

Learn to transform conflicts into opportunities which can energize your marriage and increase your love for your mate through this study.

Growing Together in Christ
by David Sunde

In these six life-changing sessions, you and your mate will begin helping each other experience the joy of an exciting, daily relationship with God. Discover all the power and joy you and your mate can find together in Christ.

Managing Pressure in Your Marriage
by Dennis Rainey and Robert Lewis

Learn how to manage stress and eliminate needless pressure in your marriage. This six-session study will help you learn how to make better choices, plan for the future, and find new solutions as you navigate through the sea of life.

Life Choices for a Lasting Marriage
by David Boehi

As a couple, learn how to deal with temptation, simplify your lifestyle, and renew your minds with the truth of God's Word. The author identifies the key choices which will keep your marriage strong against a hostile culture.

Expressing Love in Your Marriage
by Jerry and Sheryl Wunder and Dennis and Jill Eenigenburg

Begin setting aside the false ideas of love promoted by our culture and instead express God's love in your marriage. Not a fleeting emotion, God's love is a divinely inspired commitment to seek His best for each other.

FAMILYLIFE™
Bringing Timeless Principles Home
P. O. Box 23840 · Little Rock, AR 72221-3840
(501) 223-8663 · 1-800-999-8663

A ministry of Campus Crusade for Christ

For more information on these and other FamilyLife Resources contact your local Christian retailer or call FamilyLife at 1-800-333-1433. A free HomeBuilders Information Pack is also available through the FamilyLife "800" number.